Essays in Honor of Edward C. Fendt

INTERPRETING
LUTHER'S LEGACY

Edited by
Fred W. Meuser and
Stanley D. Schneider

Augsburg Publishing House · *Minneapolis, Minnesota*

INTERPRETING LUTHER'S LEGACY

Copyright acknowledgments and sources of quotations are given
in the Notes at the end of the book

Foreword

In the course of a conversation with Dr. Henry F. Schuh in 1939, he made a remark that introduced me to the name "Fendt." He observed, "There is a young professor out at the Seminary by the name of Fendt. Watch him; he is a comer."

For Dr. Schuh to make such a statement meant that he had recognized the presence of competence, devotion to the Lord of the church, and readiness to work perseveringly. What Dr. Schuh recognized back in the thirties, all friends of Dr. Fendt have come to know as fact.

The former American Lutheran Church and presently The American Lutheran Church have frequently called on Dr. Fendt to represent the church in several capacities—but particularly in intersynodical negotiations. For this work he was gifted with a wide acquaintance among his fellow pastors and a perceptive understanding of the lay constituency. His willingness to listen, his irenic spirit, and his strong convictions anchored in a lively devotion to the Gospel and Lutheran Confessions have conferred on him a special grace for this good work. It is therefore particularly appropriate that this volume of essays, occasioned by the 450th Anniversary of the Reformation, should be dedicated to Dr. Fendt.

When a man has served thirty-two years in a theological professorship, with twenty-two of these invested as administrative head of the Seminary, it is among students and colleagues that a true assessment of him may be found. Any visitor to the campus in Columbus will note that there is abundant evidence of respect, esteem, and affection. The decision of Dr. Fendt's colleagues to make this book a sixty-fifth birthday *Festschrift* in his honor bespeaks the gratitude of faculty, students, and the Board of Regents. The American Lutheran Church would like to identify itself with the seminary family in this appropriate and well deserved anniversary tribute. Thank you, Dr. Fendt, and God bless you as you carry on!

FREDRIK A. SCHIOTZ
President
The American Lutheran Church

Biographical Reflections

The title of this book, *Interpreting Luther's Legacy,* is also an appropriate description of the life and vocation of Edward C. Fendt, in whose honor it is being published.

This legacy was first imparted to him in his native city, Michigan City, Indiana. It was shared through the ministry of St. Paul Lutheran Church where he was baptized and received his early education in the parish school.

The treasures of the legacy were further opened at Capital University, Columbus, Ohio, through its Academy, College of Liberal Arts, and the Theological Seminary. While still a seminary student he began interpreting the legacy by teaching Greek and German in the College.

Following Seminary graduation in 1928, the interpretation deepened and expanded. A double ministry was successfully carried on, as pastor of Martin Luther congregation in Columbus, and assistant professor of Bible at Capital. Enrichment came through graduate work at the Ohio State University, and the Divinity School of the University of Chicago.

In 1936 he was called to succeed Dr. R. C. H. Lenski, as professor of systematic theology on the Seminary faculty. Through three decades in this role he has forthrightly interpreted Luther's legacy to hundreds of theological students, most of whom are serving today as pastors of congregations in The American Lutheran Church.

His creative leadership and administrative gifts were recognized by his election as dean of the Seminary in 1946. With the separation of the Seminary from Capital University in 1959, he became seminary president with much expanded responsibilities. Under his aggressive regime, faculty personnel has been almost trebled, a postgraduate STM degree program instituted, a three-seminary arrange-

ment of shared elective courses introduced, and a coordinating of work with several graduate schools of the Ohio State University is being developed. In its physical development, four major building projects have marked the Seminary's growth.

Beyond the confines of his own institution, he has served in many other ways as an interpreter of Luther's legacy. In 1947 he edited *What Lutherans Are Thinking*, a volume of doctrinal studies published by the faculties of all the major Lutheran seminaries in the U.S. He has represented his church at assemblies of the Lutheran World Federation and the World Council of Churches. He has served on numerous confessional and organizational committees, including those which led to the formation of The American Lutheran Church in 1960, and the organization of the Lutheran Council of the United States of America in 1967. His continuing participation on the ALC's Committee on Inter-Church Relations provides further opportunity to interpret Luther's legacy, both within Lutheranism and in the wider sphere of present ecumenical relations.

We, his faculty colleagues, have probably shared most richly in his interpretation. We know him as scholar, pastor, teacher, administrator, churchman, and friend. We happily continue to serve with him in the task of strengthening the church's ministry. In appreciation for all he has meant and continues to mean to Seminary and Church, it is our added privilege to present this book in honor of Dr. Edward Charles Fendt, president of the Evangelical Lutheran Theological Seminary, Columbus, Ohio.

To one who so productively continues to interpret Luther's legacy, we dedicate this volume, *Interpreting Luther's Legacy*.

T. S. LIEFELD
for the faculty
The Evangelical Lutheran
Theological Seminary

Editorial Preface

The essays in this volume were originally given as a special series of lectures to the faculty and students at the Evangelical Lutheran Theological Seminary, Columbus, Ohio. They were presented by the members of the faculty in commemoration of the 450th anniversary of the Reformation which occurred during the academic year of 1967-68.

Two members of the faculty at that time are not included. Dr. H. C. Leupold, professor emeritus of Old Testament, did not give a lecture. Dr. M. H. Hoops, associate professor of New Testament, was on sabbatical leave and was off campus during this time. They nonetheless share in the presentation of these papers to the public and in the honoring of a colleague.

One lecture was given which is not included here. That lecture is the one given by the man in whose honor this book is being published.

Obviously the richness of Luther's legacy is not fully exploited. It could not be. Each writer has taken some area of Luther's wide range of theological endeavor and investigated it. Some of the better known emphases of Luther and the Reformation are included only by allusion, and some not at all. In compensation for this there are insights and studies which have not been made previously.

In publishing this book there have been contributions of more than essays. The essayists wish to express their appreciation to Mrs. Edith P. Klamfoth of Columbus, Ohio, and to Mr. John C. Fendt of Michigan City, Indiana, whose generosity made the appearance of this book possible.

These lectures, offered to the Seminary in 1967-68, are now offered to a wider audience in this form, in honor of Dr. E. C. Fendt, president of the Seminary.

THE EDITORS

Contents

Part Four
Luther and the Parish

Part One

Luther and the Word

1.

Luther and the
First Commandment

RONALD M. HALS

For some time I have had an interest in the theology of Old Testament law. My concern with that theology has been twofold. First, I have been trying to get a better understanding of what law is in the Old Testament by avoiding the shallow view that sees law as a powerless offer of salvation intended by God to make a point against work-righteousness, as though God were to say: "Here is my law; if you can keep it, you can earn salvation; if not, I'll send you to hell, and that'll teach you." Second, because of the prominent way the law is an object of praise and treated as a manifestation of God's grace in the Old Testament, I have been trying to find a way to see and to set forth the depth of grace which is in the law in the theology of the Old Testament.

A natural subject seemed to be to investigate Luther on the law to see whether or not he might help in an attempt to understand Old Testament law better. At first thought that may seem to have been a pipe dream, for isn't Luther rather the one who is responsible for all the trouble in the harsh interpretation of the Old Testament law? He is the one who spoke about the "hangman's job" which the law has in the Old Testament, and it is in the Apology of the Augsburg Confession (surely reflecting the view of Luther also) that Melanchthon writes how "the law always accuses." [1] Luther can say of the lawgiver Moses that he is not just the harmless preacher of a superseded viewpoint, but that he is the deadly enemy of Christ, and remains so until the end of time. For Moses,

2

Luther has such nice names as jailer, slaveholder, hangman, and torturer.[2] And yet Luther has some very positive things to say about the law. He can call Moses the source and father of all prophets and a good Christian.[3] Perhaps the only way out of that is to admit that it is always easy to quote Luther on both sides of any question. Anybody who wrote that much generally provides material for those who wish to quote him against himself. In the instance of Luther and the law that is certainly the case.

Perhaps a better way would be to take a single Old Testament law and investigate all that Luther says about it. For this purpose one passage above all others suggests itself in connection with the law, that is the First Commandment. The First Commandment is relatively easy to examine, because, first of all, enough people have written about Luther's view of the First Commandment that the material from his writings is readily at hand. Then, as the very first of the Ten Commandments, the First Commandment is central in place. Further, as the demand of allegiance, it is central in content. Finally, it is a favorite of Luther's and thus central in emphasis. Heinrich Bornkamm observes that this one passage meant more to Luther than any other in the Old Testament.[4] What then did the First Commandment mean to Luther? To summarize this I shall present a condensation of Heinrich Bornkamm's analysis of the four meanings which the First Commandment had for Martin Luther and try to analyze each one.

I

FIRST COMMANDMENT AND NATURAL LAW

"As a command to have a god, it (the First Commandment) is a part of natural law."[5] "To have a god is not only Moses' law," says Luther, "but also a natural law."[6] Of course, the heathen have false gods, but that just proves the point. The point is that to have a god is natural, a part of natural law. In fact, the whole Decalog is just an unsurpassed summary of the natural law. Luther says, "The natural laws are nowhere so finely and orderly arranged as in Moses."[7] And for Luther it is the First Commandment which holds all the others together. In the *Large Catechism* he calls it something like the clasp or the hoop of a wreath.[8] In fact, Luther goes so far as to say that the First Commandment is the measure and judge of the others, so that when faith or love demands it the other commandments can be disobeyed. This may seem quite strange, but remember, Luther is the one who explained the First Commandment to mean that "we should fear, love, and trust in God above all things." [9] When he says faith and love may demand the disobedience of the commandments, what he has in mind is a case where God commands a man, for example, to kill another. In that case allegiance to God demands breaking the commandment against murder. Only where allegiance to God is preserved can you even speak of a legitimate use of the law.[10]

This kind of thinking makes some kind of sense. But what is the point of it? Why should Luther concern himself so much to show that the Decalog is a summary of natural law? The answer to that lies in Luther's concern as a Christian preacher. He could say, "Moses is dead; . . . not the tiniest point in Moses concerns us." [11] We are not Jews, and, therefore, Moses' law does not concern us except "insofar as it is in accord with the natural law." [12] His aim was to reach Christians. Christians do not live under the law of Moses, but all men have to do with the natural law. The natural law has as its content, as far as Luther is concerned, basically to love God and the brother.[13] The reason we are obligated to obey this natural law is not because Moses says so, but because in this natural law we with the whole world stand before another lawgiver, God himself.[14]

But even the Decalog contains ceremonial elements which are abrogated by the coming of Christ, so that the decalog and the natural law are not identical. Luther's view is that Moses is not the author of the natural law but an interpreter of it.[15] The goal that Luther has is thus that the Ten Commandments "might not be as the law of Moses bound to the range of the revelation on Sinai, but that they might be the inescapable law of God before which all mankind becomes guilty." [16] To put it in terminology that is my own, Luther, like most dogmaticians today, bypasses Sinai in order to base law in creation, thereby insuring its universal validity. But this is, from the point of view of the Old Testament, clearly non-biblical. This is not how the Old Testament sees the Law. And, perhaps not so clearly, this is dangerous. The Law the New Testament speaks about, just as much as the Savior it speaks about, is tied inextricably into the history of Israel. Bypassing Sinai is dangerous. If the Law is based in creation, for what purpose was it given? Was it really given as an impotent offer of salvation, aimed to doom all in the guilt of disobedience? That is what Paul says, isn't it? Well, yes and no. Remember, for Paul the promise comes before the Law, in Abraham. Thus Paul ties the promise to Israel and so also the Law, except when Gentiles might thereby be excluded. Paul goes back to creation not to bypass Sinai, but as a kind of minor detour. The return to creation in modern systematics as a basis for the Law seems rather to bypass Sinai completely.

II

First Commandment and the Promise

The second way in which Bornkamm analyzes Luther's use of the First Commandment is that for Luther "the prologue taken by itself is the essence of all promises." [17] Luther can stress this aspect of the First Commandment to the extreme. He calls it a "commandment in which nothing is commanded." [18] God simply offers and gives himself. He says, "I am the Lord, your God." The sense of this, according to Luther, is to teach us to rely not on ourselves but solely on his grace. And all the Psalms, which Luther so dearly loved, are for him just an elaboration of this one basic promise, the prologue to the First Commandment. [19]

Luther went further. He even saw here an attestation of how the Old Testament knows of a life beyond death. He argues this way. God himself cannot die; he is the God of the living. And therefore his people must live forever. Otherwise he would not be their God, and they could not hold fast to him when they were no longer alive. [20] We cannot accept that kind of exegesis, but the single most important result of all our form-critical comparison with Hittite treaties is to help us to see the prologue as the Gospel setting in which the demand is placed. But nobody could bring out more clearly than Luther the Gospel contained in this prologue. Characteristically, he finds in it comfort in the face of doubt. "Unbelief," Luther says, "sometimes thinks, 'God is much too great . . . to care about a poor bag of maggots like me . . . he lets angels serve him; what am I . . . a poor bubble . . . ?' Faith, though, doesn't doubt that God who created all things . . . cares about us . . . for there stands the word: I am the Lord, your God." [21] Is that the Law? No, the Law is not God's first word. That is Gospel, "I am your

God." The Law comes second in that it summons those whom God has already made his to live the appropriate life of response to his grace. Or to put it in Luther's bold hyperbole, in the Law God himself does not speak, but Moses who received it from angels. "When God himself speaks with men, they can hear nothing but pure grace...." [22]

III

Law and Gospel Alongside Each Other

But the First Commandment is more than prologue. And Bornkamm goes on to say that the third way in which Luther uses the First Commandment is as a unit showing that "it contains, depending upon whether it is directed to faith or unbelief, Law and Gospel alongside each other." [23] In spite of seeing the prologue as Gospel Luther sees both the prologue and the prohibition as belonging together as a unit. The effect of this unit when preached is both Law and Gospel. When one time he was asked how to preach to a congregation composed of both the godly and the godless, Luther answered simply, "With the First Commandment." [24] "It signifies judgment for one group, grace for the other." [25] It signifies judgment to the unbelieving who do not trust in God as their Lord, and consolation to those who hear in faith. Thus the entire commandment, prologue and prohibition, contains Law and Gospel alongside each other.

This for Luther is the background of the preaching of the prophets. For him the First Commandment is the ocean out of which the prophets have drawn both their message of consolation and their message of condemnation. [26] As he puts it one place,

> God threatens the godless who are careless and proud, and if threatening does not help, he enforces it with penalties, pestilence, famine, war, till they are destroyed. Thus he makes good the threat of the First Commandment. But he comforts those who fear God and are in all sorts of need, and enforces his comfort with aid and counsel, by all kinds of wonders and signs, against all the might of the devil and the world: thus he also makes good the comfort of the First Commandment. [27]

Before making any observations about Luther's seeing Law and Gospel alongside each other in the First Commandment, it will be best to consider the closely related fourth way in which Luther uses this commandment.

IV

LAW AND GOSPEL IN EACH OTHER

"As a command of promise for the tempted man, it [the First Commandment] contains command and assurance woven together in each other; the command comes as Gospel to him, the Gospel as command." [28] Here is the distinctive and also the disputed part of Luther's view of the First Commandment. Here God puts the command in the service of the promise. He commands that we accept his assurance. This is not really so startling, because the goal of both command and promise is the same. Bornkamm remarks that the goal of both is "naturally" nothing other than faith in the promise.[29] For my own part I can only say that I wish it were so thoroughly obvious that the goal of the command coincides with the goal of the promise. I should be a great deal more pleased with the understanding of Old Testament law that I encounter in modern writers, if they could say with Bornkamm that the goals of Law and promise are *naturally* the same.

But Luther with his flair for fervent color does even better. It is his point that God does not just allure and woo us to trust him. In order to overcome our doubt and get us to see him as our loving Father-God, he commands us to do so, using all his authoritative majesty as Creator.[30] "See what a gracious God and Father we have, who does not only assure us forgiveness of sins, but also commands concerning the most serious sin that we should believe it is forgiven, and urges us with the same command to a happy conscience. . . . " [31] For Luther, God is more offended by one's unbelief which will not accept forgiveness than by any other sin. As faith is the only and all-encompassing good work, so unbelief is the ultimate sin, the sin against the first and ultimate commandment.[32] But can such a commandment really be called law? Is the First Commandment law? What it is is decided by man's response. You could say that the *opus proprium*, the proper work, of the First Commandment is the assurance of grace, and its *opus alienum*, its alien work, its unnatural work, is the word of judgment on him who does not accept the promise. This, of course, is just the opposite of the way it is with the law whose proper work was that of the hangman; so we can say that "the First Commandment belongs completely on the side of the Gospel. It is just the most powerful form

thereof." [33] Rather fascinatingly that statement that the commandment is just the most powerful form of the Gospel is one which
was made by Karl Holl [34] and by Paul Althaus [35] a good many years
ago. That same statement, that the Law is the most powerful form
of the Gospel, is very close to what Karl Barth has more recently
written. But more of that later.

If the First Commandment can be called the most powerful form
of the Gospel, this is not to ignore the fact that the First Commandment is also the most powerful form of the Law, that is, the
threat of judgment in case we do not accept God's offered grace.[36]
Here, according to Luther, blessing and curse are frighteningly near
each other. (Bornkamm's word is *unheimlich*.)[37] God stands behind the First Commandment in a double shape. According to Luther it has a double content, his punishing as well as his forgiving
word.[38] And "it is the difficult art of faith to accept the word of
grace from the God whose judgment a man feels so deeply in his
heart." [39] It has been observed that approximately the same thing
happens for Luther with the commandments as with the righteousness of God—"What outside the Gospel can only call forth terror
in him, becomes now the strongest comfort." [40] As he was afraid of
the righteousness of God and then came to find it in God's gift to
him, so he was afraid of the commandment and came to find in it
his source of strength against his own fears. Or to put it in his own
words, "The word, 'I am your God,' . . . gives the hungry bread!" [41]

But how dare we find comfort in a demand which is never fulfilled by us! Or is the First Commandment ever fulfilled by us?
Yes, says Luther, the First Commandment is fulfilled by us through
Christ's blood. It is only thus that we fulfill God's will, love and
trust him properly.[42] All Jesus' preaching, in fact, is nothing other
than the application of the First Commandment.[43] He applies it to
himself and thus makes himself equal with the Father,[44] whom he
serves as an obedient Son, and then gives us his righteous obedience.
To summarize, "Luther finds in the First Commandment the unity
of command and promise, judgment and redemption, the care of a
father and the grace of Christ, the one God's entire giving of himself to the world." [45]

We cannot fail to be impressed by this fusion of Law and Gospel
in one who laid such great stress on their careful distinction. To
refresh your memory about the high degree of emphasis Luther

placed on the proper distinction of Law and Gospel, hear some of the things he says.

> For this differentiation between Law and Gospel is the highest art in Christianity, which all and each who boast in or accept the name Christian should know and be able to put into practice. For where this item is lacking one cannot tell a Christian from a heathen or a Jew; so much depends on this differentiation.[46]

In another place he makes it plain that by Law he means the Ten Commandments, and not just some theological abstraction about work-righteousness. He writes,

> Both are indeed God's Word: the Law, or the Ten Commandments, and the Gospel; the latter given initially by God in Paradise, the former on Mount Sinai. But everything depends on one's rightly differentiating these two kinds of Word and not mixing them together, otherwise one will neither know nor retain the correct understanding of either the one or the other; in fact, though thinking to have both, one will have neither. Therefore put the man who can exercise well this art of separating the Law from the Gospel in first place and call him a Doctor of Holy Scripture, for without the Holy Spirit it is not possible to make this differentiation.[47]

Is perhaps then this fusion of Law and Gospel in the First Commandment just a case where Luther slipped? Scarcely, since this was his favorite Old Testament passage. Or is it perhaps Bornkamm's analysis of Luther's use of the First Commandment that is faulty? After all, the very idea of Luther mixing Law and Gospel seems impossible to contemplate. But this judgment of Bornkamm's is confirmed by others. Paul Althaus observes that "The Ten Commandments, as Luther understands them, are not merely a mirror for repentance, meant to lead to Christ via the knowledge of sin. These commandments are dealt with in the first part of the Catechism; but in reality, according to Luther, their place is not only before the gospel, but also *in* the gospel, . . . "[48]

V

THE LAW IS THE NECESSARY FORM OF THE GOSPEL

Since then we cannot seem to dodge the fact of what Luther does, let us attempt to go further into this disturbing and exciting business by exploring what precisely it is that Luther does here and why he does it the way he does. To begin with, let us note

what he does not do. He does not separate the First Commandment
into a prologue of promise and a body of demand.

> This is the work of the First Commandment where it is commanded
> "Thou shalt not have other gods," that is as much as saying: Because
> I alone am God, you shall put your entire confidence, trust, and faith
> in me and in no one else.[49]
> The command is thus wrapped up in both parts of the First Com-
> mandment, in the promise and the prohibition. Therein lies the unity
> of the First Commandment. It demands of me to believe God's assur-
> ance and to recognize him alone as my God. Thereby the promise is
> the basis of the command.[50]

What Luther does do with the First Commandment is to see that
the same saving will of God is behind both Law and Gospel. God
only threatens, punishes, and even condemns, because he cares.
He only rejects because he wants to accept. In this sense his every
word is grace, because the aim of every word is to give himself to
us in love, so that we may find our true life in him. And yet at the
same time it is true that there is an unconditional demand even in
his self-giving love, for he demands to have us for himself alone.
There is no other option. We are either his or nothing. In this
sense at least it is true that the necessary form of the Gospel is the
Law.[51]

That kind of statement, of course, has some weakness as a systematic declaration. Its strength is that it maintains the biblical
flavor. That was Luther all over. But this same maintaining of the
biblical flavor at the risk of a certain systematic weakness might lead
us to compare Luther's view of the First Commandment with that
of one other who deliberately forsakes the language of the Reformation in order to be more biblical. I have reference to Karl Barth.

Barth is of the opinion that the Law is contained in the Gospel,
just as the Ten Commandments were contained in the ark of the
covenant.[52] It was the Covenant, of course, which brought God's
gracious choice of his people. Its content, like the content of the
Gospel, is, of course, grace. And since the Law is contained in the
Gospel, Barth argues that the Law too must be grace. Whenever
God speaks it is grace.[53] According to the *Barmen Declaration* Jesus
Christ is God's one word which we must hear and obey.[54] This logic
may sound rather un-Lutheran. Is it possible that it sounds un-
Lutheran but not unlike Martin Luther?

Listen again to Barth. Sin is self-will. And God's answer to sin is, "You must die." He has in mind Ezekiel 18:20, "The soul that sins shall die." Barth says this answer, "You must die," is grace. That may be the first time a death sentence has been called grace, and yet, isn't it embarrassing to find Ezekiel himself saying, just three verses farther on, "Have I any pleasure in the death of the wicked, . . . and not rather that he should turn from his way and live?" The goal of the death sentence is that the wicked turn and live. The goal of "you must die" is grace. But it does not work that way. No one submits willingly to his own death sentence. One man did; Jesus Christ did this for us, and in his obedience and submission to the Law for our salvation we find, according to Karl Barth, the true triumph of grace, that is, the triumph of God's intent in the Law.[55] Remember it was Luther who said that the First Commandment is fulfilled in us through the blood of Christ.

Listen to Barth a third time. To ask what the Law is we ought to start with the fact that Jesus has fulfilled the Law. The Law is the manifest will of God. This is what Jesus has fulfilled. He has done the will of his Father. And from what God does for us in Christ we learn what he wants of us. We learn what is the will of God. In Christ God has done all for us to make us his. He has fulfilled the Law, and that Law was, "Be mine! I am the Lord your God, so be mine!" What then must we do? According to Barth, believe! That is, we must fear and love God.[56] Shades of Luther's explanation!

According to Barth grace become manifest assumes the form of the Law, that is, of the First Commandment. Grace says, "I am the Lord your God; be mine!" The only valid claims or commands there are or can be must come from this: "I am the Lord your God." His claim is the expression in the form of the Law of the content of the Gospel. The goal of the Law is Jesus Christ, our justification. And perhaps we could see this in the Law, but we don't. Why not? Because we pervert it. We conceal the Gospel content of which the Law is only the form. We attempt to use the Law as a means to qualify for membership in God's people. We try to reverse the order God has established. We say, "I will be what you ask of me, and thus I will become yours, for I will qualify to be yours"; whereas God begins with Gospel, "I am the Lord your God" and continues with Law.[57] Is the right order Gospel and then Law? That is the order of the biblical setting of the Law.

When we endeavor to pervert the order by perverting the Law, we also thereby pervert the Gospel. When we pervert the Law into an agent by which we can save ourselves, then we pervert the content—the grace of which the Law is only the form—for we pervert the Gospel into being just that added help we need in order to make it, to qualify to be his.[58] But when we pervert the Law and the Gospel, God's claim in the Law remains. When we pervert the Law it damns us, for then it no longer has Christ as its goal. The good Law becomes then a Law of sin and death.[59] Then, says Karl Barth, the right order directed to the one misusing the Law in an attempt to save himself is Law first, the Law that means death, and Gospel second, the Gospel that means life out of death.[60] When the Gospel conquers as triumphant grace, then "the law, the form of the Gospel, is also restored out of its letters into the totality of its words, its one single word, out of the demand, 'Thou shalt!' into the promise, 'Thou wilt be!'; out of the claim upon our performance into the claim upon our trust." [61]

Is this not exactly what Luther had said, that the First Commandment is the way to preach to both the godly and the godless?[62] For to the godless it is a denunciation of their failure to trust in God, but to those who are God's it is the assurance that God wills to be theirs. Luther knew what he was doing when he thus put Law and Gospel together. And that is not just something we moderns might say about Luther. He himself reflected upon these connections that bind Law and Gospel together. "For although these two are utterly distinct, yet they must be joined completely together in the same heart. Nothing is more closely joined together than fear and trust, Law and Gospel, sin and grace; they are so joined together that each is swallowed up by the other." [63]

What is it then that we have seen? I feel it is just one more instance of a common principle that we have seen here, the principle that reality is greater than formality, that the truth exceeds our formulation of it. It is all well and good to talk about the necessity of distinguishing between Law and Gospel. And I mean that genuinely! But though such talk is well and good, it is not enough. When you seek to classify a word of God's as Law or Gospel, it is not enough to examine its content. You must go on to ask the very simple, but often so revealing, question, "To whom is this word addressed?" Luther was a master at seeing the necessity for this question. With regard to the enthusiasts' reliance on Moses as God's Word he felt compelled to say,

> God's Word   here; God's Word there! I have to know and bear in mind to whom the Word of God will be spoken. . . . One must not look just to see whether it is God's Word, whether God has spoken it, but much more to whom it is spoken, whether it refers to you. . . . There are two kinds of Word in the Scriptures. The first does not apply to me, does not refer to me. The other does refer to me. And on the basis of the one that does I'll take my chances and rely on it as a strong rock. But if it does not refer to me, then I ought to keep my mouth shut.[64]

When it comes to the First Commandment, everything depends on to whom it is addressed. The word "you belong to me" is a verdict of defeat and destruction to the man seeking to escape God, but to the man who fears that his sins have torn him away from the God whom he loves and wants to serve this same word is fullness of joy and life itself.

But even this is not enough. To see the final way in which the complexity of reality transcends the bounds of any either/or analysis, picture God as using the words of a ballad once made famous by Jo Stafford. (Why not? If the prophets can use love songs, cannot also the sons of the prophets?) In a nostalgic sequence that includes "send me photographs and souvenirs" and "the marketplace in old Algiers" there comes the line, "Just remember, when a dream appears, you belong to me." Does not this bit of lyric poetry do better to capture the meaning and function of the First Commandment than any logical analysis? We who know our weakness and vulnerability to a passing dream that would lead us astray know that with a forceful reminder we are addressed by the one who loves us as he tells us, "You belong to me!" And yet it is not a different addressee, but our same foolish and yearning hearts, which hear in these same words the rapturous assurance that he who has been, is, and will be, more to us than any dream, is saying to us, "You belong to me!" "You belong to me" is both forceful reminder and rapturous assurance. "You belong to me" is the essence of the First Commandment. No wonder Luther loved it; no wonder it was his favorite Old Testament passage. Who would not love it, once he has been helped by Luther to see that though we may truthfully call it the First Commandment and the ultimate Law, it is at the same time the greatest Gospel!

2.

Luther's Principles of Biblical Interpretation

RALPH W. DOERMANN

Of the many fruitful results of the current emphasis on Luther research, one of the most important has been an increased and renewed awareness of the vital role which biblical exegesis played in the Reformation. It has underlined the fact that the point at issue in the watchword *sola scriptura* is not just the authority of the Bible as such, but the interpretation of it.

In another chapter in this volume the relationship between Scripture and Tradition in Luther's writings is examined and discussed. In this essay an attempt will be made to deal with some of Luther's principles of biblical interpretation, and to inquire as to their significance for exegesis in our day.

There is an implicit danger in such an attempt, however, which should be recognized at the outset. Many estimates of Luther's treatment of the Scriptures have already been set forth, often with the result that he has been recast in the theological image of the one who is making the evaluation. He has been pictured both as the prototype of the fundamentalists and as the first scientific biblical critic; as the champion of a later Lutheran orthodoxy and as the breath of fresh air which eventually gave rise to the liberal movement. The reason for this wide spectrum is in part the result of theological bias on the part of the interpreters, but can also be traced in part to Luther himself, for in his writings there is such wide diversity that if one looks long enough and hard enough and is willing to take statements out of context, it is possible to find some

14

support for almost any theological position. Luther considered himself to be primarily a teacher of the Scriptures, especially of the Old Testament, but he is chiefly known as an apologist and reformer. There are numerous scripture references and allusions in his apologetic writings but often we are at a loss to know how much exegetical study or what interpretative principle lies behind them. In his polemical writings he used different emphases as occasion demanded. Against the Roman Catholics, the traditionalists, he emphasized the role of the Holy Spirit in interpreting and making plain the message of a biblical passage. Against the sects, the spiritualists, he placed a premium on limiting interpretation to the literal meaning of the text. Rules for interpretation are set forth in one place and seemingly ignored in another, without any apology at all. It often seems that Luther uses more of an intuitive approach than any set exegetical method.

This continual change of stance is itself a warning against broad generalizations based on any one aspect of his work. But with this warning in mind I propose to make a few observations in three areas: influences in Luther's exegetical development, his concept of the Word of God, and his exegetical principles.

I
INFLUENCES IN LUTHER'S EXEGETICAL DEVELOPMENT

Gerhard Ebeling, in an article entitled "The New Hermeneutics and the Early Luther," [1] has set forth several convincing arguments that the roots of the Reformation can be traced to a hermeneutical revolution—a revolution that began in the classroom at Wittenberg and was already well under way by the time of Luther's so-called "tower experience." Ebeling bases his arguments on an analysis of Luther's early lectures on Psalms delivered in the years 1513-1515. In this analysis he shows that although Luther worked mainly with traditional sources, the glosses and comments of the church fathers, and still used the allegorical method of interpretation, the surprising thing was the way in which he used them. Scholasticism believed that the peak of theological study was to be found in the systematic method, and it used Scripture and the fathers to support the system. Luther, on the other hand, though using the same sources, sought to develop his theological thinking in an exegetical manner. As Jaroslav Pelikan states, ("His exegesis sought to derive the teachings of the Scriptures from the particular statements of the Scriptures rather than from the *a priori* principles of a theological system." [2]

Already at this early stage there is a great deal of emphasis on the Word as *the* way of God's disclosure and on our faith as *the* mode of man's response.

In this exegetical emphasis Luther was not without precedent. Before coming to Wittenberg he had studied at Erfurt, where the influence of William of Occam was particularly strong. Occam had placed a high premium on exegesis and had made the statement that in order to be saved a Christian is not called upon to believe that which was not contained in Scripture or to be derived from the Scripture by inescapable logic. Further, in the interpretation of Scripture, faith is to be placed above reason. From Occam Luther also inherited an aversion to philosophical terminology, preferring the language of the Scriptures themselves. Luther was also fond of quoting Nicolo de Tudeschi, one of the conciliarists who stated that "in matters touching the faith the word of a single private person is to be preferred to that of a pope, if that person is moved by sounder arguments from the Old Testament and the New Testament." As early as 1509 in his *Marginal Notes* on Peter Lombard's *Sentences* Luther dismisses the arguments of several prominent authorities on the grounds that they do not have the Scriptures on their side. [3]

One of the most popular interpretative devices in Luther's time was the fourfold method then in vogue. In this fourfold method the literal or historical sense came first, and though increasing emphasis was placed on it in the years preceding the Reformation, it was still considered by many to be the least important of the four. This was followed by the allegorical or mystical sense in which the literal sense is disregarded and the text is made to refer to the church or to its doctrine. The tropological sense referred to the individual believer's life and conduct, while in the fourth, the anagogical, the text was interpreted eschatologically, in the perspective of the Consummation. Two centuries earlier Nicholas of Lyra had written extensively in favor of the literal and historical interpretation and had pointed out that by the use of the fourfold sense any dogma could be found in any passage, all in the name of exegesis.

Luther at first opposed Lyra, calling him a literalist and a rabbi, but in later years, especially as he began studying Hebrew and Greek, he became much more appreciative of Lyra's insistence upon the primacy of what the text actually said. In this regard Luther was also helped by the French humanist Faber Stapulensis, who had published an edition of the Psalter in which four early Latin translations were printed in parallel columns with the Vulgate. Until this time Luther had considered the Vulgate to be the inspired text, and saw little need for studying the original languages, but when he saw the many discrepancies in translation he began to feel the need to go deeper than the translated text.

Faber had also set forth the view that allegory was superfluous, because all passages of Scripture, in their literal sense, point beyond themselves to Christ. This is so because it is Christ who is actually speaking in the Scriptures.[4] Though Luther was reluctant to give up allegory completely, this "literal-prophetic" method was used by him with increasing frequency in his later lectures on the Psalms. Though to a later generation this still sounds surprisingly like allegory, it should be recognized that at that time it was a major step away from the allegorical method.

Other humanists who were influential in Luther's exegetical development were Reuchlin, with his Hebrew grammar and texts of the Old Testament, and Erasmus, whose Greek text of the New Testament was published in 1516. Luther began to study Hebrew on his own in 1509 and Greek under Melanchthon in 1518. Even though he made full use of the texts and grammatical aids furnished by the humanists, he was not convinced that language study alone could reveal God's truth. Whereas Erasmus stated that a man need only read the Bible "to learn to know that heavenly Word," Luther continued to maintain that no one can understand God's Word apart from the enlightenment of the Holy Spirit.

Luther's reason for this insistence on the role of the Holy Spirit as the interpreter of Scripture stems in part at least from what he refers to as his major exegetical discovery and what others have called his "tower experience."[5] In his study of the first chapter of Romans he was unable to come to terms with the phrase "righteousness of God."

> . . . I pounded shamelessly upon Paul's door because I hungered and thirsted to know the truth which stood behind this text. I labored over it day and night, trying to understand the relationship of the words: "In it the righteousness of God is revealed . . . as it is written, he who through faith is righteous shall live." Then I began to understand,

through God's grace, that by the "righteousness of God" is meant God's gift, through which the righteous live by faith. . . . It seemed to me as though I were newly born, and, through open gates, had entered into paradise itself. The whole scripture came immediately to have a different face. I ran through the Bible, insofar as I could remember the appropriate texts, and found similar thoughts everywhere, e.g., God's work is that which God works in us; God's strength is that by which he makes us strong; the wisdom of God is that with which he makes us wise; God's strength; God's salvation; God's glory.[6]

The force of this insight, and the transformation which it wrought in Luther's own attitude toward the Scriptures, made it impossible for him to distinguish between a "historical" and a "spiritual" exposition of the Bible. For him this was the chief message of the Scriptures; all other passages had to be judged and interpreted in its light.

II

HIS CONCEPT OF THE WORD OF GOD

Having mentioned some of the important influences in the development of Luther's exegesis, we turn now to a brief summary of his understanding of the Word of God, which many interpreters take to be the most important key to his theology and to his approach to the Scriptures.[7]

Luther regarded God as one who reveals himself through his speaking. He would remain completely unknown if he did not deign to speak. The reason that he speaks is that he wants to enter into a relationship with his people and to enable them to hear his word of judgment and grace. Both his power and redeeming love proceed from his speaking, as shown in the creation account in Genesis 1 and in the prologue to the Fourth Gospel. But the cosmic word of creation would remain meaningless and unknowable if it were not for its identification with the Living Word, the incarnate Christ.

The Word is not only to be thought of as a message, it should also be understood in the Hebraic sense of *Dabar*, as "deed" or "concrete event." In the Old Testament the Word comes to Abraham and the prophets as a message from God, but to the people of Israel as a whole it comes as concrete event in the Exodus. The Word, both as message and as event, makes known God's love and calls for acceptance in faith on the part of the people to whom it is addressed.

In the New Testament the same double emphasis is present, only now more clearly than ever. God's Word is both a redemptive act in Christ and the proclamation of this redemption. It is the same Word as that which was spoken in the Old Testament, for it is the redemptive act of the same God, but here in Christ it is the "ultimate Word," God's chief message to man. Because it is the same Word which is spoken in both Testaments, Luther is able to find the entire truth of the Gospel, though veiled, in the Old Testament. Like the New, it is full of Christ and contains the whole wisdom of God, the complete truth of Law and Gospel.[8] "There is no word in the New Testament which does not look back on the Old, where it had already been proclaimed in advance. . . . For the New Testament is nothing more than a revelation of the Old."[9] Luther could even go so far as to say, "If I take the Psalter, Moses and Isaiah into my hands and were to have the Holy Ghost, as the apostles had him, I would be able to write the New Testament."[10] Even Paul's great word in Romans concerning justification through faith is a quotation of Habakkuk—an Old Testament word now interpreted in the New.

There is a basic difference, however, between the Old Testament and the New. In contrast to the Scriptures of the old covenant the Gospel of the new, in its original form, was not a written but a spoken word. "The Gospel is really not a document, but wishes to be a spoken word, which recites the content of scripture just as Christ did not write, but only spoke. He did not call his teaching scripture but Gospel, that is, good news or proclamation. That is why it must not be described with the pen, but with the mouth." "Do not attempt to see Christ with your eyes, but put your eyes in your ears." "The Gospel should not be written, but shouted."[11]

The Gospel is thus not merely a deed in history—it is the living voice which is still heard in the church through preaching, still coming to bring men the offer of salvation in Christ. It is also present in the visible Word, the sacraments, for they too proclaim Christ and the Gospel. In this way, through preaching and sacrament, the deed of God in Christ is continually remembered in the church. This, too, is Word of God—the Gospel in action.

The only reason that the Gospel was written down at all was to preserve it from heresy. False teachers arose in the church and the sheep had to be protected from the wolves. But still the New Testa-

ment exists only to sustain the oral proclamation, which must come
forth ever anew from the written Word. Summing up Luther's
Preface to the New Testament, Kümmel writes:

> . . . Therefore we ought to approach the New Testament with the
> intention of listening to the voice of these men who do not want to
> inform us about a doctrine we already knew beforehand, but who want
> to convey to us a message that we have either not yet altogether heard
> or that ought to be reconfirmed and made more intelligible to us.[12]

From this it becomes apparent that the Scriptures are the Word
of God, but in a derivative sense, for the Word of God is far more
than the Scriptures. Luther sometimes speaks of the Bible as Word
of God but in other instances makes a differentiation between them.
He compares the Bible with the incarnation when he says,

> The Bible is God's word written, presented in letters, as Christ is the
> eternal word, presented in human nature, and just as it is with Christ in
> the world . . . so it is with the written Word of God. It is a worm and
> no book, when compared with other books.[13]

Yet as written Word of God Luther maintained that "The Bible
is the Holy Spirit's own peculiar book, writing and word." [14] "God
is in every syllable." [15] "One should tremble before a letter of the
Bible more than before the whole world." [16] From these and numerous statements the inspiration of Scripture is assumed, but no definition of inspiration is set forth, for the Holy Spirit who speaks
through the words is not limited by the words.

Yet the words which are written are authoritative, for it is through
the Scriptures that the Word is to be read and preached. It is the
Word which creates the church, not the church which disposes of
the Word. For this reason it is not for the church to decide what the
Scripture teaches, but for Scripture to be allowed to reveal what
the proclamation of the church should be. "The Holy Ghost knows
far more than St. Thomas.")

III

HIS EXEGETICAL PRINCIPLES

Luther's view of the Word sets forth his basic exegetical principle: Only that which proclaims Christ (the Word) is primary. Any
interpretation which does not follow this rule is false and must be
discarded. "If our adversaries cite Scripture against Christ, I will
cite Christ against Scripture." [17] Again, anything which contradicts

the teaching of justification through faith is excluded. "If a thousand passages of Scripture are addressed in favor of justification by works . . . I have the author and Lord of Scripture." [18]

It is on this basis that Luther gives an evaluation of the various New Testament books. In the preface of his translation of the New Testament he writes:

> In a word St. John's Gospel and his first epistle, St. Paul, especially Romans, Galatians, and Ephesians, and St. Peter's first epistle are the books that show you Christ and teach you all that is necessary and salvatory for you to know. . . . Therefore, St. James' epistle is really an epistle of straw, compared to these others, for it has nothing of the nature of the Gospel about it.[19]

In the preface to James he goes even further: "Whatever does not teach Christ is not yet apostolic even though St. Peter or St. Paul does the teaching. Again whatever preaches Christ would be apostolic even if Judas, Annas, Pilate and Herod were doing it." [20]

Luther claimed in his preface to the 1522 edition of the New Testament that he could not regard Revelation as apostolic or even as the work of the Holy Spirit, because it was so full of visions and images, and because in it Christ was neither taught nor known. Jude he questioned because he said it was derived from Second Peter. Hebrews is of doubtful authenticity because it denied a second repentance and therefore was in direct opposition to Paul. Yet he placed major emphasis on other passages of Hebrews in support of his argument for the "once for all sacrifice" of Christ. He did not eliminate any of these questionable books from the canon, as he did the Old Testament Apocrypha, but placed them all at the end of his German New Testament.

Luther employed a similar scale of values for the books of the Old Testament. Genesis was to be prized because it told how Abraham was saved by faith; the Psalms because Christ speaks in them; but Esther was worthless because there was no Gospel present at all.

Even in his translation of the Old Testament text Luther insisted that where more than one translation is possible, the one which agrees with the New Testament must be preferred. This was one of the prerequisites for proper Old Testament study. "I urge anyone who would learn Hebrew that he, before all else, should thoroughly study the New Testament and accept Christ as sun, light, and guide." [21]

But as long as the authority of Christ is maintained, critical questions can be raised freely. Thus Luther could state both that the text of the prophets was very corrupt and that they themselves were often in error; that the Book of Ecclesiastes was not written by Solomon; and that the Synoptic Gospels were not of uniform value. When Carlstadt questioned Moses' authorship of the last chapters of Deuteronomy, Luther agreed that he was probably right, but that it really didn't make too much difference. He also was of the opinion that many of the laws in the Pentateuch were much earlier than Moses.

In the treatment of individual passages Luther insisted that where points of doctrine were at stake only the literal meaning of the text, in its original context, could be used. By "original" he meant "original intent," and not just one of many grammatical possibilities. And the "original intent" was always to be derived from the message of the Gospel. There were only three possible reasons for departing from this rule: the statement of the text itself that it was to be taken figuratively; a strong indication to the same effect in another passage of Scripture; or the clash between a literal interpretation and a "clear article of faith." [22] In the controversy with Zwingli over the words "this is my body" Luther applies this rule. Nowhere is it stated that the text should not be taken literally, and there are no other scripture passages which would suggest a figurative interpretation; therefore the literal meaning must stand. Even the argument that this was contrary to a "clear article of faith," the ascension, was not convincing to Luther, and he argued at length that there was no conflict between the ascension, with Christ sitting at the right hand of God, and the doctrine of the real presence, with Christ present in the bread and wine.

But where specific points of doctrine are not involved, allegory may be used for "illustrative purposes," though it should otherwise be avoided. In his *Lectures on Genesis* he states: "The bare allegories, which stand in no relation to the account and do not illuminate it, should simply be disapproved as empty dreams. This is the kind which Origen and those who followed him employ." [23] Elsewhere he describes allegory as "monkey tricks." Yet in these same lectures Luther uses a kind of typological interpretation that comes perilously close to allegory. One of the exegetical principles that he follows consistently here is to identify the conflicts in Genesis as representative of the continuing conflict between the true and the false church. The conflicts between Cain and Abel, Ishmael and Isaac, Esau and Jacob, are but the early stages of the struggle between the church of God and the church of the devil. Esau was a bishop, a king, and a pope in his church, and he used his power to persecute Jacob, the true church. Here, as always, the true church is the one that is persecuted and oppressed.[24] This cannot really be called allegory, for the original historical sense of the passages is nowhere denied, but the danger is still present, in that the original meaning can so easily get lost in the shuffle.

Luther himself sets forth as another of his principles that the context and the historical circumstances should always be taken into consideration. In his Preface to the Book of Isaiah he urges his readers to familiarize themselves first with Kings and Chronicles, "For if one would understand the prophecies, it is necessary that one know how things were in the land, how matters lay, and what was in the minds of the people." [25] The integrity and intent of the author should always be respected, particularly when passages are quoted. ". . . the Scriptures quoted should really refer to the point at issue. I know now that it is not enough to take many passages together helter-skelter, whether they are fit or not. If this is to be the way, then I can easily prove from the Scriptures that beer is better than wine." [26] This insistence on the "historical sense," however, did not preclude interpreting a passage Christologically, for Christ is always and everywhere the total message of God.

In most of his interpretation Luther proceeds on the assumption that Scripture is clear and easy to understand. All of his translations were made in the conviction that the individual can understand as he reads, and that God's truth can become plain to a miller's daughter, or to a child of nine, if he has faith. So strongly did he feel this that he states that there would really be no need for his prefaces to the biblical books, were it not for the fact that so many false interpretations had been set forth by those who did not understand the central meaning of the Word.

Wherever there are difficulties with obscure passages—and these are bound to occur because of ignorance of words and grammar—they should be interpreted in the light of other clear passages, for *Scripture is its own best interpreter.*

Be assured beyond every doubt that there is nothing more clear than the sun, that is the scriptures. Even if a cloud passes in front of it, there is still waiting behind the cloud this same bright sun. . . . So if you cannot understand the dark passage, hold more firmly to the one that is clear.[27]

But in order for the Scriptures to come to life they must be understood in faith. Luther often repeated the axiom that the meaning of the Scriptures had to be experienced "in the heart" before they could be correctly understood. Apart from faith and the work of the Holy Spirit the words remain mere words—they do not become a message from God. A Turk can read John 3:16 and understand it perfectly, but for him it is not and cannot be the Word of God until the Holy Spirit enables him to hear the passage addressed to him personally. The same is true for the Christian. He has within himself no criterion by which he can determine what is and what is not God's Word. "He can only wait to see if God addresses him by it, if God makes it to be for him a two-edged sword which penetrates to his very heart. Luther thus distinguishes between God's Word as such and God's Word 'for me.' " [28] No one can predict when the Word will speak and no one can do anything but wait expectantly for it. But then, writes Luther, ". . . the Spirit writes within the heart the Word that is preached to us. Those who hear it are given an inner flame, so that their hearts say, 'This is true even if I should have to suffer death a hundred times for it.' " [29]

Underlying all of these exegetical principles there shines forth a profound love and respect for the Scriptures, their authority, and their life-giving power. They are the living voice of God through his church to the world, and nothing dare be allowed to prevent them from speaking clearly. In his attempt to let this voice sound forth Luther could, as occasion demanded, place the whole weight of Scripture on a single word or dismiss whole books as irrelevant. He could demand absolute grammatical accuracy in one instance and dismiss linguistic problems as "rabbi-talk" in another.

Interpreters today can look back and criticize him for making the entire Bible dependent on the interpretation of a single verse in Romans, or for his excessive use of allegory, or for failing to differentiate between "exegesis" and "hermeneutics." But for Luther there was no such thing as an objective treatment of a text. His theological presuppositions were so much a part of him that they are present everywhere, and they determine both the form and the direction of his exegesis.

While recognizing all this we still must ask what Luther has to say to us, the would-be exegetes of the 20th century. Is it possible to separate method from the spirit of the man? Or can we systematize that which defies all of our systems? If this is what we are looking for, perhaps we should turn to some of his successors, who made rules aplenty but lost many of his insights.

Certainly he can give us some directions. One of these is the way in which he manages to stress both the importance of the scriptural text and the duty of the exegete to examine it critically. Emil Brunner states that Luther was the first major theologian to represent a biblical faith which could be combined with biblical criticism.[30] Kurt Aland adds that Luther has demonstrated that critical consideration of scriptural externals, of the earthen vessels in which we have the Gospel treasure, has nothing to do with belief or unbelief.[31] He goes on then to say that it is precisely the importance of the message that demands the critical work of scholarship, making it an essential part of exegesis.

Brian Gerrish suggests that perhaps it would be possible to retain Luther's Christocentric understanding of scriptural authority and to discard the remains of medievalism that still cling to his thinking.[32]

And here, I believe, is the vital point. It cannot be denied that Luther used whatever methods were necessary to find Christ behind every bush and beneath every stone. But he did this because he had first heard the living voice addressing him. Regardless of method Luther continually pointed beyond himself to the Living Word who speaks when and where he will through the Scriptures. And as he invited the men of his day so he would invite us to *listen*—rather than trying to tell the Scriptures what they have to say.

3.

Scripture and Tradition, in Luther and in Our Day

THEODORE S. LIEFELD

In some four centuries of Reformation observance Protestant churchmen have celebrated a long list of principles and values growing out of the sixteenth century movement associated with Martin Luther and the other Protestant reformers. From one generation to another the spotlight has highlighted different ideas, as the problems of society and the concerns of the church have shifted. But over all these centuries a consistent prominence has been given to the so-called "solas" of the Reformation: *sola gratia, sola fide,* and *sola Scriptura.* This essay is concerned with certain aspects of the third of these, which is commonly labeled the formal principle of the Reformation: *Sola Scriptura*—by the Scriptures alone.

I
Luther and Scripture

Several reasons call for some sort of reexamination. One is the ambiguity, or variation in meaning, we seem to encounter in Luther on the scriptural principle, depending on whether he is debating with Roman Catholic opponents at Worms, or with other Protestants at Marburg. Another reason is the stereotyping and distorting which in time took place in Protestantism, so that what for Luther was a living expression of faith-attitude and interpretive procedure became frozen for some into a confessional object of veneration or lip-service. A third reason for some rethinking in this area is that in the ecumenical developments of our day—especially as this increas-

26

ingly involves both Roman Catholics and Orthodox—it is crucial that Lutherans (and Protestants generally) rediscover their confessional posture on *sola Scriptura*—particularly as this relates to Tradition.

Father Paul Verghese, of the Syrian Orthodox Church of India, has written an article for the *McCormick Quarterly* on the topic "Authority in the Church." He concludes:

> The churches of the Reformation could, by moving closer to the Reformers, come closer to the authentic tradition of the Church. If the 450th anniversary of the Reformation can lead to the understanding of the Reformers themselves as searching for the authentic tradition in the community of the Universal Church, then the Protestant-Orthodox-Catholic dialogue can help us forward to the true uniting Reformation.[1]

"Scripture and Tradition, in Luther and in our day" is a title that risks promising much more than a single chapter can deliver. More modestly, I limit this inspection to particular aspects of the Scripture-Tradition problem which call for historical reexamination and fresh reflection today.

Many of the mistaken notions (or half-truths) which have developed concerning Luther's role in the sixteenth century have resulted from oversimplifying the picture of his day, with the result that some facts get concealed. This applies particularly to the question of Scripture and Tradition.

For example, Luther is sometimes credited with starting a "back to the Bible" movement. It is not likely that he himself saw it that way. For one thing, he was quite aware that others before him over a number of centuries—men like Roger Bacon and John Wyclif—had issued the *sola Scriptura* call. This was not new to him or his contemporaries; he did not "invent" it. Furthermore, there were many in the church of his day who subscribed to the declaration of Occam, that "what is not contained in the Scriptures, or cannot with necessary and obvious consistency be deduced from the contents of the same, no Christian needs to believe." [2] In fact, this was the view which marked Luther's own theological training in the cloister at Erfurt.

Father Yves Congar, a French Dominican priest and one of the most influential Roman Catholic theologians of our time, is particularly respected for his extensive research and balanced appraisal of the factors that shaped the developments of the sixteenth century. In his volume *Tradition and Traditions* Father Congar builds an impressive case for the idea that not only the early fathers, but also the medieval theologians, recognized the sufficiency of the Scriptures.[3] Specifically in Thomas Aquinas he finds Scripture as the "rule of faith, to which nothing can be added, from which nothing can be deleted." [4] And he points out that Luther "was very strongly convinced, as a result of his teaching, of the absolute primacy of Scripture over all other authority, and in that he was completely Catholic." [5]

I believe we have no serious quarrel with Congar, or Rome, at this point. As a trainee of the church, Luther already had the Bible, and as a faithful churchman, in common with many others of his day, he already recognized its authority. Well, then, what made the difference? What "set him off" on a reformatory program?

A number of factors could be cited. But from the particular point of concern here, two things must be noted. First—Luther's discovery of the Gospel, and thereafter his application to the reading of all Scripture of the Gospel principle: *was Christum treibt* (that which is directed to or speaks of Christ). In other words, his major achievement was not the recovery of the Bible, but of the Bible as the bearer of the Gospel. In the words of Jaroslav Pelikan, "The church did not need a Luther to tell it that the Bible was true. But it did need a Luther to tell it what the truth of the Bible is." [6] Second— Luther's growing conviction, contrary to the position of Rome in his day, that the teaching of the church and the teaching of Scripture are not necessarily or inevitably the same. These two insights must be further examined in order to understand the Scripture-Tradition problem as it developed for Luther, and as it confronts us today.

May we remind ourselves of a few basic things which should already be familiar to us? Protestants and Catholics alike, whether in the 16th or the 20th century, have agreed that Luther's theology was a theology of the Holy Scriptures. And almost all of his interpreters recognize the primacy in his thought of the Word of God. But far fewer understand that while Scripture and Word were inseparable for Luther, they were not always interchangeable or synonymous in his thinking.

He understood the Word of God as the speech of God—his active, historical speaking to man. Both his creating power and his redeeming love proceeded from him through his speaking. In his "Commentary on Psalm 90" Luther writes:

Everything was created and is preserved through the Word. Moses employs such language in order to give prominence to the greatness of the Person who with one word destroys and establishes all things. What appears to be more meaningless than a word? And yet when God speaks a word, the thing expressed by the word immediately leaps into existence.[7]

In the words of Jaroslav Pelikan, "Luther contended that whatever God might be in and of Himself apart from the created world, in the creation He had put relations between Himself and the world upon the foundation of the Word of God." [8]

In other words, Luther's conception of the Word was not mainly in the categories of existence and being, but of act and deed. The Word, historically, was the concrete action of God; all his acts in human history were his words, designed to fulfill his purposes of redemption and revelation. And both of these Word-deed purposes find expression as Gospel in the Old Testament, as well as in the New. The word of the exodus in the Old Testament was a redemptive act of God; but it was also the anticipation of the exodus of God's ultimate redemptive deed in Jesus Christ. So the Word which was in Christ unites the Testaments—anticipated in God's redemptive acts in the Old, and realized in the historical Jesus in the New. And in the whole of the New Testament record of this life, Luther heard the Word, through both Jesus' words and his deeds. But God's clearest action-speaking was through the crucifixion and the resurrection, which together accomplished and revealed the redemption of mankind.

All of this is basic and familiar to us. But it is equally important to recall that for Luther this Word-act of God in the person of Jesus Christ did not stop with that moment in history. In its being remembered and recited by his community of followers, it continued as the same active Word. And when the Word of God was spoken in the church of later centuries it was not another Word but the same Word in Christ that was spoken in the first century. So God's identical Word continued to communicate redemption from generation to generation, through his redeemed and redemptive community; it began already before there were New Testament documents, or a canon, and it continues to the end of time.

Here, by the way, is a significant point at which the Church of Rome, both in the 16th century and ever since (and including

Father Congar), seems to lose its way in Luther and make false
accusations. Luther many times had occasion to declare, as in his
tract *On the Abuse of the Mass,* "The Church does not make [or
create] the Word, but [the Church] is made by the Word." [9] On the
assumption that Scripture can be equated with Word as here used,
Congar asks: "Can this polemical form, in which the Church is
derived from Scripture, be maintained despite the fact that the
Church existed prior to *all* the writings of the New Testament and
[prior] to the drawing up of the canon of these writings, which itself
was the work of the Church?" [10] Quite obviously, biblical and later
church history give the answer, and it is negative. But Luther did
not say that the church was created by written words of the New
Testament Scripture, but by the Word in Christ, the redeeming
Gospel. In such context he himself objected to this biblical identifying of "Word" with the text of Scripture.

What I have been saying is a reminder that Luther gave large
and important place, in the continuing life of the church, to the
Word of preaching—the oral Word. In his characteristic way he declared in the *Church Postil* of 1522, "The church is not a pen-house
but a mouth-house." [11] And preaching meant, not recitation of Scripture, but its exposition and proclamation in such a way that the Gospel might be heard, and understood, and appropriated. So we find
that while Luther minimizes the importance of the clerical priesthood, at the same time he exalts the ministry of the Word. It was not
just because preaching in his day was so bad, but because in his
view of the life-giving Word preaching was so important, that Luther gave so much of himself to providing exegetical resources for
the church. This, the proclamation of God's Word in Law and Gospel, was the primary responsibility of the church.

But for Luther no proclamation could claim to be the "Word of
God" unless it soundly presented the deeds which were the "Word
of God." And the only reliable and authoritative record of such
deeds was the Bible. Therefore for him Word always depends on
Scripture, and in a derivative sense the Scriptures *are* the Word of
God.

Without the written Word, the church's proclamation has nothing
to sustain it, nothing to maintain its vitality. Furthermore, it is only
by the written Word that the spoken Word can be preserved from
error. Yet Luther was enough of a historian to realize that virtually

every major heresy that had afflicted Christendom had supported itself by appeal to Scripture. Recognition and use of the Bible, and even claim to the "Word of God" did not guarantee soundness and purity.

II
LUTHER AND TRADITION

What did? The Roman Church found the answer in the church, the hierarchy—the Tradition. Where did Luther stand? Was his scriptural position radically anti-Tradition?

In an over-all evaluation, the only justified answer seems to be "No." But in arriving at that, one encounters on the way so many partial "yeses," as well as "noes," that there is no avoiding here one of the major paradoxes in Luther and the Lutheran Reformation.

For example, in his 1519 debate with John Eck at Leipzig, he plainly declared that he was setting the authority of the Scriptures against and above the authority of the Tradition of the church. The Scriptures, he insisted, and not the church fathers, should decide a theological controversy. And on the interpretation of "rock" in the Matthew 16:18 passage he said that even "though Augustine and all the fathers were to take the 'rock' to mean Peter, I should withstand them all alone by the authority of the Apostle, that is, by divine right, as he writes (1 Cor. 3:11): 'No other foundation can anyone lay than that which is laid, which is Jesus Christ.' " [12]

But it is not many years later that we find him defending the Tradition of the church against those who, in the name of Scripture as they read it, wanted to set aside the liturgical and other forms developed in the church's Tradition. In his 1528 controversy with fellow reformers over the Lord's Supper we hear him defending the medieval church and his interpretation of the church fathers against Carlstadt and Zwingli.[13]

We encounter a great deal more of the same (ambivalence?) in Luther. Recall how he challenged his opponents to show him one church father who had not erred. And if there was none without error, then the Tradition of the fathers did not belong on the same level as the teaching of the Scriptures.[14] But in another context he pays them this tribute: "The beloved fathers wanted to lead us into Scripture with their writings, but we use them to lead ourselves out of it." [15] Luther's own exegetical writings frequently cite early fathers of the church, and especially Augustine, in support of his interpretation of passages of Scripture. In regard to church councils, he repeatedly calls attention to their fallibility, and to the mischief that sometimes resulted from their decisions. Yet he defends the first four ecumenical councils (Nicaea, Constantinople, Ephesus, and Chalcedon), all on the same ground that they were primarily concerned, not with introducing something new, but with clarifying and preserving an ancient article of faith, grounded in Scripture, against some threatening heresy. With regard to the church, Luther vehemently opposed every evidence of institutionalizing and claiming of absolute authority; yet in the *Large Catechism* he called the church his mother, the source of his spiritual life, "outside of which there is no forgiveness," [16] and "apart from which no one can come to the Lord Christ." [17]

III
WHAT IS TRADITION?

Church fathers, church councils, the church exercising authority through its episcopacy—all of these are active agents and institutional elements in the development of Tradition. But what is "Tradition" itself? The term is elusive and flexible. When we consult a responsible spokesman for the Roman Church, like Father Congar, we find that throughout some 500 pages he is constantly introducing new facets of meaning. But he offers a fairly definitive statement in the following:

> *Tradition:* this presents three—or even four—aspects or meanings:
> (i) The transmission of the whole Gospel, that is, the whole Christian mystery, in any form: Scripture, the [spoken] word, confessions of faith, sacraments and acts of worship, customs and prescriptions—all these together with the reality which they convey or produce. This transmission may further be taken either in its objective sense as the content transmitted; or as the act of transmitting.
> (ii) In the content thus transmitted, which is the truth of the Christian mystery or of the covenant in Jesus Christ, we may distinguish between things as such (Scripture, sacraments, and institutions; but especially Scripture) and their interpretation or meaning. In this sense Tradition is the interpretation or meaning given to realities transmitted within the group to which they have been committed, a community living and sharing them.[18]

Father Congar later adds a distinction always recognized by Catholicism, which became quite crucial for Martin Luther—the distinction between apostolic and ecclesiastical tradition. "Apostolic tradition is the tradition that has the apostles as its transmitting subjects." [19] It finds its principal expression in the apostolic writings—the canonical Scriptures—but it includes also an "oral" apostolic tradition, passed on independently of texts or otherwise than in writing (presumed to deal with teaching, rules of conduct and discipline, matters of worship, organization, etc.).

And the second, ecclesiastical or ecclesial tradition, "is that which has the Church in its historical life as its originating subject." [20] Congar adds, " 'Originating subject' is important." And certainly I must add that for Luther and the Protestant reformers this was one of the most objectionable features of medieval traditionalism: the church's claimed authority for initiating or innovating teaching and practice without clear warrant in Scripture, and even contrary to the Gospel.

Right at that point Father Congar provided considerable illumination in his historical tracing of developments, especially in the Middle Ages. He declares that the men of the Middle Ages generally held that Scripture contained all the truths of faith necessary for salvation. But he adds that "everyone knew, and stated quite happily, that many things . . . were held and observed by the Church which were not to be found [explicitly] in Scripture." [21] And for some point of Catholic doctrine whose formula could not be found in Scripture, "there was no hesitation in calling on an oral tradition." [22] On the other hand, he acknowledged that "Medieval writers had no difficulty in finding everything in Scripture, since their principles of exegesis provided them with the necessary means" [23] (that is, allegory).

> It is a fact that the prestige of "Holy Church," the affirmation of her power and privileges, have never been as strong as they were in the fourteenth and fifteenth centuries. . . . The Church, guided by the Holy Spirit, could not be deceived in what related directly to salvation. Vigorous in their religious convictions, their attention was focused on the indefectibility of faith as a subjective virtue, an indefectibility which had been promised and which remained permanently guaranteed to the Church. They were convinced that the Church could not be mistaken, animated as she was by the Holy Spirit continuously at work in her, to make known to her the truth. So that what she approved would carry the same force as sacred Scripture or the creed.[24]

Congar also acknowledges that for the Reformers, such a self-assured position on the part of the church was tantamount to attributing to men an infallibility and authority which should be reserved to God.

It is interesting to observe that Catholics and Lutherans alike commonly seek to clarify the matter of Tradition by quoting Martin Chemnitz, the orthodox interpreter of Luther. In his *Examen*, written in reaction to the Council of Trent, about twenty years after Luther's death, Chemnitz lists seven senses of the word tradition, or types of tradition, which he broadly allows as scriptural, or in conformity with Scripture, but which the Roman Church has been confusing. In condensed form these are:

1. The message of Christ and the apostles, in original living voice form.
2. The books of sacred Scripture, as transmitted by the Church.
3. The articles of faith expressed in the apostolic creed.
4. The legitimate and proper interpretation of the text of Scripture (i.e., the apostolic exegesis).
5. Dogmas not explicitly formulated in Scripture, but clearly drawn from Scripture (as the doctrine of the Trinity).
6. The catholic consensus of the fathers.
7. Ancient rites that are ascribed to the apostles.

With these seven aspects of tradition Chemnitz finds in Luther no major quarrel. But in the light of Trent's formulation, he adds an eighth sense of tradition, as an item of radical opposition:

8. Attributing to unwritten traditions (pertaining to both faith and morals) a right to the same reverence and piety as sacred Scripture itself.[25]

In the words of Father Congar, this for the Reformers meant making "tradition a formal principle different from Scripture, if not autonomous." And a little later he provides an even more sympathetic interpretation by stating:

The Reformers were doubtless victims of the bad formulation of the question prevalent in the fourteenth and fifteenth centuries, itself the fruit of excessive exaggeration of ecclesiastical machinery and especially of papal authority. Many thought, or at least expressed themselves in such a way as to give the impression, that "the Church," in practice the pope, gave Scripture its "authority" by approving it and declaring it canonical.[26]

Perhaps these things will clarify for us much of the distinction that prevailed in Luther's mind, and the protest that resulted. He opposed, not Tradition itself (certainly not in many of its ancient forms), but the *abuse* of Tradition—especially some of the late medieval perversions, such as are cited in the Augsburg Confession: "human traditions, instituted to placate God, to merit grace, and to make satisfaction for sins." [27] He saw the Tradition of the church featuring moralism, with unbiblical stress on asceticism and celibacy, and the interpretation of Scripture increasingly perverted by Aristotelian philosophy. He was convinced that the church which had the Scripture was less and less obedient, subservient to it. Episcopacy was making itself the arbiter. In effect, the church was sitting in judgment on the Scripture, rather than always being judged by it. The answer to all this was *Sola Scriptura*—primary recourse to the Scriptures, as source and norm for all matters of faith and life, and authoritative standard for all forms of tradition. But Tradition itself he did not reject, rather maintaining toward it a critical reverence. Luther took history and the church seriously. The continuing work of the Holy Spirit—the development of the church, the canon of the New Testament, the ancient creeds—these and other expressions of the Tradition he recognized and treasured. In that connection, it is significant to note that in his Smalcald Articles, when he contends against "human traditions," he supports his case with testimony from both the ancient church councils and a half-dozen or more of the early fathers (Origen, Cyprian, Chrysostom, and especially Augustine)—all of whom are also part of the Tradition in the broad sense.

Many within Protestantism have great difficulty understanding the Scripture-Tradition controversy of Luther in its sixteenth-century terms. In fact, in many quarters it no longer exists in the form it assumed at the time of the Reformation. Subsequent history has had a lot to do with that, and for many Lutherans seventeenth-century orthodoxy gets in the way. It is not being unsympathetic to observe that in its eagerness to defend Lutheran doctrine, orthodoxy reverted to the medieval scholastic method and largely obscured Luther's central insights concerning the living Word and the core of the Gospel in Christ, freezing them into a rational system. Ironically, some Lutherans in that day even described Aristotle's logic as "God's own logic"—no doubt causing Father Luther to turn over in his grave! [28]

Some of their lineal descendants are still quite vocal. On the one hand, they approach the Bible as a collection of truths, laws, prin-

ciples, rather than a channel of God's speaking to us in Christ. On
the other, they use favorite phrases from confessional statements
to determine what the Scriptures say, rather than letting the whole
Scripture sit in judgment on man's formulations.

IV
TODAY'S PROBLEMS

But we are living in a time when we must acknowledge our own
traditionalism and come to terms with the Scripture-Tradition issue
in a way that essentially reflects Martin Luther himself. I believe
it is the working of God's Spirit that this is being pressed on us by
present ecumenical developments.

We may arbitrarily select two items, of the many (almost daily)
ecumenical developments, as aids toward re–finding ourselves on
this matter. One comes out of Roman Catholicism—specifically the
Dogmatic Constitution on Divine Revelation, promulgated by the
fourth session of Vatican II (November 1965).[29] It is most interesting to note that in four years of consideration and revision, this
document underwent a complete overhauling in both approach and
language. The first draft was philosophical in language and began
with "Two Sources of Revelation" (Scripture and Tradition), thus
perpetuating the medieval competition between authorities. It was
so severely criticized by the Council that it not only was sent back
to committee but placed in the hands of a new commission for
recasting. What finally was adopted is more biblical and historical
in language and emphasis, and affirms not two sources of revelation,
but only one, namely God, who reveals himself and his purposes.
Four of its six chapters expressly deal with Sacred Scripture.

The *Dogmatic Constitution* is by no means a Protestant statement. It leaves many crucial questions unresolved, and cites "the
Scriptures together with sacred tradition as the supreme rule of
faith." [30] But at least it seems to offer much clearer possibility of
Rome's recognizing the testimony of canonical Scripture as the
judge and arbiter of the teaching and practice of the church.

At that point the clearest reassurance comes from the first inter-
national Lutheran–Roman Catholic dialogue, held in November
1967 in Zurich, Switzerland, on the subject "The Gospel and the
Church." The joint statement issued from this meeting declares

agreement "that the Word of God is supreme and that the authority of the Church stands in its service." [31]

The other trend with which we must reckon comes out of the ecumenical Faith and Order movement, both on a world and on a more regional, interdenominational level. At the 1963 Faith and Order Conference (Montreal) a study report was presented, revised, and adopted on "Scripture, Tradition, and traditions (small t)," which seeks not so much to distinguish between these terms, as to relate and associate them. On the basis of the New Testament study and early church usage (i.e., *paradosis,* tradition), it declares that "We exist as Christians by the Tradition (capital T) of the Gospel." [32] In the dynamic sense here used (that of transmission), there is no problem, either, with reference to the essential Gospel message in the oral tradition period, or even its communication to us today. But the term was altogether too appealing to some, as an escape from the Scripture-Tradition bind, and was expanded to the point where *sola Scriptura* was almost forgotten. In fact, one enthusiastic subsection at Montreal even proposed a new formula for our day: "sola Traditione." The plenary floor reaction was loud and negative; and the proposal was quickly and overwhelmingly thrown out. But since then some of the same churchmen seem to be getting used to the substitute idea.

In our own country the Consultation on Church Union (commonly known as "COCU") now involves nine major Protestant communions which together are investigating the possibilities of denominational merger. Many studies have been produced as bases for theological discussion. One of these is known as the Oberlin Report on "Scripture, Tradition, and the Guardians of Tradition." In its pattern of approach, and use of language, it is clearly related to the Faith and Order report referred to above. The term "Tradition" is used almost wholly in a functional way, with no clear distinction between Tradition and Scripture, or between act and content. Here it would appear that what is potentially the largest segment of American Protestantism is threatening to abandon *sola Scriptura*—at least as a reformed and evangelical formula. "Tradition," says the Oberlin Report, "is the whole life of the Church."

I believe there is ground for uneasiness about this reformulation. It seems to embody Scripture so completely in a contemporary process as to minimize the uniqueness of the historic biblical witness, and the real authority of the canonical Scriptures, both as source and norm for Christian faith and life.

V
CONCLUSIONS

Finally, what does all the foregoing say to us?

1. *Sola Scriptura*—when it is used as a prescription, or an argument, for deliberately ignoring all the insights of previous centuries —is not authentically Lutheran, for it repudiates the church and denies the ongoing working of the Spirit.

2. *Sola Scriptura*—even when used as a description of our Lutheran position—can be unrealistic. In fact, it may not even be honest if it claims that each of us listens to the witness of Scripture totally divorced from our own conditioning, from one another, from the church and its history and confessional consensus. It is no more possible for us than it was for Luther to get out of our historical skins (and those skins have been a long time developing!). Oscar Cullmann observes that "we have begun to break away from that strange conception of Church history and Christian thought which supposed that between the second and the sixteenth centuries there was, with the exception of certain sects, a complete eclipse of the gospel." [33] The past thirty years of Luther research, and now a great deal of Protestant study of the church fathers, are eliminating many blind spots.

A Lutheran like Ernst Kinder can accept the idea that "Tradition (in its best sense) is the unfailing life of Scripture in the Church under the Spirit's influence. Tradition is the Church's life of listening to the Holy Spirit repeating the Word of God ever anew." [34] I take this to say that the church of *sola Scriptura* does not actually live by the words of Scripture alone—for the church inevitably reads Scripture within a total, ongoing tradition. In this sense, may we need to recognize the realism of Dr. Albert Outler's phrase *Scriptura numquam sola* (Scripture is never alone)?

3. But finally, this neither eliminates nor makes obsolete the formal principle of the Reformation—either for Luther or for us today. Rather, it underlines all the more the need to let the Word of Scripture sit in judgment on all that we think and say and do—so that the Lord of the church and his Spirit may be sovereign in us, and speak clearly to and through us. So we reaffirm "*sola Scriptura.*"

Part Two

Luther and His Interpreters

4.

The Changing Catholic
View of Luther

FRED W. MEUSER

A profound restudy of Martin Luther is under way in modern Catholicism in spite of the fact that its official excommunication of him in 1520 still stands. Some Catholics and Protestants have suggested that canonization of Luther might be the quickest way to undo the great schism of the sixteenth century, or at least to make rapid strides toward Protestant-Catholic reunion.[1] Although few Catholics actually favor such a step or see any possibility of it, a great many Catholic writers speak of him in terms very different from those of just a few years ago.

The traditional attitude to Luther has by no means disappeared; in fact, in some segments of Catholicism it has not even been tempered. For too long Luther was belabored as a demon to be exorcised from the body of the church for any modified spirit to gain a quick hearing. The destructive attack that simply damned Luther on the basis of the inherited prejudices has not disappeared from seminary instruction, parochial schools, or tract literature, any more than has the adulatory naiveté of some followers of Luther. But change is definitely in the wind. A few examples of the old attitude may be in order as background for the changing spirit.

I
A Demon to Be Exorcised

A great deal of the portrayal of Luther as a "demon" has relied heavily on John of Wendelstein, better known as Cochlaeus, a contemporary of Luther. This priest, who had at first been rather sympathetic to Luther, soon turned against him and wrote the first Catholic biography of Luther[2] for the express purpose of setting straight anyone who might be tempted to believe that Luther was a virtuous man. He refers to Luther as a child of the devil, the fruit of a union of Satan with Luther's mother who later regretted not having murdered him in the cradle. His fellow monks knew him as a demon-possessed quarreler who lusted after drink and sex, without conscience, ready to use any means to further his own plans. Demonic monstrosities boiled out of his powerful but perverted mind. At Luther's death, this "father" appears to drag him off to hell. Although recent Catholic scholarship has shown Cochlaeus to be terribly prejudiced and unreliable, most Catholic writers into the twentieth century relied heavily on him. His charges, "sources," and characterizations were reprinted, circulated, and accepted in much of Catholicism.

In the next generation John Pistorius the Younger, a convert from Lutheranism to Catholicism via Calvinism, continued the polemical attack with even greater zeal.[3] Having read through the works of Luther three times, he prepared a list of quotations from Luther to prove that their author was possessed of a host of evil spirits— the sensuous, blasphemous, slovenly, erroneous, insolent, proud, fraudulent, and traitorous. His portrayal of this "hellish person" also nourished controversial Roman Catholic literature for several centuries.[4] Pistorius' use of Luther quotes is a perfect example of what can happen when one reads the works of an opponent for the sole purpose of gathering polemical ammunition. It is bald polemic masquerading as history.

In the late 19th and early 20th centuries, the works of three very capable historians fanned the Catholic revulsion of Luther, and thereby stimulated more capable Protestant Luther research. Johannes Janssen, historian at Frankfurt, made out an impressive case for the claim that Luther and his followers choked off a rich and promising flowering of church life, art, and science that had been developing for several centuries. Dazzling in his use of medieval literature, objective in tone, Janssen gave documentary "proof" for all his claims.[5] His influence can be surmised from the fact that the volumes dealing with the Reformation went through twenty editions and were to be found in the library of almost every rectory.[6] They were received with great enthusiasm in Catholicism and along with other historical stimuli of the late 19th century caused many Protestants to reconsider their own evaluation of the Reformation.[7] The most important sign of the new interest of Protestants was the effort to publish a critical edition of Luther's works, the now-famous Weimar Edition, whose first volume appeared in 1883.

Even more important than Janssen's work was Heinrich Denifle's *Luther und Luthertum.*[8] A very capable medieval scholar, Denifle pursued the question of Luther's relationship to medieval theology, especially to Thomas Aquinas. His conclusion: the Reformation was based at least in part on Luther's woeful ignorance of classical Roman theology. As for the causes of Luther's reformatory views, Denifle found them in what he called Luther's unbridled sensuality, his uncontrollable lust, thirst, and appetite. Justification by faith then became the cover-up for his own sins. The composite picture of Luther is that of a glutton, a forger, a liar, a blasphemer, a drunk; a vicious, proud, unprincipled, syphilitic man whose communion with God ceased entirely before his death, which may have been self-inflicted. Denifle's greatest positive effect was the stimulus he gave to deeper study of how and why the young Luther became the reformer, especially by Protestants like Otto Scheel and Karl Holl. Within a few years Denifle's angry, two-fisted attack was followed by a calm, but even more devastating, psychological repudiation from the pen of a Jesuit professor, Hartmann Grisar. His huge, three-volume work [9] presents Luther as a man who was physically, mentally, and spiritually ill, a psychopath who should have been hospitalized. Grisar invites the reader to pity Luther, but his own malice shows through very clearly.[10] Luther is a wholly impure, deeply immoral individual. As in Denifle, the doctrine of justification is an excuse for sinful living. The shock of the thunderstorm accentuated deep basic maladjustments in Luther's personality. He entered the monastery as a neurotic and ended up a pitiable psychopath. In a 1926 one-volume summary of *Luther* Grisar thought he foresaw the time when no one would take Luther seriously.[11]

A much more popular treatment of Luther, and perhaps a more influential one with non-scholars, at least in the English-speaking world, was Patrick O'Hare's *The Facts About Martin Luther.*[12] Published in the 400th anniversary year of the Ninety-five Theses, it claimed to show by extensive quotation of the sources what kind of man Luther really was. O'Hare makes no effort to understand Luther. Instead he heaps up quotation upon quotation from Luther to prove that he was an absolutely immoral, mentally and spiritually deranged man. All of Luther's weaknesses and misjudgments (such as the case of the bigamy of Philip) are paraded in a spirit of angry outrage. "The cesspool," he says, "seems to have been the garden that furnished his choicest flowers of rhetoric."[13] Martin and Katie are the Adam and Eve of a new gospel of concubinage. His purpose was to deify indecency, decry celibacy and virginity, dishonor the married state, sanction adultery, prostitution, and indecency. He was a drunkard who went for beer to the Black Eagle, theologized in taverns in the midst of alcoholic fumes surrounded by revolutionary comrades. He was "a blasphemer, a libertine, a revolutionist, a hater of religious vows . . . the father of divorce . . . and the propagator of immorality and open licentiousness."[14] His Gospel was directly opposed to the Gospel of Christ; he fabricated justification *sola fide*, perverted the Word of God, founded his own church out of hatred of authority and love of disorder. He was a deformer, not a reformer, an Antichrist, the enemy of God and man.[15]

Even the philosopher Jacques Maritain falls into this category of those who see Luther as the demon.[16] To him Luther adds up to be the man of total self-will, who brooks no restraint and no authority. By his emphasis on paradox and his mistrust of human reason "Luther brought a deliverance and an immense relief to humanity. . . . He delivered man from the intelligence, from that wearisome and besetting compulsion to think always and think logically."[17] To him Luther is the egocentric par excellence, obsessed with indecency, who convulsively forces trust in Christ to save himself. For such a man Maritain has only a feeling of deep disgust.

Less violent works, marking the faint signs of a change are Joseph Clayton's *Luther and His Work* (1937), Frantz Funck–Brentano's *Luther* (1939), and Philip Hughes' *History of the Church* (1947). Although they repeat many of the familiar charges, they usually do so without bitterness and they are able to see a good side of Luther. But the combination still adds up to a most distasteful whole—a genial, friendly, charming, magnanimous man of great ability who turned out to be neurotic, foul, and a false prophet who put man and not God into the center of the spiritual life, deliberately wrecked the church because of his own pride and then gloated over it. These authors and others of similar spirit, in spite of their occasional kind words about Luther personally, are unable to have any sympathy for his thought, his theology.

A somewhat new variation of an old theme has been advanced recently by the Franciscan Reinold Weijenborg, who says that Luther became a monk because he wanted to be able to study literature and philosophy in peace. To get permission from his father, he invented the story of the thunderstorm and took a monastic vow which put him into a state of mortal sin. Unwilling to repent of his error, he cut himself off from the salvation to be found in the church and invented his own doctrine which was supposed to bring peace to his conscience.[18]

The pamphlet literature on Luther and the Reformation, which is far too extensive and repetitious to explore here in any detail, reiterates the "demon" theme with very few exceptions. A frequent tactic is simply to pick up Luther quotations, or judgments from antagonistic authors that paint Luther in unrelieved black. Documentation of the Luther quotations is usually absent or so vague as to be valueless. Cochlaeus, Pistorius, Denifle, O'Hare, and even Grisar were thus channeled into the thinking of Catholics who were never exposed to the full works of such authors. It is safe to say, at least about Catholicism in America, that, until the ecumenical mood of the mid-twentieth century began to make some inroads, seminary instruction, education of nuns, parochial school instruction, and pamphlet literature affirmed uncritically the view of Luther as a demonic figure who brought only pestilence into the church. Small wonder that many Catholics were honestly puzzled about how people who revered such a man could claim to be Christians.

II

A MAN TO BE UNDERSTOOD

Decades before the ecumenical spirit officially caught hold in Catholicism, some Catholic authors begin to insist that Luther was not being fairly dealt with by Catholic scholars. Instead of prejudging him because of his revolt and smearing his character wherever possible, a few theologians asked for a more objective approach. Whatever his views and their consequences, Luther was surely entitled at least to a respectful hearing. In their zeal to counteract his influence, antagonistic Catholic writers had forgotten their primary responsibility of trying honestly to *understand* him as a man, a Christian, a theologian. The feeling gradually picked up momentum in Catholicism that the traditional approach was totally unsatisfactory and unchristian on two counts. First, because it was not interested in doing justice to Luther, only in destroying him. Secondly, because it lacked the basic Christian attitude of love, without which it is impossible to understand anyone. When Catholics began to try to understand Luther, revision of the traditional picture became a possibility.

Among the many pioneers of the changing spirit between World War I and World War II were Sebastian Merkle, historian at Würzburg, Franz Kiefl, dean of the cathedral at Ratisbon, and Anton Fischer, dean of the chapter of Cologne Cathedral. In a 1917 article Kiefl criticizes both Denifle and Grisar for failing to do justice to Luther's deeply religious motives and to the theological causes of the upheaval.[19] He faults Denifle for seeing in Luther's protest no more than a libertine's revolt against the church. He tries to understand justification by faith and rejects the *a priori* judgment that it must undermine any serious attempt to live the Christian life. At the heart of Luther's thought he finds a deep appreciation for the sovereign grace of God, but concludes that an overemphasis on this truth led Luther astray on depravity, free will, imputed righteousness, and the church's role in mediating salvation.[20] Kiefl respects Luther's genuine piety, his literary genius, and his profound understanding of much of the Christian faith. According to Richard Stauffer, this article "opened up the way for all conscientious Roman investigators to grasp the theological significance of the events of the sixteenth century." [21]

In 1929 a collection of articles on Luther, *Luther in ökumenischer Sicht*,[22] gave considerable further impetus to the new approach. Sebastian Merkle's "Gutes an Luther und Übles an seinen Tadlern" sketched some guidelines for Catholic historians of the Reformation: They must recognize the basically spiritual character of the Reformation; they should recognize Luther's religious motives, stop belittling and detracting from him, and perceive that he was in no sense a modern free-thinker or revolutionary. Anton Fischer's "Was der betende Luther der ganzen Christenheit zu sagen hat" praises Luther as a man of prayer from whose biblically-centered prayer life Catholics can learn to pray more effectively. The other two essays, on Luther's "evangelicalism" and his "subjectivism," examine the Christocentric character of his theology with considerable appreciation.

Of similar spirit in the 1930's was the young historian Hubert Jedin, now well known through his writings on the ecumenical councils of the Roman Church. His *Die Erforschung der kirchlichen Reformationsgeschichte seit 1876* and a series of lectures in Berlin in 1938 (the manuscript of which was destroyed in the Russian invasion of Berlin) tried to counteract the influence of Denifle and Grisar and to do justice to the religious concerns of Luther as reflected in his early writings.[23]

Important as these voices were in paving the way for greater justice to Luther, none of them presents a full new picture of Luther. The first comprehensive reinterpretation of Luther appeared in 1939-40—*Die Reformation in Deutschland*[24] by Johannes Lortz, then of the University of Münster. The tone is clearly irenic. "Reformation" is not a bad word. The issues are not black and white. Luther is no longer a demon who had to be exorcised, but a fellow Christian to be understood.

Lortz begins with a frank criticism of the church at the eve of the Reformation. Papacy, theology, church life needed reformation at many points. He even speaks of Roman Catholic *guilt* for the state of affairs in the church. He regrets the fact that Rome was too rigid to allow the protest and reform which are necessary for any healthy organism.[25]

Although his treatment of Luther is by no means always favorable, his desire to understand him is evident on almost every page. Luther was above all *homo religiosus,* to whom Christ crucified and risen is everything, whose religion is all grace. Lortz deeply admires his profound trust in God, his deep personal appropriation of Scripture, his attitude toward confession and the Presence of Christ in the Lord's Supper, the powerful way he could preach and the effective way he could teach men to pray, and much more about this creative but very complex man.

Yet at some very crucial points Lortz is sharply critical of Luther without, however, impugning his integrity. In spite of his Christocentric faith and theology, Luther was too subjectivistic. This is Lortz's basic thesis, that "he took his own highly personal convictions, based on a very exceptional experience and perhaps valid for himself personally, and made them into a binding requirement for all." [26] Luther wanted to be faithful to Scripture, but because he always interpreted it in terms of his own personal needs he over-emphasized some aspects of it and neglected others. He was not really a fully attentive listener, a *Vollhörer* of the Word in its full-ness because he allowed some aspects of Pauline thought to over-shadow everything else.[27] He intended only to purify the church but his rejection of the church's necessary teaching authority brought a great schism. Even so, the actual schism was also partly the fault of the pope and others in authority who were not willing to take the evangelical concerns of Luther and his followers seriously.[28]

Although some Catholic and Protestant authors have subsequently criticized Lortz for some of his judgments on Luther, there is general agreement that his Reformation history opened up the possibility of real dialogue between Protestants and Catholics on Luther. The fact that the book did not appear in English translation until 1968 is at least part of the reason why the Catholic re-evaluation of Luther began much later in England and America.

Very different from Lortz but just as important in the changing attitude toward Luther was Adolf Herte's *Das katholische Luther-bild im Bann der Luther-kommentare des Cochlaeus.*[29] Probably because of its great size—three large volumes—and technical schol-arly character it has never been translated into English, a fact which also helps to explain the relative tardiness of the Luther re-evalu-ation among English-speaking Catholics. Herte's purpose was sim-ple—to examine the influence of Cochlaeus on Catholic literature through the centuries and to evaluate Cochlaeus' portrayal. On the former point he showed that almost all Catholic biographies of Luther (including Denifle, Grisar, Maritain, and many others) leaned very heavily on Cochlaeus' evidence and interpretation. In regard to Cochlaeus' reliability he concluded that the whole por-trayal was a caricature reflecting the author's own deep aversion to and hatred of Luther. Not that Cochlaeus was completely false. He knew the extant Luther literature as no one else of his time. He helped to preserve some valuable original materials. He admit-ted that Luther's New Testament translation stimulated the religious hunger for the Word of God among the people. Yet, the composite picture of Luther was thoroughly unreliable because of Cochlaeus' deep personal antipathy which predetermined what he could see in Luther.[30] Herte's careful scholarship has helped to free modern Catholic historians from bondage to the traditional picture and given great impetus to the modern search for a more accurate understanding of Luther. It will take considerable time, however, for Herte's influence to purge Catholic consciousness and literature of the assumptions that have been building up for centuries.[31]

Another part of the respectful encounter with Luther which seeks to understand him as man, Christian, and theologian has been a deeper wrestling with the content of his theology. Whatever the historians may conclude about his character, the exact balance of the guilt for the schism, the reasons why he was what he was, Catholic theologians sense much more clearly than ever before that theology must take Luther seriously. A few references to this aspect of the changing attitude to Luther must suffice.

An institutional expression of it is the beautiful and well-equipped Johann Adam Moehler Institute at Paderborn, Germany. Supported by an organization under the leadership of Archbishop Lawrence Jaeger, its purpose is to encourage the study of non-Roman Catholic theology, especially that of Luther and the Reformation. It attracts Catholic and Protestant scholars from many lands. In 1960 its director, George Brandenburg, published a study of Luther's 1513–15 lectures on the Psalms under the title *Gericht und Evangelium*.[32] Of particular interest to him was Luther's understanding of the Word of God, especially the Holy Spirit's testimony to the veracity of the Word in the heart of the believer. What Brandenburg sees in the young Luther convinces him that Luther seriously endangered the objectivity of the Word and that Rudolph Bultmann and Gerhard Ebeling, in their view of the Word, stand in the general theological tradition of Luther.

Stephanus Pfürtner's *Luther and Thomas on Salvation*[33] is an examination of what each has to say on the question of "Christian assurance." Although Thomas focuses on hope and Luther on faith as the locus of assurance, Pfürtner finds them to be not as different from each other as had been assumed.

Many other recent Catholic authors have tried to rise above the old antagonism to Luther's theology.[34] Two such are Yves Congar and Louis Bouyer. Both of them reflect much of Lortz's spirit toward the church of Luther's day and toward Luther's spiritual struggles.

And like Lortz, they both fault Luther, without passion or rancor, for what they regard as basic weaknesses that led him and his followers astray. On justification Congar sees his doctrine as a one-sided Galatianism which led to schism because Luther failed to take the full biblical and ecclesiastical tradition seriously and because he impatiently expected rapid change in the church.[35] Bouyer has special appreciation for Luther's stress on grace, on Christ, and on Scripture but finds Luther and the Reformation deficient because of what he regards as the unjustified extremes to which they pushed these doctrines. Grace was distorted into total rejection of all significance to man's own acts and decisions; the stress on Scripture into complete rejection of the authority of the church.[36]

III

A BROTHER TO BE WELCOMED

The change from the polemical to the historical stance in regard to Luther undoubtedly marks one of the great watersheds in Catholic twentieth-century scholarship. Even though it has been too drastic a step for some Catholics, others have gone considerably farther in their own appreciation of Luther and his importance for the Roman Catholic Church. A few of them are hailing him as a brother to be welcomed, personally and theologically, into their fold.

One of the most favorable of all published Catholic treatments of Luther is *Luther in katholischer Sicht* by Johannes Hessen,[37] philosopher of religion at the University of Cologne. To Hessen, Luther stands in the line of the Old Testament prophets, a man with a divine mission to overcome a great falling away from the Gospel and to restore the Gospel to its proper place in the church. His own agonizing struggle about a "gracious God" was the same path Paul had trod, and it brought Luther to the same childlike trust in the undeserved grace of God. Not pride or ego but God and his grace were the basic forces at work in Luther. His experiences, although subjective in form, were actually an objective confrontation with God. Because Luther's faith was grounded so completely in Christ and grew so completely out of Word and Sacrament Hessen disagrees thoroughly with Lortz's charge that Luther was subjectivistic to the core.[38] He sees no similarity at all between Luther and modern subjectivism or individualism.

Hessen also makes every effort to understand and appreciate Luther-ideas which even his objective colleagues had attacked. For example, in the area of free will, depravity, and good works, Hessen sees that Luther's invective against human works and merit is not philosophic determinism but a way to emphasize man's absolute dependence upon God and to eliminate the possibility of any pride on man's part.[39] On the sacraments he sees the reason for Luther's attack to have been a virtual ignoring by Roman doctrine and practice of the need for a direct relationship between the individual and God. Luther's attack on the church's hierarchy and institutionalism meant to stress the same need for inner union with Christ rather than mere membership in an institution.[40] On these and other points Hessen believes that Luther was affirming the true Catholic position, even though he often allowed the heat of the controversy to push him into extremes. The extremes, says Hessen, should be rejected by Luther's followers, but the criticisms should be heeded by Catholicism to which they are still addressed.[41] Thus Luther can help Catholicism to overcome its perennial tendencies toward intellectualism, moralism, sacramentalism, and institutionalism.[42] It was Hessen's hope (writing in 1947) that Protestants and Catholics would be able to come to a common understanding of Luther and that an effort to do this would be "the way to the *Una Sancta.*"[43] Like the works of Lortz and Herte, Hessen's had no appreciable influence on English Catholicism for want of a translation.

Not until 1961 did another equally favorable Catholic work on Luther appear. That year Thomas Sartory of the ecumenically active Niederaltaich abbey in Bavaria gave a series of four radio talks with the same title as Hessen's book.[44] The significant thing about these essays is not so much what they said, because much of it is found in Lortz and his forerunners, but in their wide audience —that of the Southwest German Network.

Sartory looks at Luther from four angles: the psychological, the historical, the theological, and the ecumenical. In the psychological section he examines and rejects as completely inadequate the approaches of Cochlaeus, Denifle, Grisar, and Weijenborg. The more recent psychoanalytic interpretations of Luther are not rejected out of hand but are put into perspective:

> For anyone who like Luther has experienced in his own life the reality of the angry and the merciful God, it is no wonder if the tiny

human vessel develops cracks and leaks, or even if it breaks apart. One can analyze the phenomenon of *Angst* in Luther's life psychologically and yet know very little about it, unless one also takes into account the God of wrath and man in the totality of his sin. But what wrath of God and sin really are, neither psychology nor medicine can tell us.[45]

Recognizing that many aspects of Luther's personality will probably never be solved, Sartory focuses on the question whether Luther did not have a God-given mission for his time.

Theologically Sartory sees Luther's one great concern as the living God and the individual face to face with him. Luther, therefore, could not think of God abstractly but only in terms of his relationship to man, to Luther. Yet, says Sartory, "Luther would very likely turn in his grave if he should hear that he was a defender of a subjectivism or a religion of conscience in which man is morally autonomous, free from all bonds to a superior reality." [46] The force which must control conscience is not, however, the church but the Bible, specifically the Bible's Gospel of salvation by grace alone. Sartory's most pointed challenge to Luther (and to Lutheran theology) is to ask Lortz's question at this point—whether justification really is the center from which all the rest of Scripture is to be understood. Sartory believes that it does not take seriously enough the resurrection, the lordship of Christ, and their significance for the New Testament church.[47]

Historically and ecumenically, Sartory is encouraged by the fact that the Council of Trent did not condemn Luther by name or completely close the door to conversation with Protestants. He commends the pioneers of the restudy of Luther. He points to Luther, with all his strengths and weaknesses, as a promising subject for ecumenical discussion. In love, Catholics should seek and listen to the truth which Luther affirmed, should try to see him as God sees him, to perceive what God did for him and through him. He sees that Luther's personal practical religious approach can help Catholicism overcome its tendency to philosophical speculation.

> The Luther who speaks of man's Christian existence, who verbalizes his personal experience of God, who explains Scripture and proclaims the word with unprecedented power, who gives expression to his worship in his hymns—this Luther is the spiritual man, the pastor and preacher, whom we in the Catholic world do not want to miss out on.[48]
>
> For centuries we Catholics saw in him only the apostate monk, the polemicist against the church. For centuries we Catholics learned the

catechism against Luther, to our own loss. We shall certainly not make the mistake of taking him more seriously than he wished to take himself or than the church which bears his name takes him. Luther is not the Gospel, either for them or for us. Nevertheless, in spite of all our reservations, in spite of the "No" which the church has spoken to him, we Catholics wish to hear his word in so far as it is a witness to the Gospel, so that we too may be inflamed with the love which burned in him for God.[49]

The last work which we shall note is one in English, John M. Todd's *Martin Luther*.[50] It is a sensitive and moving biography by a Catholic layman who has done his homework on Luther very well. His purpose—"to take advantage of the recent cooling of temperatures [between the confessions] to give a brief record of his life . . . doing justice to the central religious issues, without being merely dissectionist on the one hand or partisan on the other" [51]—is achieved to a remarkable degree. He leaves one with the impression that he has not merely met and analyzed Luther but has also lived and struggled with him, e.g., on Luther's turmoil, his terrible sense of "coram Deo," his irritation with the medieval system, his struggle to grasp the promises of God, his trouble with authority, his tendency to depression, his physical ills, his occasional extremes in language.

Todd touches on most of the important doctrinal issues, not in a profound analysis, but adequately enough to demonstrate that he has read widely and sympathetically in many of Luther's works. One can sense this in the way he deals with Luther on justification, faith and good works, the sacraments, the will of man. Without approving of Luther's addition of the word "alone" to the Romans justification passage, he presents Luther's reasons fairly, and lets it go at that. At points where Todd might have been sharply critical of Luther he desists. Luther's temper, his attitude to monasticism and marriage, his role in the Peasants' War and in the Philip of Hesse affair cannot be ignored, but Todd has no intention of using these to build some kind of case for serious spiritual or mental deficiency in Luther. Typical of his touch is this comment:

> As his way of life became established [after his marriage] he became more relaxed and jollier; and his criticisms became even less restrained than before. He grew fatter, until he was very large; he drank much and boasted of it; two characteristics being almost disconcertingly common in Catholic tradition.[52]

Rome is frankly criticized for its whole approach to Luther. Instead of taking his concerns seriously it opted for the "easier" route, ecclesiastical pressure to silence him. The curia was blind to the theological issues, unable to believe that a critical German was really trying to work for the good of the church. Yet Todd is not on a pro-Luther crusade. He is as fair with Luther's opponents, e.g. Cajetan, as with the Reformer.[53]

Though Todd does not claim to be a technical Luther scholar he does not hesitate to criticize the scholars, both Catholic and Protestant. Ronald Knox's evidence to prove that Luther was an "enthusiast" is worthless.[54] Louis Bouyer is criticized for charging that Luther teaches a salvation which does not draw man out of sin at all.[55] Philip Watson and Heinrich Boehmer are charged with failing to investigate Catholic teaching adequately and, therefore, with seeing tension between Luther and the Catholic Church where there really was none.[56]

To Todd, Luther's great positive achievement was a new Christian vision, directly based on the Bible, with a renewed conviction of the sovereignty of God, of man's life as built on faith in him; a new face for religion, expressed in the people's language, taking them up into its practice in more democratic fashion.[57]

> Luther's message was not solely the rather austere theology of justification [*sic*] but a return to the New Testament themes of the Fatherhood of God, the sending of the Son, and the Son's message of forgiveness and love for all men. Beneath the polemics and the theology lay this concern for man, the personal appeal. He spoke of Christ the man who had suffered for them, and had taken on the bitter life of the world. Luther himself lived out his life as one who shared all things with others, an ordinary honest man.[58]

The setting of the book is openly ecumenical. He wants Catholics to see Luther with sympathy and to listen to his message. He wants Protestants to recover much of the real Luther and to take seriously the possibility that the kind of "reformed Church of Rome" which Luther hoped for is now coming about. Todd has written an excellent book; it goes to the heart of many of the issues. It ought to help many Catholics shrug off the unworthy notions of the past so that they,too, may see in Luther a brother.

Yet the best even Todd can say about the key issue of the Reformation, the centrality of justification, is that history is today showing that the essential Lutheran insights and expositions are ultimately able to be integrated into the Catholic tradition; the Catholic tradition is sufficiently flexible to be able to be modified and enlivened by Lutheran theology.[59]

That statement pinpoints the most significant issue which the changing Catholic approach to Luther poses for those who follow him. The important question is not whether Rome will take him back but whether the doctrine of justification is *the* key to the understanding of Scripture, *the* heart and center of all Christian theology. Almost every one of the current Luther scholars in Rome raises this question in one way or another. They do so not out of hatred or misunderstanding of Luther, but in love for him and the church. In this ecumenical age will we to whom it is addressed have the courage and the faith to let the Catholic question drive us back into a deep study of the Scriptures? Is the Luther emphasis really true to the whole of the biblical revelation? Who is the really attentive and faithful hearer of Scripture? Did he, and have we, played off justification against other biblical emphases? Is there really such a "core" to the scriptural revelation? Is it true that in his (and our) concentration on justification and the closely related doctrines of sin, atonement, and forgiveness he failed to do equal justice to the reality of the resurrection, the new life, the Holy Spirit in the believer and in the church? All of the Catholic re-evaluators, even the most friendly, believe that Lutheranism needs the constant stimulus and corrective of the "fuller Catholic and biblical tradition" to bring balance to our theology.

To raise such questions does not mean to assume that the Catholic position is correct.[60] It only means to say that a church which stands on the formal principle of the Reformation ought to listen to this Catholic word with respect, without prematurely regarding it as another expression of anti-Luther prejudice, and to respond to it by the kind of biblical and theological effort which it invites. Joint Catholic-Protestant work of this type is an important dimension of ecumenical life today to which the restudy of Luther has contributed much.

5.

A Positive Response to
Erik Erikson's *Young Man Luther*

LELAND ELHARD

Luther was a charismatic personality. Over and above the favorable accidents of history which thrust more leadership upon him than he or Roman Catholic Christendom had bargained for, Martin Luther was a powerfully magnetic man. Even today his life story and his words stir and lead people. This ongoing interest seems deeper than the thrill of meeting a charmer or the worship of a dead hero or the propagandist emblazoning of a convenient extrinsic figurehead on a movement which has intrinsically left him behind in spirit long ago. Rather, across the centuries the spirit of the man himself still touches us and hints at a gift of power which is from the heart of things. People may be for him or against him, but they find it difficult to be indifferent to him. He attracts attention from historians, theologians, philosophers, sociologists, psychologists, capitalists, and communists. Certainly, many different reasons are at stake. But for these people and for most ordinary people Luther the man is impressive. Somehow the psychological depths of Luther touch our depths. As Erik Erikson says:

> Obviously, when this monk spoke up he presented in his words and in his bearing the image of man in whom men of all walks of life were able to recognize in decisive clarity something that seemed right, something they wanted, they needed to be. Whatever theological rationale unified Luther's teaching as an evangelist was transcended by his influence on men in his own and other reformers' churches, in his and in other countries, and even on the Catholic Church's own counter-reformation.[1]

This essay attempts to present a case for making responsible use of Erikson's study of Luther, and other studies of similar calibre which may appear, in our constructive appropriation of the Gospel which made him a great and faithful man. It does not hope to take possession of Luther's charisma by analyzing it. It proceeds on the intuition that great believers and great men with varying shapes of faith seem to be like him in some deep way. It is not afraid that shining the light of psychology on him will necessarily evaporate God's gifts of faith and greatness displayed in Luther. It assumes that a humble, responsible psychology cannot only help clear away mistaken views about a hero but can also confront us with the central unmistakable genius wrought by God in one of his human servants. On the basis of a thorough understanding of all of Erikson's authorship as well as of *Young Man Luther*, I find Erikson to be a man who has also been grasped by Luther's charisma and who reverently seeks to know it together with himself better.

Erikson is strangely attracted by Luther and is interested in his greatness. He describes his reasons for writing *Young Man Luther* in the preface, which he concludes:

> I have attempted in this preface to give a brief rationale for writing this book; I doubt, though, that the impetus for writing anything but a textbook can ever be rationalized. My choice of subject forces me to deal with problems of faith and problems of Germany, two enigmas which I could have avoided by writing about some other young great man. But it seems that I did not wish to avoid them.
>
> When speaking about Freud to the students at Frankfurt and at Heidelberg, I remembered an event in my own early years, a memory which had been utterly covered by the rubble of the cities and by the bleached bones of men of my kind in Europe. In my youth, as a wandering artist, I stayed one night with a friend in a small village by the Upper Rhine. His father was a Protestant pastor; and in the morning, as the family sat down to breakfast, the old man said the Lord's Prayer in Luther's German. Never having "knowingly" heard it, I had the experience, as seldom before or after, of a wholeness captured in a few simple words, of poetry fusing the esthetic and the moral: those who have once suddenly "heard" the Gettysburg Address will know what I mean.
>
> On occasion we should acknowledge emotional debts other than traumatic ones. Perhaps, then, this study is a tribute to a spring morning in that corner of Europe from which Schweitzer came; and an attempt to grasp something essential in that reformation which stands

at the beginning of our era, something which we have neither completely lived down nor successfully outlived. Such is the material of psychoanalysis.[2]

I agree with Philip Woolcott Jr. of the Menninger Foundation that Erikson does not adequately fulfill his implicit promise of understanding Luther's greatness and the charisma which grasps us personally.[3] In the end he is enticed by the conflicts and the symptoms, especially of "old man Luther," enticed by his life-long experience as a clinician of dealing with people who are sick and not also great. So, as he somewhat reluctantly admits, I think, "It is obvious I have charted the decline of a youth, and not the ascendance of a man. Another book would have to do that."[4] For myself I must say that I earnestly wish Erikson would write that other book. However, I doubt if Erikson can do it. I think that someone from within the church must do it, someone more completely nurtured on Luther's greatness than Erikson, yet detached and dispassionate enough about it to analyze it.

Furthermore, I must assert at this time that whoever writes this book will have to use as basic tool and resource Erikson's *Young Man Luther*. Having lived with his book for ten years, I conclude that it is one of the most significant books written in our time. I recognize that this conclusion is a "minority report" in contrast to the majority of theologians.

The reaction to Erikson's book among Luther scholars has been almost universally negative. The best one can say is that the book has been noticed. Some of them have read it. Some have obviously skimmed it and concluded it is no good because a psychologist wrote it and even suggest in print that they know what it is about by muttering something about a "split father image" and "anti-mother complex," terms, incidentally, which Erikson does not use. A few haven't bothered to look up the man's name; they spell it with a "c," but still make public judgments about him. Most of them seem afraid of the book. Roland Bainton's review of it is a classic in conflict about it. He admits it is a needed work completely done, but finds it impossible to admit its powerful implications.[5]

Because Bainton's reaction to *Young Man Luther* represents so well in one place all the major points mentioned by Luther scholars in disagreeing with Erikson, this essay will be focused on it. I do not, by any means, imply here that Bainton is the most critical of

Erikson. In fact, his review is very appreciative and reasonable in comparison with some oral and written reactions.

The scholars indicate the point of difficulty as methodological. How Erikson proceeds, what evidence he admits, how he organizes the material, how he draws conclusions—these they object to. What method *does* Erikson employ? He uses a combination of anthropology and psychiatric case study. Those of you who have ever sat on a psychiatric case study know it can be a bewildering experience. Especially in the team approach emerging today, evidence is brought in from every angle. Testimonies of everyone are seen as worth while. Even prejudiced testimony is useful. Carefully evaluated, it throws light on attitudes and the kinds of relationship in the situation. Nobody is wholly right or wrong. The confusion is allowed to build until a configuration begins to emerge. This configuration is surprisingly very much like the picture of a real human being such as we know our relatives and friends to be. The subject under investigation is allowed to be a believable human being because he, in his confusions and incompleteness, is seen as embedded in his interactions and contexts and not abstracted from them. Facts, interpretation, personal responsibility, and various determinisms are not as easily sorted out into white and black boxes as they are in detective stories. When the case study is completed, you find yourself agreeing with a majority of the participants that some judgments about it ring true and others do not. You have discovered together a process, a direction, a configuration, which makes up your diagnosis and prognosis. You, perhaps, are not sure of any one bare fact in the person's life; too many people may have their questions about it from their informed perspectives. Yet out of the whole experience you know the *person* and what he is likely to do much better than if you have a hundred unimpeachable bare facts which do not add up to a picture of a human process. Erikson is a master at such configurational analysis. He insists on contexts and backgrounds. He never goes in a straight line, introducing point one and finishing with it before point two. He insists on going around and around the subject, viewing it from every angle. Every statement is qualified. He does write books which are impossible to grasp unless you are willing to enter into the situation he presents.

One of the passions in all of Erikson's work is to widen the scope of history to include childhood. He says, "One may scan work after

work on history, society, and morality and find little reference to
the fact that all people start as children and that all people begin in
their nurseries." [6] He insists on a continuity between the experience
and training the child has and the history he later makes as an
adult. All of our childish irrationalities do not suddenly disappear
the day we are old enough to vote or buy a car. Ask any politician
or salesman. Nearly every alert adult will observe how politics and
infantile experience reverberate with each other in any year of the
presidential election, but some historians do not catch on. With sad-
ness I quote Roland Bainton in his review of *Young Man Luther*,
"It seems to me that Luther's theological development might have
been just the same if he had been left an orphan in infancy." [7]

Erikson does not mean that we are to reduce history to childhood
writ large. He says,

> We can no longer abide the one-way proposition which explains the
> behavior of leaders and of masses on the basis of the childhoods they
> had or had shared. In *Young Man Luther* I used Luther's childhood
> and youth to show that a reformer and his childhood and the to-be-
> reformed and their childhoods, as well as the political actuality which
> brings them together in one decisive historical deed, are all aspects of
> an epoch's style of adaptation and readaptation. [8]

He sees an essential difference between the dynamics of individuals and that of group political action. There are never direct equa-
tions between them. Yet the way individuals and their institutions
interact always has a relation to the way children first relate to their
social world.

> All of this [the matter of influence and authority in adult life] has its
> antecedents in childhood and in identification with the first counter-
> players in individual life. Every new beginning in later life, and every
> new attachment and involvement, reverberates in the childhood strata
> of our images and our effects where all kings and leaders are fathers or
> big brothers and all countries and ideas, mothers. [9]

Luther himself understood this well when he related the Fourth
Commandment to *all* the authorities we encounter in every age of
life.

Erikson's whole view of man includes the continuity between
emotions and the body. He suggests that Luther's "tower room experience" includes simultaneous freeing of the channel of encounter
with God and a certain channel of elimination in the body. This

should make sense to us in the light of our own physical reactions to some overwhelming experiences we have had. As Erikson connects Luther's discovery of grace with the toilet, it is a "part of the plot," as the movie censors would say. It is unfortunate that many people confuse Erikson with John Osborne whose play *Luther* is a distorted fragment of Erikson's thought. Osborne's sensationalistic play distorts the man by putting the focus on an aspect of him as if it were his center.[10]

Another aspect of psychoanalysis which is, at once, its method and the center of its contribution to the understanding of people is its principle of conflict. Luther himself pointed to it in his doctrine of man as being *simul justus et peccator,* simultaneously saint and sinner. Man is not "either-or." He is "both-and." The best and the worst in a person are two sides of a coin. To Erikson Luther is neither only sick nor only great. He is a great young man, sickness and all.[11] Erikson loves Luther. He says, "There is no triumph in showing that these remnants [of childhood repressions] exist, even in a great man. We have come to take it for granted that any greatness also harbors massive conflict."[12] Psychoanalysis finds illustrated in Luther's life and theology that man lives and *grows* in terms of crisis and conflict. To a large extent, Luther was a greater man *because,* not in spite of, his inner conflicts. He was a "weller" man because he was a sicker man. For most of us, to say a man is sick finishes him as a human being and to say a man is great is to say there isn't anything at all wrong with him. For most of us a man either hates or loves, not both. James Atkinson, the British Luther scholar, has rightly said that Luther loved his father.[13] There is plenty of evidence for this assertion. As far as Atkinson and many others are concerned, Luther then could not possibly also hate his father and, therefore, in this "bind," be a very troubled soul! Also while he has a number of positive things to say about the relationship, Erikson nowhere says right out that Luther loved his mother. Therefore Bainton concludes in his review that Erikson says that Luther hated his mother. I can find no place where Erikson comes close to saying simply that. In fact, Erikson nowhere says that Luther had but *one* simple feeling for anyone close to him. He is far too sophisticated a student of us complex human beings for that.

Some people may react to this obvious emphasis on emotion with some disbelief. Even though a man has feelings, as a grown man, he

can and ought to know how to control them. Surely a great man
like Luther did, did he not? Nevertheless, it has been the discovery
of psychoanalytic psychology that he who is made to control his
emotions too rigidly is controlled most rigidly by them. Luther
experienced the power of emotions and said some pretty sensitive
and insightful things about them. For example, about the influence
of lust on the whole person, "By the time it is noticed it is too late.
Once it burns . . . the eye is blind." [14] In one of his letters he is sad-
dened and somewhat amazed that he, the most gifted of God in
the church for a thousand years, should be so captive to the feelings
of grief he experienced after his daughter died.[15] He describes these
feelings in a way which reminds one of Erich Lindemann's classic
study of grief. At times he counseled people to do battle with their
emotions, e.g. you can't keep the birds from flying over your head
but you can prevent them from making a nest in your hair. But he
always saw this battle as occurring within the victory of Christ and
he always took seriously the feelings people brought to him. From
his own experience he learned that one can't "think away" one's
struggles and he would agree with Shakespeare that everyone can
master a grief but him who has it.

One is led toward the conclusion that Erikson has written a book
so subtle and difficult that a non-psychologist cannot understand it.
However, it is then amazing that Bainton should publicly and cas-
ually presume to understand Erikson's use of the word "ego" in the
sense of "hybris," as inflated self. Anyone could look up its precise
psychoanalytic meaning in any up-to-date dictionary. Erikson comments on Bainton's review as follows:

> And even where the psychoanalytic concept of the ego has perme-
> ated, it has been immediately drawn into the imagery of man's "lower
> nature," and into the popular meaning of ego, namely, an inflated self.
> Thus a church-historian, in one of the best of our academic journals,
> could suggest that a psychoanalytic study of Luther's identity crisis
> was meant to show that Luther started the Reformation merely "for the
> satisfaction of his ego." To that extent has the popular "ego" as a desig-
> nation of modern man's vain sense of a self-made Self (a precarious
> sense, subject to sudden deflation by the pricks of fate—and of gossip)
> penetrated the vocabulary even of the learned. But it happens to desig-
> nate the opposite of the psychoanalytic meaning; therefore, in all but
> the most specialized circles, it is still necessary to say what the ego
> is not.

The psychoanalytic meaning of ego designates it as an inner-psychic regulator which organizes experience and guards such organization both against the untimely impact of drives and the undue pressure of an overweening conscience. Actually, ego is an age-old term which in scholastics stood for the unity of body and soul, and in philosophy in general of the permanency of conscious experience. . . . The ego in psychoanalysis, then, is analogous to what it was in philosophy in earlier usage: a selective, integrating, coherent and persistent agency central to personality formation.[16]

Therefore, it is clear there are some links between the psychoanalytic "ego" and the biblical term "living soul," the life of the whole person. The ego refers to man's drive to become an integrated human being in the midst of the forces which would destroy him as a person. It was Luther's great discovery that by faith man could *live*, live as a man before God. Understood correctly, Luther's struggle "for the satisfaction of his ego," as Bainton puts it, really is his struggle for faith, for a sure and honest center for his life.

The real points of contention in any discussion have to do with the assumptions upon which people operate. I wish to mention the two which seem to be present in this controversy. First, I presume to tell historians how they write history. I contend that they always write about the past in the light of their experience and understanding of the present. Certainly there is a "vice-versa" here, but we can simply admit it and go on without distorting anything. Bainton begins his critique of *Young Man Luther* by quoting affirmatively the president of the American Historical Society that the next dimension of history to be explored is that of psychological depth. Bainton says, "The claim is valid that whatever casts light upon the present should be thrown upon the past." But he goes on: "Yet one must recognize that the task is one of extreme difficulty because the dead cannot be summoned for examination." [17] Thus Bainton closes the door to a psychological dimension to history by assuming that the only way psychology can function is through personal psychiatric interview. Yet, if historical science applied to all its tools this rule of direct observation and accumulation of bare facts, which are interpreted only after they have been put on the tray before us, it could say very little about anything. Rather, historians are in a constant process of looking back in terms of their experience now. Facts, as Collingwood suggests, are always *interpreted facts*.[18] They are constantly "rediscovered" in the light of the new slants we put upon them. Always we see the past in terms of what we need to see. This does not mean that history is only ideology. It means that we must keep at the historical task and that we must use the tools which keep us honest. Psychoanalysis is, after all, a tool for honesty. Furthermore, we always use some kind of psychology in our study of history. Usually it has been an implicit, undisciplined psychology which can easily betray us. For example, Otto Scheel, in his study of Luther, is using a psychology, implicit of course, without benefit of personal interview, when he describes Luther as "simple, hardworking, earnest, straightforward, dutiful." [19] Who says that Scheel's old and very bad static psychology is all right to use on Luther and not Erikson's informed, dynamic psychology? One can speculate that it is the people who are more comfortable with Scheel's cover-up than with Erikson's insights. But it makes for bad history, a history in which present and past are not in contact.

Like it or not, we are, as Philip Rieff says, living in the era of psychological man.[20] We cannot veto it. It has happened. Erikson suggests that Luther had a hand in spurring it along. Whether it is used as a tool of healing or a weapon of destruction, psychology is deep within the bones of every man who is modern. This is the way we try to understand man as he lives now. Whether we admit it or not, we also look back at every event and person in the past with our psychological lenses. Because we do, we discover new facets in old facts. Because we do, the past is continuously discovered to be in continuity with the present and helps us to make sense of the present. One may object that the past is not amenable to such renewed interpretation, that because they did not have psychologists then, but had demons instead, there is no way of bridging the two world-views. But then one is forced eventually into saying that all study of history is impossible because there is no continuity, no basic human stuff which has to do with both demons and psychologists and somehow connects the two. As a matter of fact, historical science operates on the basis of continuity and uses the present to see the past. Today this means that responsible history now must use psychological insights. This is how Erikson operates. His *Young Man Luther* is a book about all human beings, as well as about a single great man. Throughout his book he sketches various psychological insights into human nature. He then goes back to Luther and fits them into the information, sometimes sketchy, which has been preserved. More times than not, the scheme fits, it explains, it pulls facts together. Most of all, it makes Luther come alive for us today. This is what the historian wants!

Whether Luther actually had a "fit in the choir" has been the subject of concern. Erikson accepts the legend as having some validity. He can do so because, in his understanding of youth and its crises, events something like the so-called "fit" have a dynamic place in the life of a troubled genius like Luther. Crises like these are far, far closer to the normal development of a gifted man in a situation like Luther's than they are to insanity or demon possession. Whether or not it happened, for Erikson, the "fit" accords with other more substantiated events in Luther's life. As far as I am concerned, the "fit" probably happened, and it doesn't diminish Luther an iota.

The second assumption is the most decisive of all. It is eminently theological and has ramifications in every theological direction. We remember Bainton saying that Luther's theological development might have been just the same if he had been an orphan. At another point he objects to Luther's theological development being portrayed in terms of his struggle to achieve independence from his parents, sometimes as "a projection of this struggle upon the cosmos," sometimes "as a rationalization," sometimes as "a device for solving a personal problem." [21] Assuming this is an accurate portrayal of what Erikson does with Luther's theology, we must ask Bainton (and many others) what the assumption is behind the objection. May I suggest a formulation of the assumption? If one views Luther, or anyone, as a "patient," if one, even in a responsible way, understands him psychologically, then one cannot understand him theologically as well. In other words, to psychologize is automatically to dehumanize a man or to view his life as pathological or to explain away his faith. Certainly there are psychologists who would reduce a man to "his diagnosis" in their particular psychology, but surprisingly, many theologians make the same reductionistic assumption. They do so when they anxiously hold that to admit that psychology has something to say in the inner sanctum of man's religious experience means that theology is bankrupt. Erikson does not attempt to explain away Luther's faith by reducing it to a psychological reaction only. He views Luther's experience multi-dimensionally. Psychology and theology together throw light upon Luther and upon each other.

Over and over again Erikson makes sober judgments about Luther's experience. He never gets carried away with psychoanalysis, e.g., the way Puritan historian Preserved Smith did. Erikson is very critical of Smith. Smith takes to Freudian notions the way a child tries out a strange new toy on everything. He says of Luther, "Luther is a thoroughly typical example of the neurotic quasi-hysterical sequence of an infantile sex-complex so much so, indeed, that Sigismund [sic] Freud and his school could hardly have found a better example to illustrate the sounder part of their theory than him." [22] Erikson never piles up psychoanalytic terms in shibboleth fashion in his study of historical personages. He denounces the recent publication of a psychological caricature of Woodrow Wilson written by an ambassador and a dabbler in psychoanalysis named William Bullitt, supposedly in collaboration with Freud when Freud was, in fact, dying of cancer.[23] He shows how Freud could not have taken an active part in it, even though in his terminal illness in gratitude to Bullitt for many kindnesses he was thrust into giving his name to its authorship. In other places Erikson repeatedly criticizes psychoanalysts for using their tools as weapons and as cloaks for a lack of integrity. He suggests that the scientific state of mind needs analyzing as much as any religious attitude.[24]

About Luther's faltering at his first mass, Erikson says, "I would not be willing to give exclusive precedence to the theological conflict (as the professor does) or to the personal-neurotic one (as the psychiatrist does) in this condensed, intensive experience." [25] Certainly, Erikson sees the relationship of strain and attachment between Luther and his father as having great influence. Luther presents enough evidence for Erikson to make a strong case here. Nevertheless, Erikson's central judgment about Luther's anxiety before the altar is the same as many theologians have made. "He had no living concept of Christ." [26]

Theology has come along to the place where it views God the Creator as working through and not merely around the regulations of his physical universe. In relation to natural science we have given up the picture of God retreating before every new discovery as if more and more of his mystery and power were being taken away by science. We realize that the God of the "gaps" is hardly the almighty, active Creator of the world and Lord of history portrayed in Scripture. On the other hand, we have not moved so far in relation to the sciences of man. There we still play a theology of the gaps. We fail to see that surely God is Lord "in, with, and under" psychological regulations and patterns too. Also, many theologians, on this question, are hidden Apollinarians who imagine that God in Jesus assumed our physical nature but not our psychological nature. Our starting point must be that Christ is the active Lord in our psychological universe also. According to the model of the incarnation, in the experience of the child Luther and of the young man Luther, God was once again bringing forth his salvation and revelation in and through a man in *all* his creatureliness. With psychology we are helped to understand God's giving of the Gospel to Luther. At the same time we are helped better to understand the Gospel in our own experience.

As every responsible psychologist knows, there is plenty of mystery left in man and in his relationships after psychology has done its best. Precisely at the point of our greatest understanding we are confronted with God's secret of being Lord of the man he frees. There is no need to separate psychology from a man's relationship to God. Even Paul Tillich, the great synthesizer, fails at one point here. At the end of *The Courage to Be*, Tillich posits a "God above God"—one above the ambiguities of our earthly father images.[27] Evidently Tillich is pointing to a mystical immediate relationship with God where we see him face to face, *totally apart* from any of the faces which have given us psychological trouble. If I read the incarnation rightly I see rather a God who continues to come to us through the face of the man Jesus and through the faces of those imperfect fathers who have seen him. Thus we dare to investigate the personal conflicts of Luther's life, and of our lives, trusting that we encounter there the Creator and Redeemer of reality, including the reality of man.

Part Three

Luther and Theology

6.

The Smalcald Articles
and Their Significance

JAMES L. SCHAAF

Perhaps the least known of all the documents contained in the *Book of Concord* is the Smalcald Articles. It is unfortunate that this writing has been so neglected by students of the Reformation. Aside from the two catechisms, which actually are more didactic than confessional in nature, the Smalcald Articles are the only one of the symbolical books of the Lutheran Church from the pen of Martin Luther himself. In them he intended, as he put it, to give "those who live after me . . . my testimony and confession . . . to show where I have stood until now and where, by God's grace, I will continue to stand." [1]

Yet more than their authorship by Luther makes the Smalcald Articles worthy of our consideration. In contrast to the conciliatory nature of the Augsburg Confession, which attempts to show the points where Lutherans and Roman Catholics were united, the Smalcald Articles deliberately intend to point out the areas of disagreement where no surrender to the Roman errors is possible. They have been called the Lutheran "declaration of independence." [2] J. T. Müller, who in 1848 edited a version of the *Book of Concord* [3] which was the standard edition in Germany until the critical jubilee edition superseded it in 1930, [4] saw the Smalcald Articles as forming a terminal point in the development of Lutheran doctrine. He wrote: "They form with the earlier Symbols a complete whole, yet have . . . an independent value, because in them the Lutherans for the first time, expressly and at large, define their relations to the Pope and the Papacy. We may say that in and with them the Reformation closes, and the final separation from Rome is pronounced." [5]

In an age, however, when we are beginning to talk about the possibility of overcoming the separation of the past four centuries, do the Smalcald Articles stand as an insurmountable obstacle in the path toward Christian unity? Is it not something of an embarrassment, to say the least, to have in the confessional writings to which we pledge ourselves, a statement such as this: "The pope is the real Antichrist who has raised himself over and set himself against Christ . . . "? [6] Must we overlook the sentiments of the prayer with which Luther concluded his preface to these articles?

> Dear Lord Jesus Christ, assemble a council of thine own, and by thy glorious advent deliver thy servants. The pope and his adherents are lost. They will have nothing to do with Thee. But help us, poor and wretched souls who cry unto Thee and earnestly seek Thee according to the grace which Thou hast given us by Thy Holy Spirit, who with Thee and the Father liveth and reigneth, blessed forever. [7]

The purpose of this essay is not to propose the Smalcald Articles as a basis for reunification of the church or even to exegete away all these difficult and offensive passages. Its intention is much more modest, merely to serve as an introduction to this remarkable writing which so clearly sets forth what the Reformation was really all about. I shall attempt to sketch, first, the reasons why the Smalcald Articles were written, then explore briefly their contents, and finally indicate how they attained confessional status and what their worth is today.

I

The Reasons for the Smalcald Articles

In tracing the history leading up to the composition of the Smalcald Articles one might well go back to the conflict between conciliarism and curialism which plagued the church during the Middle Ages, for this document was originally designed to be used at a general council. For the present, however, one must pass over the manifestations of conciliarist thought in both Catholic and evangelical ranks and merely recall the many times during his early reformatory work when Luther appealed to a free, Christian, general council of the church to vindicate his doctrine. The confessors at Augsburg offered "in full obedience, even beyond what is required, to participate in such a general, free, and Christian council," [8] and the recess of the Reichstag in 1530 promised that a council would be held within six to twelve months from the adjournment of that assembly.[9]

For political reasons, however, the promised council failed to materialize. Not until 1534, when a successor to Clement VII ascended the papal throne, was the subject of a council to be considered seriously and, after discussing the matter in Rome with Emperor Charles V in the spring of 1536, Pope Paul III on June 2, 1536, issued the bull, *Ad Dominici gregis,* summoning a council to assemble on May 23, 1537, in Mantua, a city in the territory of the Republic of Venice.[10] The bull itself contained nothing of an unusual nature, merely stating that the purpose of the council was to serve the peace of the church by eliminating all heresy,[11] but another bull issued in September, while not referring specifically to the council, gave the evangelicals cause for concern since it listed as a heresy to be eliminated "the pestilential Lutheranism." [12]

Meanwhile, following the hard line taken by the emperor and the Catholic estates at Augsburg, the evangelical territories had organized a defensive alliance in December 1530 at a meeting held in the Saxon village of Schmalkalden, which took the name of the Smalcald League. The strength of the Smalcald League managed to preserve an uneasy balance of power in Germany, prevent civil war, add new territories to the league, and allow the evangelical faith to flourish in lands which belonged to it.

When Paul III's announcement of the council reached the elector of Saxony in July 1536 he was confronted with a difficult decision. Experience had taught John Frederick that action favorable to the evangelical cause could hardly be expected at the council, yet to refuse to attend would be to abandon the long-standing demand of the Reformers for a church council to settle the religious controversy raging in Germany. If he and the other leaders of the Smalcald League were to boycott the council, it could easily be claimed by their Roman opponents that all their talk about willingness to submit to the decisions of a general, free, Christian council was nothing but sheer propaganda designed to mask their stubborn heresy.

The elector, on the other hand, had no desire to participate in such a council, for to do so, he felt, would be to acknowledge the pope as the head of the council and of the church, a thought at which his evangelically instructed conscience rebelled.[13] Far from possessing the divine authority to convoke a council, the pope was the chief enemy of the church whose invitation to participate—or whose demand to appear, for it was not yet clear which—at the council must be rejected. The chief problem confronting John Frederick was not whether to attend the council or not, but how to say "No" most diplomatically to the papal legate he expected would soon come to Germany bringing the official summons to the council.[14] The elector even began to revive his plan, rejected by his allies three years earlier, of calling a genuinely free, Christian counter-council under Luther's auspices, to which the pope, the emperor, and all Christian rulers would be invited.[15]

To aid him in his task he enlisted the assistance of his theological and legal scholars at Wittenberg in providing him with an answer to the problem of the papal council. However, this opinion of the scholars, written by one of the lawyers and revised somewhat by Philip Melanchthon, proved unsatisfactory to the elector, for it recommended that if the pope invited the evangelicals to participate in the conciliar proceedings, they should go, with the understanding that they expected it to be a free Christian council and that they did not acknowledge the pope as their judge.[16]

Luther himself, who was one of the participants in the group which drew up this opinion, was eager to attend a council. It was his belief that the papists were afraid of the truth and would like nothing better than to have the evangelicals decline to participate in the council. Thus they could boast that they had overcome the Lutherans and proceed to condemn them *in absentia*.[17] He said,

> They would like to frighten us into refusing it; for then they could safely say that we had prevented it. Thus the shame would not only cleave to us, but we would have to hear that, by our refusal, we had helped to strengthen such abominations of the Pope, which otherwise might have been righted.[18]

His advisors' opinion was highly unsatisfactory to Elector John Frederick. He rejected it on the grounds that the scholars had not framed it with the diligence appropriate to such an important matter and ordered his chancellor, Dr. Gregor Brück, to confer personally with the group of professors in Wittenberg and request from them another statement on the matter.[19] This meeting, at which were present Luther, Melanchthon, Johann Bugenhagen, professor and city pastor, and Caspar Creutziger, professor and preacher at the castle church, took place on August 30, 1536.[20]

Four days later Brück reported in a letter to the elector, then in residence at his castle in Torgau, that he had accomplished his prince's mission. In his letter Brück also stated:

> I also delivered to Doctor Martin the credentials which Your Electoral Grace gave to me, and thereupon also spoke with him in accordance with the command of Your Electoral Grace. He promised to be obedient in every way. It also appears to me that he already has the work well in hand, to open his heart to Your Electoral Grace on religion, which is to be, as it were, his testament.[21]

This statement presents to us a mystery in connection with the origin of the Smalcald Articles. It seems obvious that Brück had delivered a special communication from Elector John Frederick, ordering Luther to prepare a statement on religion which might serve as something like a last will and testament. We possess no more information than this about any special instructions Luther received from the elector in addition to the task laid upon all the theologians. Is then this "testament" on which Luther was diligently working to be identified with what later became known as the Smalcald Articles? A literary argument on this question filled the pages of the *Zeitschrift für Kirchengeschichte* about ten years ago in which Ernst Bizer, professor at the University of Bonn, said "No," while Hans Volz said "Yes." [22] Although the evidence is not absolutely clear-cut and incontrovertible, I tend to prefer the position represented by Volz for several reasons: (1) We have no other document from Luther's pen dating from this period which can be identified as the "testament" he was writing. (2) The Smalcald Articles themselves clearly have the character of a "final word" on the subject of Luther's teaching. (3) Luther frequently made use of documents prepared for one purpose in other ways, e.g. taking the Schwabach Articles and converting them into the Marburg Articles. (4) The state of Luther's health in 1536 was so poor that several times he felt his death was imminent, so it would not have been something extraordinary for the elector to request him to prepare a "testament" for posterity.

As for the official opinion requested of the theologians by Brück, its composition was postponed until Melanchthon returned in November from a two-month trip through southern Germany.[23] At the beginning of December the elector made a trip to Wittenberg and during his stay there took the opportunity to convey a memorandum to his theologians. Elector John Frederick wrote, in his own hand:

Although, in the first place, it may easily be perceived that whatsoever our party may propose in such a council as has been announced will have no weight with the opposition, miserable, blinded, and mad men that they are, no matter how well it is founded on Holy Scripture, moreover, everything will have to be Lutheran heresy, and their verdict, which probably has already been decided and agreed upon, must be adopted and immediately followed by their proposed ban and interdict, it will nevertheless be very necessary for Doctor Martin to prepare his foundation and opinion from the Holy Scriptures, namely, the articles as hitherto taught, preached, and written by him, and which he is determined to adhere to and abide by at the council, as well as upon his departure from this world and before the judgment of Almighty God, and in which we cannot yield without becoming guilty of treason against God, even though property and life, peace or war, are at stake. Such articles, however, as are not necessary, and in which, for the sake of Christian love, yet without offense against God and His Word, something might be yielded (though, doubtless, they will be few in number) should in this connection also be indicated separately by said Doctor Martin. And when Doctor Martin has completed such work (which, if at all possible for the Doctor, must be done between the present date and that of the Conversion of St. Paul [January 25], at the latest), he shall thereupon present it to the other Wittenberg theologians, and likewise to some prominent preachers whose presence he should require, to hear from them, at the same time admonishing them most earnestly, and asking them whether they agreed with him in these articles which he had drawn up, or not.[24]

John Frederick's plans for an evangelical counter-council had not been completely abandoned, for he mentions them later in the memorandum, but the emphasis here is primarily on having a document prepared for use at the council announced by the pope. It is to be a document setting forth clearly the most important Lutheran teachings on which no compromise is possible. And who better was there to compose such a statement than Martin Luther himself, the mighty leader whom God had raised up to proclaim the Gospel and whom God might at any moment call home? Luther's articles, so the elector ordered, were to be approved by the theologians at Wittenberg, put into both German and Latin,[25] and then discussed at the forthcoming meeting of the League set for February 7, 1537, in

Schmalkalden.[26] Each prince and representative would be asked to bring two or three of his theologians to this meeting to examine the articles to see if they might serve as a unanimous presentation of all the evangelicals should the members of the Smalcald League decide to attend the council.[27] At Elector John Frederick's order, expressed officially in a letter dated December 11, Luther set to work.[28]

II

AN EXPLORATION OF THE CONTENTS

That Luther worked carefully in preparing these articles during the month of December 1536 is evident from a glance at his original manuscript which since 1584 has been in the library of the University of Heidelberg.[29] It is filled with changes, phrases crossed out, words written between the lines and in the margins, and shows that he was giving careful consideration to each statement in these articles which as yet had no title. A noteworthy characteristic of this manuscript is that only the first 16½ pages of the 22-page document are in Luther's handwriting. This is explained by the fact that he was forced to interrupt his writing after suffering a severe heart attack on the evening of December 18. He managed to complete the task by dictating the final portion to two secretaries; this is the reason for the relative brevity of the last twelve articles. That he intended to elaborate on them later when his health permitted seems evident from the fact that the last two pages are only half-filled with text and that two blank pages are attached to the end of the manuscript.[30]

While this is not the place to go into a general discussion of Luther's illnesses, it might be appropriate, remembering the testamentary character of these articles, to note that the condition of his health was quite bad during the entire year of 1536.[31] Already the previous year, 1535, he had been forced to interrupt his teaching and preaching for several periods of time. In January and February 1536 he suffered from a severe cold; on February 22 he experienced a fainting spell in the Wittenberg church; on March 25 he wrote that for a period of two weeks he had been compelled to take to his bed. At Easter, which fell on April 16, he believed he was about to die.[32] Recovering from these severe afflictions, he was again forced by illness on December 10 to cease preaching and could not resume until mid-January. Thus even before his heart attack he was suffering great pain at the very time he was writing these articles for the elector. His suffering became even more intense at Christmas.[33] This may help us to understand the frame of mind of the man who at the conclusion of his articles writes in the first person: "These are the articles on which I must stand and on which I will stand, God willing, until my death. I do not know how I can change or concede anything in them." [34]

Luther divides his writing into three main parts. "The first part of the Articles," he says, "treats the sublime articles of the divine majesty." [35] "The second part treats the articles which pertain to the office and work of Jesus Christ, or to our redemption." [36] The third part Luther heads in this way: "The following articles treat matters which we may discuss with learned and sensible men, or even among ourselves. The pope and his court do not care much about these things; they are not concerned about matters of conscience but only about money, honor, and power." [37]

Part I is divided into four articles which are so brief that they scarcely deserve the name of articles, all but the fourth being only one sentence long. This is as it should be in regard to articles dealing with the divine truths of the Holy Trinity, the incarnation of the Son of God, and the statements of faith in the Apostles' and Athanasian Creeds, for, says Luther, "These articles are not matters of dispute or contention, for both parties confess them. Therefore, it is not necessary to treat them at greater length." [38]

Part II contains four articles pertaining to the office and work of Jesus Christ, entitled Christ and Faith, the Mass, Chapters and Monasteries, and the Papacy.

Part III, consisting of subjects which may be discussed with "learned and sensible men," contains fifteen articles on these themes: Sin; the Law; Repentance (after writing this Luther suffered the heart attack); the Gospel; Baptism; the Sacrament of the Altar; the Keys; Confession; Excommunication; Ordination and Vocation; the Marriage of Priests; the Church; How Man Is Justified Before God, and His Good Works; Monastic Vows; and Human Traditions.

Anyone familiar with the earlier Lutheran confessions, the Augsburg Confession and its Apology, will immediately recognize that Luther's articles deal with some matters which were completely ignored in the two symbols written by Melanchthon. The times had changed. No longer was the task to show that Lutherans were loyal members of the Catholic Church; now was the time to speak out boldly against the errors of Romanism which could not be tolerated by those who had rightly heard the Gospel. And, of course, this is the mighty reformer, Martin Luther himself, speaking, not the irenic scholar, Philip Melanchthon. These articles were intended neither to replace nor to supplement the Augsburg Confession and its Apology, but to speak to a different situation. Now was the time for strong words. Altered circumstances brought forth a different kind of document.

According to the elector's instructions, the Wittenberg theologians assembled shortly after Christmas 1536 to discuss Luther's articles. Joining Luther, Melanchthon, Bugenhagen, and Creutziger at this conference was Justus Jonas, professor at Wittenberg and at that time rector of the university, who had been absent from the city when the earlier deliberations had taken place. Three other pastors from outside Wittenberg had been invited by Luther on December 15 to participate in this meeting and were present at the time, Nicholas Amsdorf, pastor and city superintendent in Magdeburg, Johann Agricola, pastor in Eisleben and director of the Latin school there, and George Spalatin, pastor in Altenburg. Spalatin, who also held the position of Electoral Librarian, served as secretary of the conference.[39]

At this conference, which because of Luther's illness lasted several days, all the articles prepared by Luther were discussed in turn and adopted by the group.[40] The only significant change undertaken was to add a paragraph concerning the invocation of saints in the article dealing with the mass.[41] It is impossible to determine at whose suggestion this addition was made, but Luther assented to it. Additional proposals, most probably made by Melanchthon, to include an article on both kinds in the sacrament, an addition to Luther's article on ordination, and a statement on adiaphora, were rejected by the group.[42] After finally approving the document on December 28 or 29 substantially as it had come from Luther's hand, the men instructed Spalatin to prepare a formal copy for presentation to the elector.[43] To this document the eight men signed their names. On January 3, 1537, Spalatin carried it, along with a covering letter from Luther, to Elector John Frederick in Torgau.[44]

Extremely grateful for the receipt of the articles, the elector wrote to Luther:

We give thanks to Almighty God and to our Lord Christ for having granted you health and strength to prepare these articles in such Christian, true, and pure fashion; also that He has given you grace, so that you have agreed on them with the others in Christian, also brotherly and friendly unity. . . . From them we also perceive that you have changed your mind in no point, but that you are steadfastly adhering to the Christian articles, as you have always taught, preached, and written, which are also built on the foundation, namely, our Lord Jesus Christ, against whom the gates of hell cannot prevail, and who shall also remain in spite of the Pope, the council, and its adherents. May Almighty God, through our Lord Christ, bestow His grace on us all, that with steadfast and true faith we abide by them, and suffer no human fear or opinion to turn us therefrom! . . . After reading them over for the second time, we can entertain no other opinion of them, but accept them as divine, Christian, and true, and accordingly shall also confess them and have them confessed freely and publicly before the council, before the whole world, and whatsoever may come, and we shall ask God that He would vouchsafe grace to our brother [his step-brother, John Ernest, with whom he shared authority] and to us, and also to our posterity, that steadfastly and without wavering we may abide and remain in them![45]

III

Confessional Status

Pleased with the unanimity of his theologians, the elector took steps to secure additional signatures. Gabriel Didymus, pastor in Torgau where the electoral residence was located, subscribed, and John Frederick announced his intention of making several stops on his way to the meeting at Schmalkalden to secure additional signatures, but did not find it possible to carry out this plan.[46]

The show of unanimity, however, had already been slightly marred and was soon to be more seriously damaged. When Melanchthon subscribed the articles he qualified his stand by writing:

I, Philip Melanchthon, regard the above articles as right and Christian. However, concerning the pope I hold that, if he would allow the Gospel, we, too, may concede to him that superiority over the bishops which he possesses by human right, making this concession for the sake of peace and general unity among the Christians who are now under him and who may be in the future.[47]

The quiet reformer was still hoping, long after Luther, the other theologians, and even the elector had abandoned all their illusions, that the pope might be persuaded of the truth of the Gospel. While Luther's articles deny that the pope is head of the church by divine right, Melanchthon would be willing to permit him that position by human right in order to preserve peace and tranquillity within Christendom.

In February the princes, representatives of the free cities, and theologians gathered at Schmalkalden for the meeting. Although it was the intention of the Saxon elector to have Luther's articles adopted as the evangelical statement for use at the coming council, his plan was thwarted, due, in part at least, to Melanchthon's machinations behind the scenes. Privately Melanchthon convinced Philip of Hesse that the position on the Lord's Supper in the articles had been influenced by Bugenhagen and thus was sharper than that of the Wittenberg Concord, which only nine months earlier had produced a modicum of agreement between the South Germans and the Wittenberg theologians on this vexing subject, and suggested that the evangelical estates declare their intention to make no further statement than had already been made in the Augsburg Confession and the Wittenberg Concord.[48]

Although we possess at least seven accounts of the action taken by the Smalcald League in its public sessions on February 10-12, 1537, our knowledge of the motives of the participants is quite fragmentary.[49] Rather than explore this extremely interesting subject, we shall confine ourselves to the league's decision, which was that no statement should be made indicating what could or could not be compromised at the council. The Augsburg Confession would be presented as the evangelical statement of faith on which they intended to stand or fall. However, it would be well to ask the theologians present to examine the Augsburg Confession and its Apology and furnish the league with biblical and patristic citations reenforcing the statements in these two documents. Also, because there was nothing in these earlier documents relating to the authority of the pope, the theologians would be requested to prepare a careful exposition of papal primacy.[50]

Because of the lack of library facilities at Schmalkalden it was impossible to undertake the work of providing proof texts for the Augsburg Confession and Apology, but the group of approximately forty theologians at the meeting did produce the required statement on the papacy. The task of writing it might well have been given to Luther, but at that moment the Reformer lay in his quarters at death's door. As he did not improve until he had begun the trip back to Wittenberg, hoping thereby to be granted his last wish of dying at home, the theologians were forced to proceed without Luther.[15] The final statement, entitled Treatise on the Power and Primacy of the Pope, was instead written by Melanchthon who completed it on February 17. The representatives of the League approved it the following week and in the final recess of the meeting listed it as an official document.[52] Thus instead of the articles which had been prepared by Luther, the Smalcald League approved Melanchthon's writing, although in the popular mind the document was considered "Compiled by the Theologians Assembled in Smalcald in the Year 1537," [53] and Melanchthon's authorship was forgotten for a time and not even noted in the editions of the *Book of Concord*.[54]

This was not the end of Luther's articles, however. At the end of the meeting of the league the theologians assembled at the request of Bugenhagen and Amsdorf, against Melanchthon's wishes, to discuss the original articles Luther had written. Luther could not be present at this meeting on February 24, but his statements were discussed, and those theologians who agreed subscribed. All but five, including Martin Bucer, affixed their names. The same day Melanchthon's Treatise on the Power and Primacy of the Pope was presented to the same theologians, all of whom declared that they were in agreement with the teaching of the Augsburg Confession, the Apology and the Treatise itself and signed their names. Luther, of course, was ill, so his signature was not included, although there is no reason to suppose that he would have objected to anything in Melanchthon's Treatise.[55]

The articles that Luther had written, which he took with him on his trip back to Wittenberg and which were signed by ten more pastors in Erfurt during Luther's stop in that city, never were used for their intended purpose.[56] The council never met in Mantua; in April 1537 a papal bull postponed it,[57] and it was to be eight years before a council actually did meet, and then in Trent, by which time there was no question of the Protestants needing a document to present.

Luther, however, had invested too much effort in these articles to allow them to remain in the elector's files. In June of the following year, 1538, he published them as a private writing, furnishing them with a preface indicating why they were written and conveying the misinformation that they had been officially accepted by the representatives of the Smalcald League.[58] Although historically this was not exactly true, the articles did express the convictions of the majority of the theologians and representatives present at Schmalkalden, and they generally became known, after 1554, as the Smalcald Articles.[59] In this first edition of 1538 Luther made extensive emendations, corrections, and additions to his manuscript, and it is this version of the Smalcald Articles, not the original text, which is included in the *Book of Concord*.[60]

We do not know if Elector John Frederick instructed Luther to prepare his articles for publication in 1538, but we have proof that in 1543 he ordered them to be reprinted.[61] It was largely due to the influence of John Frederick that the Smalcald Articles took on confessional status in the Lutheran Church. In his own last will and testament in 1553 he declared his faith in "God's pure Word, gospel, and religion, as, God be praised, it is found in the Augsburg Confession and the articles which blessed Martin Luther, doctor of the Holy Scriptures, presented . . . at the meeting in Schmalkalden in 1537" and exhorted his three sons to remain steadfast in the same faith.[62] Under the reign of the elector's son, also named John Frederick,[63] pastors in Saxony were required to pledge themselves to the Smalcald Articles as well as to the earlier Lutheran confessions,[64] and when the new university in Jena was established in 1558 all professors and students were obliged to adhere to it.[65]

Gradually, therefore, the Smalcald Articles came to be acknowledged as an expression of, as we have said, Lutheran independence from Rome. For this reason the framers of the Formula of Concord could write:

> We also commit ourselves to the Articles which we prepared in the great assembly of theologians at Smalcald in 1537 and there approved and accepted . . . as an explication of the Augsburg Confession, to which the electors, princes, and estates were resolved by God's grace to remain faithful. In these articles the doctrine of the cited Augsburg Confession is repeated, several articles are further explained on the basis of God's Word, and in addition the grounds and reasons are set forth at necessary length for renouncing the papistic errors and idolatries, for having no communion with the papists, and for neither expecting nor planning to come to an understanding with the pope about these matters.[66]

Returning to the initial subject, the value of the Smalcald Articles today, their chief importance is that they deal with essentials in faith. It is noteworthy that Luther, in attempting to summarize his faith, does not begin with any of the doctrines we customarily associate with him. At the very outset stands, not *sola Scriptura,* nor *sola gratia,* nor *sola fide,* but the simple statement of the divine majesty, that there is one God in three persons. Then after this he writes, in the first article of the second part:

> The first and chief article is this, that Jesus Christ, our God and Lord, "was put to death for our trespasses and raised again for our justification." He alone is "the Lamb of God, who takes away the sin of the world." "God has laid upon him the iniquities of us all." Moreover, "all have sinned," and "they are justified by his grace as a gift, through the redemption which is in Christ Jesus, by his blood." . . . Nothing in this article can be given up or compromised, even if heaven and earth and things temporal should be destroyed. . . . On this article rests all that we teach and practice against the pope, the devil, and the world. Therefore we must be quite certain and have no doubts about it. Otherwise all is lost.[67]

This is why Luther includes so many other topics in Part II of his work, the section which pertains to the office and work of Jesus Christ, or to our redemption. The practices introduced by the papal church must be opposed because they conflict with the first article, because they do injury to the teaching that Jesus Christ is the only Redeemer. "The mass in the papacy," Luther writes, "must be regarded as the greatest and most horrible abomination because it runs into direct and violent conflict with this fundamental article." [68] Invocation of the saints "is in conflict with the first, chief article and undermines knowledge of Christ." [69] Chapters and monasteries are attacked because in them men through "dangerous and needless effort" claim to be superior to the ordinary Christian and thus also detract from Christ's redemption.[70]

A more substantial problem, as much so in our day as in Luther's, then comes under attack, the papacy. Says Luther:

> The pope is not the head of all Christendom by divine right or according to God's Word, for this position belongs only to one, namely to Jesus Christ. . . . Manifestly . . . the papacy is a human invention, and it is not commanded, it is unnecessary, and it is useless. The holy Christian church can exist very well without such a head, and it would have remained much better if such a head had not been raised up by

the devil. The papacy is of no use to the church because it exercises no Christian office. . . . The pope is the real Antichrist who has raised himself over and set himself against Christ, for the pope will not permit Christians to be saved except by his own power, which amounts to nothing since it is neither established nor commanded by God.[71]

Here is Luther dealing with essentials. Whatever detracts from the honor due Jesus Christ as the only Redeemer of sinful man must be abolished. If the papacy, the mass, human ceremonies, or anything else obscures Christ, it must go. Nothing can be tolerated if it conflicts with the first and chief article, that Jesus Christ, our God and Lord, "was put to death for our trespasses and raised again for our justification." In this Luther is not just delivering a manifesto to the corrupt church of his century. He is also directing a reminder to those today who call themselves by his name, asking them constantly to examine their teaching to see if in it Jesus Christ is really the first and chief article.

7.

Luther's Understanding of Heaven and Hell

HANS SCHWARZ

When we inquire about Luther's understanding of heaven and hell, the first question is to what extent the classical three-decker universe, with heaven above, the earth in the center, and hell below, influenced Luther's understanding of heaven and hell. If we come to the conclusion that this world view had no influence on Luther, then we have to ask further whether Luther attributed to the terms heaven and hell any other spatial meaning. The last but not least important question, however, must be what theological significance Luther connected with the terms "heaven" and "hell." In the course of this discussion we shall first inquire about the dimension of "heaven," then about the dimension of "hell," and, finally, about the dimension of the "intermediate state."

I

THE DIMENSION OF HEAVEN

Heaven as a spatial concept. It is well known that in defending the omnipresence of God against Zwingli Luther did not allocate a certain definable place as a residence for God. Regarding the concept of "heaven," the problem cannot be so easily solved, because Luther was aware that even in the Bible the term heaven is very often used in a local way. Thus, for instance, in the story of the flood we read of the "windows of the heavens" (Gen. 7:11). Luther, however, interprets this phrase as meaning openings of the heavens. He insists that this cannot be understood literally, because

83

it only seems to us as if, through the openings of heaven, water is poured down with great force.[1] Luther discovers that even the horizon as the apparent demarcation line between heaven and earth is called heaven in the Scriptures.[2] Thus the whole firmament is named "heaven of all heavens," because in it all horizons are summed up including, for instance, the horizon of the people in France, who have a different heaven or horizon than we do.[3] When Psalm 8:8 mentions the "birds of heaven" (RSV: "birds of the air") Luther interprets "heaven" as the air in which we live.[4] Luther also uses heaven in an astronomical sense, e.g., when he speaks of a threefold movement of heaven.[5] First, with an immense velocity, the whole firmament revolves around itself once within 24 hours. Second, there is the motion of the planets in the sky and, third, Luther mentions a recently discovered motion in the sky which was still very uncertain for him. When the Scriptures say that something is "above us," or "far away," or "in heaven," or "beyond the sea," there are, according to Luther, no human or divine dimensions expressed with these terms. They are only spatial measurements, which indicate that something is away from us, or to the right, to the left, or in back, or in front of us.[6] In this way heaven is seen as part of the world of space and time that is known to us.[7] Besides that, however, there is another heaven which belongs only to God, in which he lives and which he alone knows. Our heaven, which we see, has a different spatial dimension from the heaven of God [8]; thus the visible heaven, or the sky, is entirely different from the heaven of God, which is accessible only to God.

Heaven as the realm of God. Luther realizes that in the Old Testament God was frequently described as residing over the cherubim and over Jerusalem which God had elected as his dwelling place.[9] Therefore Daniel turned to Jerusalem when he prayed to God. But with Christ's ascension we can no longer hold to this local and national understanding of God, because God is everywhere, so that everybody under the sky can pray to God. However, Luther knows that the "Schwärmer" still understand God's dwelling place in heaven in a local way. Because the visible heaven or sky is constantly moving, Luther concludes that this would mean that God could not sit still for a moment.[10] Luther thinks it absurd to understand God's realm in a local way so that one thinks of God as sitting on high somewhat like a stork in its nest.[11] Luther agrees with the Scripture that heaven is the throne of God and earth is his footstool,[12] but this does not mean for him that a piece of heaven is his throne and a piece of earth his footstool. Rather, God's throne extends as far as the heavens do. And all of the earth, whether the bottom of the sea or the grave of a dead man, is his footstool.

This kind of interpretation shows how Luther forsook all ideas of God being at home only in the visible heaven or the sky. God fills heaven and earth so that he is not far removed from his creation, but near and everywhere present,[13] in death, in hell, in the midst of his enemies and even in their hearts.[14] This is so because he has made everything and rules it by his very presence. Yet Luther knows that God is not present in a visible way.[15] As Paul says, God dwells in an inaccessible light.[16] Thus we cannot reach God by our own means. Even if he is omnipresent and even if his heaven is everywhere, we cannot see or notice his heaven and his omnipresence. Though God is omnipresent, Luther can say that through his Word God has his dwelling place in heaven from where he reigns. Through his almighty will he reigns everywhere as far as the earth extends.[17] Thus Luther's understanding of the omnipresence of God does not lead to an identification of God and the world. Because in his very presence God lives in heaven, he is transcendent for the world. Heaven does not here mean a place which could be determined by a spatial reference system. "What is in and before God" is determined only by the presence of God who is in heaven.[18]

Heaven is not a place beyond, separated from our earth in a spatial way.[19] Its dimension is different from that of our earth, a dimension founded in and determined by the presence of God. Heaven is present in the same way as God because it is present wherever God is present. This sentence is irreversible, because God's presence determines heaven and not vice versa.

Heaven as the Christian state of being. Luther, however, does not understand heaven exclusively as God's presence but also as the Christian state of being. This can mean that heaven is something which a Christian is in, or which comes to a Christian, or into which he will be received. Thus, on the one hand, heaven is understood as the dimension in which Christians already live when God, who is in his realm or in heaven, reigns in them.[20] On the other hand, the realm of heaven can be on earth now, because, somewhat like the angels, Christians are simultaneously both in heaven and on earth.[21]

Luther defends himself against the charge that he would conceive of heaven as locally definable by his understanding of it as the dimension which expresses the immediate closeness of God. In the same way he says, for instance, that Word and Sacrament are the entrance to heaven,[22] which means the beginning of the immediate communion of God with the believers.

To this interpretation of heaven as a present state of being it must be added that one lives simultaneously in the dimension of the world. Being in heaven or in the realm of God does not exempt the believer from being under the obligations of the earth and from being subject to its limitations. But in denoting the present state of being of a believer as the realm of heaven it cannot be only a temporary existence and then pass away, because heaven or the realm of heaven does not pass away.[23] Moreover, heaven as the Christian state of being is not understood as merely transitory in nature, for its presence is based on the presupposition that it is already created as the new or future heaven.[24] Thus heaven is ultimately futuristic or dynamic because it tends towards its fulfillment and completion. Thus we wait in hope and have redemption only through faith. But when the new heaven comes in its full reality we will live exclusively in that dimension and not simultaneously in that of the world. Then all the limitations to which our heavenly existence is now subjected because of our simultaneous existence in the world will be abolished. God will talk to us directly without the necessity that his Word be revealed to us,[25] and we shall hear him, see him, and be happy. Then the revelation of God *sub contraria specie* will be abolished and we shall see and understand him in his immediate glory, so that preachers will no longer be necessary.[26] This means that the step from the present to the future form of heaven is characterized by the transition from mediate to immediate communion with God in the glory of the Father when the dimension of the world is abolished.

Ascension as Christ's inauguration to power. We have seen that Luther's understanding of heaven as the state of being of God or of the Christians is independent of any world view, not because his conception of heaven would require a sacrifice of the intellect, but rather because heaven as the ultimate state of being of God is an entirely different dimension than our rationally determinable world. In the same way Luther's understanding of Christ's ascension does not conflict with any world view. The ascension of Christ is his exit from these earthly limitations and his entrance into the godly omnipresence [27] by which his kingdom exceeds the Jewish limitations and becomes as universal as his presence.[28] When Christ was here on earth he could only be present to a numerically limited group of people.[29] But when he entered the universal state of being of his Father, because of his Father's omnipresence he became present to all men. However, the new being of Christ which began with his ascension cannot be understood statically, as if he would fill the world like an ether, but rather his omnipresence is dynamic in that he creates and governs everything by his very presence. Through the ascension the body of Christ, which has been tied to our earthly space, becomes the omnipresent body of the Lord who is no longer limited to space and to whom the omnipresence of God is attributed.[30] Thus after the ascension the body of Christ is beyond all creatures because he is exalted above them and can no longer be understood in spatially determined categories.[31]

At the same time, however, he is in all creatures because he works from within them and sustains them. Here Luther emphasizes that, because of his ascension, Christ's spatial limitations are removed and he is closer to us than before.[32] This does not mean that he is nearer to us in a local sense but rather that he governs and sustains us from within when he permeates and embraces our earthly state of being with the dimension of his godly being. He does not sit lazily in one spot after his ascension but God gave him the lordship and power to sustain and govern the whole universe.[33] Luther realizes that it is impossible to explain in a rationally convincing way the transition from our state of being to the state of being of God that has taken place in Christ's ascension. Thus he admits that Christ's ascension is an article of faith and inaccessible to reason.[34] This, however, does not mean that this article is contrary to reason, because what is not rationally convincing need not be rationally impossible.

II

THE DIMENSION OF HELL

We have seen that Luther does not conceive of heaven as something above or beyond our earth. The dimension of heaven comprises and permeates our world without being spatially determined.

But how does Luther understand hell as the "lowest" level of the classical three-decker universe? Does he understand it spatially or as a certain state of being of man?

Hell as temptation and as the wrath of God. First we notice that Luther uses the term "hell" metaphorically. In his exegesis of the Old Testament he realizes that God seems to send men into hell and to call them back again.[35] Thus, for instance, he assumes that according to Scripture many saints go into hell because the word "Sheol" is used very often to express the ultimate anguish and pain of the dying.[36] When Jonah came into the belly of the fish it seemed to him as if he had gone into hell.[37] Going into hell while one is still alive can also express the climax of temptation under the wrath of God,[38] because man actually thinks that he has to perish before God. The experience of God's judgment, the despair concerning election, and the realization of being abandoned by God or of being far away from him are typical ways in which man "experiences" hell.[39] Unlike theologians of the Middle Ages, Luther does not understand hell as a subterranean place of anguish and despair, but rather as an existential situation so that everybody has hell within himself. In our time this can be experienced as the pain of despair under God's judgment.[40] Being in hell means also to exclude oneself consciously from God's life and to be excluded from it.[41] Thus there is both an active aspect of hell, namely, turning away from God, and a passive aspect, namely, being pushed into hell and away from God. Because he sees the passive aspect, Luther, like the psalmist (143:7b), can call to God: "Do not turn away your presence from me that I will not be like those who go into hell." [42] This indicates that hell as temptation and as being under the wrath of God can be overcome by loving God even in hell [43] and by trusting that he will lead us out of hell again.

Hell as eternal damnation. However, Luther does not interpret hell as an exclusively present state. For him hell is also the future state of those who are damned. Thus he distinguishes between hell before the last judgment and after the last judgment. He is not positive what hell is now; however, it is evident for him that it cannot be a specific place where the souls of the damned are now tortured as the artists paint it.[44] His exegesis of the Scripture leads him to the assertion that hell signifies the being of man in and under the wrath of God.[45] Thus he can understand pain as "the gate and entrance into eternal sin and punishment which means death and hell" [46] because pain leads to death and death to hell. He who suffers feels no great distinction between hell and death because death is the bitter separation from life. Hell, moreover, means that death is accompanied by the feeling that this punishment is at once unchangeable and eternal.[47] The soul is so captured that it cannot feel anything else but that it is eternally damned. Thus, Luther even calls hell the tomb of the soul.[48]

Pain, death, and hell, as the feeling that the punishment is unavoidable, however, still belong to the realm of the present experience of hell. Although they are irrevocable in the sense that whoever experiences pain and death cannot ever be exempted from them, they are not insurmountable. Devil, death, and hell are overcome for him who believes in the reconciliation in Christ, that he has given his body and his blood for our sins.[49] Thus, for instance, Luther can understand the words of the institution of the Lord's Supper as words of life and eternal bliss because in those words the whole redemptive event is summarized. "For him who believes in this all sins are forgiven by such a father and he is a child of life and has conquered hell and death." [50] This does not mean that he will never again experience pain, death, and hell as temptation but he will experience only their present dimension, not their dynamic drive toward hell as the place of eternal damnation.

Hell at judgment day is fundamentally distinguished from hell as a present state, because the future hell will be a certain place where all the damned will be gathered and placed under the eternal wrath of God.[51] However, Luther does not go into detail about hell as the place of eternal damnation because he constantly emphasizes that no matter how horrible you picture it, it will be much more horrible than anyone can imagine or portray it to be. Yet it is important for us to know that Luther understands hell at judgment day as a distinct place, because at judgment day the *evident* separation will take place between the believers and the unbelievers. Then a special realm of being has to exist for the unbelievers. But even this understanding of hell as a special place cannot conflict with any world view because the last judgment implies the abolition of our present world by the new imperishable world.

III

THE DIMENSION OF THE INTERMEDIATE STATE

A real point of conflict with the modern world view, however, could be caused by a spatial understanding of the so-called intermediate state or the world of the dead. Therefore we have to ask how Luther understood this intermediate state and how he understood the terms that are connected with it, such as the descent of Christ into hell, purgatory, and Abraham's bosom.

Location of the souls of the dead. Because Luther believed that through death the soul was separated from the body, the question arose for him: Where would the soul stay until judgment day? Luther was especially interested in knowing where the souls of the saved would be, because they are not yet in heaven and, of course, not in hell.[52] Yet he was convinced that God had a special place where the elect rest without death, pain, and hell. However, Luther does not indulge in speculation. He admits that no one knows either the name or the location of this place, though he is sure that it exists. All he can definitely say is that the "place" in which the soul of man remains and rests until judgment day is the Word of God.[53] Luther reminds us that we should not look at the "place" as such. We should, rather, look at the Word and the almighty power of God, because if God marks the heavens with a span and encloses the dust of the earth in a measure (Isa. 40:12) then his Word is much mightier and comprises much more than we can ever assume.[54] Therefore the Word or the promises of God are the receptacle of the souls in which they rest. When we faithfully grasp the Word and die in that faith our soul comes into an infinite space. In this way Luther has abandoned the idea of a specific location for the souls of the blessed dead, because an infinite space can only be of a dimension different from that of our present world.

This is seen more clearly when he determines further what the Word of God or the promises of God mean in this context. Thus he calls the state of being after death the bosom of Abraham to denote the place into which all are received after death.[55] However, the bosom of Abraham no longer exists, because in the resurrection it was replaced by the bosom of Christ into which the souls of believers now enter at death.[56] Of course, Luther means nothing spatial by these terms, because the bosom of Abraham signifies only the promise that in him all generations will be blessed (Gen. 22:18).[57]

Luther finds another term for the "place" of the souls of the dead in his exegesis of the Old Testament.[58] He translates the Hebrew *Sheol* with "hell" or "infernus" and interprets it as either the grave of the body or the receptacle of the soul.[59] According to Luther *Sheol* usually means grave, because the Scriptures mention no place into which the dead will be received.[60] Luther realizes that the Old Testament is concerned only about the body of the dead and not about the continued existence of the soul. Thus, he concludes that in Hebrew hell, as the place to which body and soul will go, is usually described in such a way that only the body is mentioned.[61] For us it is important here to see that Luther does not understand the receptacle of the soul in a local way. After death the soul does not rest in a spatial place [62] but in the Word of God. One could say that, according to Luther, the abode of the soul is simply within the dimension of God.

The problem of purgatory. An investigation of Luther's understanding of purgatory raises the question whether he thinks of it in any kind of local fashion. However, we also must consider here that Luther accepted the concept of purgatory only in his early years. Later on he rejected it as an article of faith. Then he realized that the idea of purgatory had no foundation in Scripture and served only as a pecuniary resource for the church.[63] In his early years he described purgatory as a punishment which is much stronger than all punishments on earth because it lasts into eternity.[64] Many who are alive have already been subjected to this punishment but in purgatory this punishment will be much more severe.[65] Luther's understanding of purgatory as a present state is similar to his understanding of hell as a present state [66] which, as we have already discussed, signifies temptation and the wrath of God. However, Luther also understands purgatory as something yet to come and so he cannot escape the question as to where this assembly of souls of the dead is located. He is not willing to agree with Thomas Aquinas that it is beneath the earth. He suggests that we should rather follow Augustine's proposal that we have no knowledge of its location.[67] Therefore Luther gives no certain answer to this question. He becomes even more suspicious about the locality of purgatory when he realizes that it is not necessary to believe in a purgatory because God's judgments are not an object of faith.[68] He admits that there could be a purgatory for a few but only those who

experience it know about it. Again a local understanding of this
kind of purgatory remains questionable.

Descent of Christ into hell. The question of Christ's descent into
hell poses further difficulties. The local understanding of hell which
such a descent requires is possible only after judgment day. Before
judgment Luther views hell as being only temptations and the wrath
of God. So if Christ descended into hell, it means that he was exposed to the wrath and the temptations of God, as in his passion,
especially on the cross. It is claimed, indeed, that this was Luther's
understanding of the descent into hell.[69] However, this interpretation
does not do justice to Luther. Though he knew Duns Scotus' claim
that the descent into hell cannot be proved by scriptural passages,[70]
Luther still was convinced that Christ experienced a real descent
into hell and not just some kind of existential exposure to the wrath
and the temptations of God. Nor is justice done to Luther by some
scholars who try to show that there are actually two lines in his
understanding of the descent.[71] Their argument goes like this: On
the one hand, Luther teaches that Christ's descent *coincides* with
his death in which he gained the victory over hell, and, at other
times, he teaches Christ's descent into hell *after* his death, in accor-
dance with the Apostles' Creed. His real conviction, they say, was
the former, namely the identification of Christ's descent with his
passion in Gethsemane and at Golgotha.

But what did Luther actually say? First, it is evident to him that
Christ did not suffer after his death, because descent into hell means
that Christ has been made the Lord of everything.[72] Descent into
hell thus cannot be connected with sufferings or temptation but
only pertains to the triumph and exaltation of Christ. For Luther it
is an article of faith that Christ descended into hell,[73] even if he has
trouble accepting the classical references (1 Peter 3:18 ff. and 1
Peter 4:4) as proof texts.[74] Luther asserts that in its substance the
soul of Christ descended into hell, but he admits that it has not been
revealed sufficiently what this descent was like.[75] Thus Luther faces
two difficulties here—first what the descent into hell means and
secondly how we can conceive of it.

Through his descent Christ gained the victory over everything
that can threaten us, the future wrath of God, anxiety, judgment,
and hell.[76] In his descent he shows that he has become Lord over
everything, that he has all power,[77] and that even the patriarchs can

be saved by him. In a very picturesque way Luther describes how Christ took the thief on the cross with him when he went to hell to redeem the patriarchs.[78] Thus the descent of Christ is the completion of his redemptive act, because even those who have lived before Christ are thereby included in his redemption. This is analogous to his ascension and exaltation, where his kingdom becomes universal for all who live from that time on. Thus Luther understands Christ's descent into hell neither as a descent into the future hell of judgment day, nor as a descent into the present hell of temptation and of the wrath of God. He sees hell as the dimension of existence of the souls of the dead as he did in his allusions to Old Testament ideas.

Luther does not object to a very picturesque understanding of the descent into hell and of the redemption of the fathers. He argues that no one can perceive these events without picturing them, albeit in an inadequate way.[79] To man's reason these events remain hidden, and therefore it can only be silent or speculate.[80] Thus it does not make sense to ask whether Christ was in hell according to his substance or according to his efficacy.[81] Hell is beyond our phenomenal world. When our thoughts deal with it they deal with something which lies beyond this world. To Luther the event of the descent is inaccessible to reason, not because it refers to a locality which is too far away to be reached but because something is expressed by it which is beyond our rational and phenomenal world. The descent of Christ leads to a realm which is in a dimensional relationship to our phenomenal world. It does not contradict it, but it is no part of it either.

IV

SPACE AS A FORM OF OUTER INTUITION

Our effort to discover how Luther understood the dimensions of heaven and hell has shown that Luther did not understand them in a local way. Heaven and hell are not locally determinable places beyond us, high above or deep down.[82] However, we cannot just spiritualize them either. Luther's understanding of heaven and hell is not a part of a certain world view and thus it cannot offend our modern world view.[83] Heaven and hell are determined in a strictly theocentric way,[84] and thus like God they cannot be described in spatial categories. Space is only the form of our sensual perception or of outer intuition.[85] Luther knows very well, for instance, that hell is not built of wood or bricks and that it does not have gates, windows, locks, and bars as a house does here on earth.[86] Nor did Christ destroy hell with a flag of cloth in his hands. But Luther affirms that "we have to grasp all things which we do not know and with which we are not acquainted in pictures even if they do not coincide or if the reality is not precisely as one paints it." [87] Pictures are necessary means of perception and intuition because they show us convincingly what Christ has done for us. Thus we can generalize with Luther that all spatial categories regarding the terms heaven and hell are only means of intuition which we have to use to express what is meant by these terms, or else we have to remain silent. However, despite the fact that Luther's understanding of heaven and hell is still meaningful for us today, it seems an exaggeration to assert, as some scholars do, that Luther had an almost unpredictable impact on the development of the modern world view when he abandoned the naive spatial understanding of heaven as the realm of God [88] and replaced it by a profound theological interpretation. Especially do the latest theological debates about the question of the modern world view show that Luther's understanding of God's relationship to space has unfortunately not become well known among theologians and even far less among scientists.[89]

8.

Concern for the Person
in the Reformation

HAROLD H. ZIETLOW

Who is Lutheran today? What marks Lutheran identity? What is the unique content of Lutheran religious self–consciousness? A unifying motif relevant today which marks Reformation theology and ethics is concern for the person.

I

CONCERN FOR THE PERSON IN THEOLOGY

Luther did not intend his criticisms of indulgence abuse to become a spectacle before the whole world. He considered his earlier "Disputation against Scholastic Theology" of September 1517 to be more important. Scholastic theologians had become too impersonal in their speculation about how many angels could sit on the point of a needle. The church's canon lawyers abused reason by calculating why a priest needed a cook but not a wife. They were accused of confusing the people. Scholastic theology rationalized the Christian faith to such a degree and removed it so far from the authentic religious needs of the common person that their priest-centered theological activity has been compared to sharpening a pencil so much that the point breaks off.

Adolf Harnack criticized the impersonal speculation of early church theology, e.g., its distinctions between *homoousios* and *homoiousios,* and observed that the masses of common laymen had to turn to bones and relics to satisfy their religious needs. Could not this same historical judgment account for the common people seeking religious satisfaction among Frederick the Wise's collection of relics in the Castle Church in Wittenberg, which included over 19,000 holy bones and a twig from Moses' burning bush? Frederick had a type of pragmatic fund-raising theology as the basis of his relic display. He was trying to raise money to build a bridge over the Elbe river.

So the first issue upon which Luther broke with Rome involved *theological method* itself. Scholastic theology placed too much emphasis on man-centered reason. Luther criticized reason as an untrustworthy prostitute and turned theological method away from speculation to the *God-centered* authority of the Bible. Here he and his followers could find a personal God reaching out to help his people in concrete, historical deeds. People could identify with the needs of those whom God helped in the events of the Bible and could find their own identity in relationship to the personal God revealed in the Bible.

The biblical revelation of a *personal God* becomes the second identifying mark of Reformation theology. While there has been disagreement among Lutheran theologians on the conservative–liberal spectrum, one thing they have all agreed upon is the unique personalism of Luther's emphasis on the biblical "I-Thou" relationship between man and God.

Already from the time of his early lectures on the Psalms Luther saw the twofold nature of God as hidden and revealed. Many theologians have affirmed these two qualities, but Luther's development of them unfolds in a dramatic, personal wrestle.

In the *Bondage of the Will* he describes God's hiddenness as what God is in himself. Personally Luther felt this to be the naked being and justice of God which demanded so much that Luther felt his bones were turning to ashes. Since the mystery and depth of what God is in himself intrinsically were neither revealed nor comprehended, Luther at times could think of God as an enemy. Luther's personal wrestle with the austere majesty of God placed an important item on the succeeding theological agenda, including our modern discussions. That item is the reality of God. God is not a product created by man's research, but sought and found in praying people with their humbled heads bowed to the dust. In a *Sermon on Preparation for Death* Luther said we should let God be God.

The living God also reveals his fatherly heart in Jesus Christ. God clothed in the love of Christ is the God "for us," said Luther, pointing up his personalistic theology. He said that God's living Spirit reveals to us the awesome Creator as a "friendly Father" who is present and active in all space and time. Luther's personalistic language says that man always runs in God's hand.

Christ himself was described by Luther as *one, true person,* personally united to God and man in his own life. Luther said that in Christ man is God and God is man. Christ is ubiquitous, everywhere present, bringing forgiveness and meaning to persons seeking his comforting nearness and forgiveness, as in the Lord's Supper.

Luther's trust of the heart in God's personal presence provided courage for him. When he alighted from the carriage for his trial before the Emperor in Worms, some evangelical-minded priests who agreed with Luther's biblical theology rushed to him and warned him to flee or recant lest he be killed. "God will be with me," Luther said. The *coram Dei* has unusual personal power in Luther's thought.

Still more important for showing the personal concern in Reformation theology is a third doctrine of the new theology, the *theology of the cross.* Again, Luther criticized the man-centered "theology of glory" of scholastic theology and put over against it what God does *for us* as described in the "theology of the cross." Adolf Harnack said that the one unifying work which all Lutherans have in common is Luther's *Small Catechism.* Having known the joy which came when he personally discovered the saving grace of God in Christ's cross when he was studying St. Paul's Epistle to the Romans, Luther underscored the personal work of God in his explanations to each of the three articles of the Apostles' Creed. God has "created *me*"; Christ has "redeemed *me* . . . bought and freed *me*"; the Holy Ghost has "called *me*" into faith. We trust that we shall live and reign with Christ through all eternity. Nowhere in the history of the church's theology can we find a more certain and dramatic assurance of personal salvation through Christ's cross than in Luther's justification doctrine.

The fourth component showing personal concern in Reformation theology is dynamically inseparable from saving love. It is *faith.* Luther sees faith as trust of the heart in the God who personally speaks to man through the Bible, sermons, Christ, and sacraments. The personal presence of God's Holy Spirit calls man to trust through the Word of God. Therefore when Luther was asked to discontinue writing and speaking about his grace and faith doctrines he said he could not in order that people might have a chance to hear the Word, accept its grace in Christ, and be saved. This same life-and-death issue of salvation motivated his personal concern to get the Bible translated, catechisms written, and schools increased and improved.

Many personal benefits came to the people through the unfolding of the new biblical theology. What an excitement it must have been for masses of peasants and artisans to hear the emancipating and empowering message of Luther's doctrine of the "priesthood of all believers" in his 1523 sermon on 1 Peter 2:9, "you are . . . a royal priesthood." Up to that time they knew nothing of royalty or priesthood. The royalty or patrons of the churches sat in honored box seats near the altar, and priests were portrayed rowing their boat to heaven through the waves of the stormy sea while the laity were drowning. Luther told the people that the spiritual values which they shared with Christ through faith and baptism were far more precious than the crowns of the nobility and the insignia of authority hanging on the pope. In all events, the personality of Luther himself dramatized his concern to make the God-man relation so real and personal in theology that it would communicate meaningful help and hope to people.

From a historian's viewpoint Ernst Troeltsch saw Luther's charismatic personality as an example of how history can be directed by a person in the context of freedom which contradicts the Marxist emphasis on economic-determined history. Harnack wrote that the dynamic person of Luther was one of the four causes of the break-up of the Middle Ages and the initiation of the modern era. Both of these men criticized some of Luther's ideas, and stimulated discussion at the time of the 400th anniversary of the Reformation, which led to the so-called "renaissance of Lutheran theology" in the twentieth century. In Germany Karl Holl, through historical research, defended Luther against detractors by reconstructing the context in which Luther made his decisions.

Meanwhile the renaissance in Lutheran theology through historical research and systematic construction was growing in Sweden. Söderblom applied Lutheran theology to missionary witnessing and ecumenics. He was a personal friend of the Hammarskjöld family.

Dag Hammarskjöld later wrote about the meaning of the theology of the cross for one whose efforts as leader of the United Nations confronted him with the possibility of imminent death. Anders Nygren developed the doctrine of God's love, *agape*, and Gustaf Aulén provided us with a modern Lutheran interpretation of the atonement in his book *Christus Victor*. In Denmark, Regin Prenter reconstructed Lutheran theology following the lines laid down by Luther himself.

Two trends continue in Lutheran theology's influence on the modern mind. One is that of the biblical-historical piety which shows its concern for persons primarily in missions of witness and mercy and pastoral teaching, preaching, and care of congregations. The other is an intellectual movement. Immanuel Kant, in his effort to use philosophy to "make room for faith," stimulated theology most by his *Critique of Practical Reason*, which stated the Golden Rule in a philosophical personalism. In the late nineteenth century Albrecht Ritschl developed this personalism for the human community. This moral theology had a great creative influence, for example at the Boston School of Theology, where it was again related to biblical theology by the president of the school, himself a professor of biblical studies, Albert C. Knudson. Here and elsewhere the personal meaning of Christianity reached out to people through a strong emphasis on pastoral counseling and social action.

The ideas and person of Luther were never lost in the modern concern to help people. Martin Luther King Jr., a Baptist, received his doctorate at Boston. When he and his father, who were so concerned to help people, changed their names to "Martin Luther" King they did it out of honor for the Reformer who they felt was at all times willing to give up his life to minister God's help to the needs of his people.

II
Concern for the Person in Ethics

William Ernest Hocking wrote about the need for a "reconception" of one's religious faith in his book *Living Religions and a World Faith*. He studied the encounter of the world religions and said that one of the four marks of the faith which will persuade the world to accept its truth will be "ethical personalism."

How does our understanding and expression of the Christian ethic measure up to this modern criterion of *personal concern?* If we were to eliminate the Christian church from the coming civilized community what would actually be missing?

A few of the major Lutheran motifs demonstrating concern for the person are: (1) the very being of the *person* defined as dependent upon a faith relationship to the love of God in Christ which motivates man in a new obedience; (2) the will of God made known through the Word in Gospel and Law; (3) the Commandments interpreted as love to God and neighbor; (4) the guidance of man into a life of tolerable ethical structure by the orders of creation; (5) the personal concern for natural human fulfillment in marriage as set against the separation of clericalism and secularism; (6) the mutual responsibilities of parents and children; (7) the role of the family and state in education; (8) the inclusive relevance of servanthood in free responsibility; (9) the illustration of all of these in the person of Luther himself.

According to the experience of the church's renewal when it made the transition from the Middle Ages to the modern period, the two elements which the Christian faith communicates to man are *Gospel and Law*. The Reformers listened to the living God speak his Word to their times in a personal manner. The ultimate personal concern was heard in these words, "You shall love the Lord your God with all your heart, and with all your soul, and with all your mind, and with all your strength. And the second is this, 'You shall love your neighbor as yourself'" (Mark 12:30-31). Luther brought this personal concern of love into his Christian interpretation of the Ten Commandments. He correlated the Gospel of God's love for man with the First Table which made up the first three Commandments. Man finds his personhood when the living God speaks his renewing covenant word, "I will put my law within them, and I will write it upon their hearts; and I will be their God, and they shall be my people" (Jer. 31:33; cf. also Heb. 8:8-12).

Each of the Commandments is explained in a personal and positive manner to show how it helps man. Luther introduces each of them with the words, "We should fear and love God. . . ." The fear and love of God correspond to the mystery and revelation in Luther's doctrine of God. He explained "fear" as honor or respect. Christians reverence God because of his holiness, goodness, and greatness. The fear shown toward God is like the honor shown to parents in the Fourth Commandment. God speaks to us through the Commandments out of fatherly concern for our welfare. Children should not be led to believe that this is the kind of fear which we have of the hangman, said Luther. Luther was convinced that man can face his ethical obligations because of the new strength received through justification by grace.

Luther fortifies the motivating persuasiveness of the first three Commandments with his theology of the cross. In his personalized Christian teaching of the meaning of Christ's sacrificial love he found man's power to say "I." His *Lectures on Galatians* (1535) based the courage to say "I" on the righteousness revealed on the cross. "I have been crucified with Christ; it is no longer I who live, but Christ who lives in me; and the life I now live in the flesh I live by faith in the Son of God, who loved me and gave himself for me" (Gal. 2:20). There can be no "neutral" position, says Luther. We are either alive in Christ or dead in some form of impersonal legalism. Luther says we are cemented together with Christ, as closely knit as the bones in our body.

When twenty-one years old Luther returned home to Erfurt University and lightning struck near him, whereupon in fear he vowed, "St. Ann, help me! I will become a monk." The vow which he took in the Augustininan monastery articulated his search for a gracious God.

Luther did not find a gracious God until his discovery of the forgiving righteousness of Christ in his biblical studies at Wittenberg. Luther had done his best as a monk, but his best was not good enough for a right relation to God. Only the love of God revealed in Christ's cross could say to Luther, "It's all right." In view of Romans 6 he interpreted the dying to sin and the birth of a new courage each day. Each day God says to us, "It's all right."

"Where there is forgiveness of sins there is life and salvation," Luther said, showing the relationship between the cross and courageous life. The one who receives the gift of Christ's healing forgiveness can affirm life. He can say, "I live." For whatever gift he has received to affirm life he thanks God. He drinks from God's fountain of love to find strength for the demands of a new day.

Here the law is personalized by seeing it as a loving command to help us. The person of Jesus Christ reveals the fatherly heart of God. The loving command is more personal than a condemning, punishing law. The key passage for interpreting the Law as a structure and power influenced by Christ for making known to us the will of God was Galatians 3:24-26: "So the law was our custodian until Christ came, that we might be justified by faith. But now that faith has come, we are no longer under a custodian; for in Christ Jesus you are all sons of God, through faith." Christ enhances God's personal concern for us and invites us to be his brothers and sisters, sons and daughters of the Father.

A letter which Luther wrote to Coburg Castle to Justus Jonas on June 30, 1530, provides us with his positive interpretation of the relationship between Christ and the Ten Commandments. He wrote:

> I have become a new student of the sacred Ten Commandments. Again like a child I learn them word for word and discover that it is true that their wisdom is unlimited. I have concluded that the Ten Commandments are the dialectic of the Gospel and the Gospel is the rhetoric of the Ten Commandments. And Jesus Christ has everything that is in Moses, but Moses does not have everything that is in Christ.[1]

By this imagery Luther suggests that the Ten Commandments teach God's wise will for us by instructing our reason, while the Gospel adds to the rational appeal for persuasion of Christ's saving love which convinces our emotions and will.

We accept Christ as the Exemplar and Prototype of one willing to do the will of God. The Holy Spirit leads us to surrender to God's will by the gift of a decision to accept the invitation to the marriage feast of grace (Matt. 22:1-14). The personal God invites us into the covenant of grace.

The Second Table, the last seven Commandments, deal with our love to our neighbor. Luther taught that the Fourth Commandment, "Honor your father and your mother . . . ," provided the foundation for moral order in society. Therefore, he said, God has attached an earthly reward to those who obeyed it.

The Fourth Commandment makes known the will of God for the *family*. In his catechisms, sermons, and articles on monasticism, marriage, and related subjects Luther introduces an evangelical sex ethic. These writings accomplish two aims.

a. They criticize the weaknesses of the existing medieval church's canon law which put the unmarried priests and nuns at a higher level of meritorious life than the married laity. Luther charged that the abuses of Roman sex laws were intolerable. He contended that the casuistry of scholastic laws, based on pagan reason, was contrary to the Word of God. For example, the church would agree that the priest needed a housekeeper, but forbade priest and cook to sleep together. Luther compared this to mixing straw and fire. When some priests slept with their housekeepers the church charged the concubines a financial penalty which enriched the bishops' treasury. When others were caught sleeping together they were told that sex relations would be going too far. This is like putting dry wood on the fire and telling it not to burn, complained Luther. In comparing human sex passions to dry straw or wood, Luther would quote 1 Cor. 7:9, "For it is better to marry than be aflame with passion."

Luther exposed the fallacy of priests thinking that they could continue celibate after ordination if they burned out their lustful passions by an orgy of fornication before ordination. Instead, said Luther, they became accustomed to it and came to enjoy it and could not avoid it after ordination. Existing immorality led to guilty consciences on the part of those involved.

b. After criticizing the practical failures of an impersonal and unrealistic canon law, Luther pointed to the Word of God as teaching a wholesome sex ethic in marriage. He dedicated an elaborate treatise on monasticism to his father and confessed that entering into a vow of monastic celibacy was less pleasing to God than Martin thought when he was a young man entering the Erfurt cloister against his father's wishes.

Luther himself demonstrated a personal concern for monks, priests, and nuns who were victims of an unfree vow of celibacy by counseling them into the conviction that they could make a free decision on marriage. The police force enforced the church law holding monks and nuns in their convents, but many were escaping the police, among whom was Katherine von Bora.

Her life gives us insights into the change from the old ethic to the new. She had been placed in a celibate, institutional life by her parents at the age of ten. Later she sought the personal freedom of decision on marriage in evangelical Wittenberg where she and Martin Luther were betrothed on June 13, 1525. She bore six children in ten years, took care of orphans, housed students, and cared for the garden and a farm. She fell from a wagon while fleeing Wittenberg when it was invaded after Martin's death. She suffered severe injuries from which she died.

Luther expanded his evangelical ethic to apply its personal concern to parent-child relations. He told parents that their children were precious. Mothers who wake to care for their babies, wash diapers, and nurture and discipline their children are performing honorable deeds in God's sight, because they are called to show God's loving care to their children.

Remembering that he was once spanked until he bled for stealing a nut and frequently paddled for not knowing his Latin lessons, Luther advised parents to apply love with discipline in training their children. Give the child an apple as well as the rod, he advised.

The issue of personal concern to improve family relations led Luther to appeal to both the parents and the state to step up efforts for better education of children. Reform of the church brought with it social reform, especially in education. Luther appealed to the biblical doctrine which states that God created the world. In this manner Luther replaced the philosophical ethic and old natural law with a God-centered sanction for obedience. He said that God wrote his will for man in *orders of creation,* such as the family and state. God works under the masks of these institutions.

Luther pleaded with the parents that they send their children to school and instruct them in the Ten Commandments, the Lord's Prayer, and the Creed in the home. You are the apostles, bishops, and pastors of your children, he said. He admonished parents to imagine that their children had two sacks. Into one the parents must put faith and into the other love. This humble, imaginative incident summarizes Luther's whole personal concern in evangelical ethics, faith active in love.

Luther also magnified the role of the schoolmaster in the work of humanizing and civilizing a community by Christian-motivated education. Likewise he reminded governmental rulers that the new church reforms would save them a lot of money which in the past had leaked to Rome. He suggested that this be used to improve the schools. The church of the Reformation which appealed to the Word of God required an educated people. Luther cried out to Germany that the money spent for guns and armies could be better invested in the education of her children.

The goal of Luther's biblical, personalistic ethic which appealed for help to educate children was the better *service of society.* Better educated people could contribute more as servants of the common welfare. In a sermon on Luke 2:22-32, Luther said: "A father sends his child to school . . . that he should study in liberal arts, learn decency, honesty, and good morals, that he may become a fine person, fit to serve land and people." [2]

The personal concern of Luther's biblical ethic was motivated by Christ's setting us free. Luther speculated whether his own family name developed from the Greek word for the one freed by Christ, "eleutheron." He summarized his ethic of free responsibility in his strategic essay of 1520, *The Liberty of the Christian Man*, by quoting from 1 Cor. 9:19, "Though I be free from all men, I have made myself a slave to all . . ." The modern meaning of this is: to be free is to be a person.

Luther also appealed to man's direct personal moral responsibility to the will of God as made known by the Holy Spirit. In his *Lectures on Galatians*, 1535, Luther wrote, "The physical Word which I speak is not the word of the flesh; it is the Word of the Holy Spirit and of Christ." [3]

But once Luther freed man from the external legalism of Rome, libertines arose, pleading that the Holy Spirit gave them a right to act lawlessly. They were called "antinomians," which means that they were opposed to laws. The danger of irresponsible lawlessness led Luther to write against the Antinomians in 1538, affirming voluntary responsibility under the universal law of God. Luther's emphasis on the positive function of the law should be heard in our day of autonomy and secularism. He calls us back under the authority of a personal God working in two ways. First, God extends his helping right hand of "proper" love to us through the church's means of grace, i.e., the teaching of the Word and administration of the sacraments. Second, with his left hand God reaches out to help us survive in an orderly, tolerable fashion in spite of our sins. "God is clothed with human masks *(larva humana)*, hidden in the prince or judge. Behind the masks I must see God or God's function." [4]

Of all Luther's contributions to personal concern in spheres of ethics, his own example of active involvement is perennially inspiring. His sermons and writings on a biblical ethic for marriage and the family edify us, but his example as a husband and father helps us even more as we seek for ideals to reconstruct the family in our modern context of dehumanization and disintegration.

Luther was intensely concerned for a fulfilled life for the persons of his family. He honors his father by his own initiative toward reconciliation. He loves his children by filling their lives with love and faith. Notice the intensity of his witness of God's personal love and promise to his dying thirteen-year-old daughter.

"My little Magdalene, you would like to stay with your father, but you are also willing to go to your Father in heaven?" he said after his prayer.

"Yes, dear Father, as God wills," she said.

She died in his arms. Luther was grateful to have had the joy of being a father, and found comfort in God's promise of everlasting life reaching into his sorrow. He said, "Dear little Lenie, you will rise and shine like the stars and the sun. How strange it is to know that she is at peace and all is well, and at the same time feel so sorrowful." [5]

Part Four

Luther and the Parish

9.

Luther's Liturgical Surgery

EUGENE L. BRAND

What is your picture of Martin Luther? Fearless reformer? Great preacher? Formidable theological debater? Stinging polemicist? Teacher and catechist? Bible translator? Hymnist? In addition to all of these Luther was a liturgical reformer, a role seldom considered. Though this phase of his work comprises a tiny fragment of the total output, it has exercised an influence all out of proportion to its own size and to Luther's announced intention.

For Luther did not turn to this task naturally, equipped with vast knowledge and singular literary skill. His influence upon Lutheran liturgical life is quite different from that of Thomas Cranmer in the Church of England. Luther was forced into the task, almost, it would seem, against his will. He knew it had to be done; he thought others were doing it badly; thus, he had little choice but to try his own hand at it. He was not motivated by any disgust with the form of medieval worship. In fact, he had a great love for it, especially its music. From long years of monastic life the rhythm of masses and offices had become part of him. His motivations were two: theological and pastoral.

Certain things in the medieval mass were contrary to Luther's theological convictions, and they could not be permitted to remain. But the mass also had to become clear to the people so that they could understand it and participate in it. That required a change in language from Latin to the vernacular; it required a simplification of the redundant ceremonial; and it required a musical form which was popular.

108

The language in Luther's reform did not achieve any official status as did that of Cranmer's *Prayerbook*. Since he allowed room for great variety in ceremonial, his own ceremonial pattern did not become particularly significant. The musical form of his *Deutsche Messe* did have a lasting influence, resulting in the so-called *Liedmesse* or "Hymn-mass." But even here most of the music was composed by others.

Viewed from the vantage point of four and a half centuries and in the perspective of the whole church, it would seem that what has been most influential about Luther's liturgical reform is not the recasting of traditional elements, but the omission of certain ones. In other words, it is not what he put in but what he left out that has stamped Lutheran worship ever since. There were two families of Church Orders in the 16th century. One followed the tradition of the *Formula Missae* (1523). The other was more like the *Deutsche Messe* (1526), but with few exceptions all members of both families bear the scars of Luther's surgery at two points: the offertory and the canon (the prayers surrounding the Words of Institution).

My purpose is to look more closely at this surgery, trying to understand the reasons for it. Then I shall try to note some of the things that have happened to our worship as a consequence. We shall examine the patient after 450 years to see what the surgery accomplished and whether we are satisfied to continue with the good Doctor's procedures.

I
LUTHER'S CONSERVATIVE REFORM

Compared with the programs of Zwingli and Calvin, Luther is always called a conservative reformer of the liturgy. Whereas they tried to abolish the mass and return to what they considered to be a reconstruction of the worship of the primitive church, Luther wanted simply to rid the mass of objectionable elements and put it into a form which enabled popular participation. Following Luther, the Augsburg Confession makes it a point to insist that the mass had not been abolished (Art. 14).

But viewed from the standpoint of the tradition of both Western and Eastern churches, Luther's reform did not look so conservative. In the *Formula Missae* (1523) any Christian would have felt quite at home during the Office of the Word. Here only minor changes were made and the Latin was retained (perhaps even for the lessons).[1]

But after the sermon his ease would have been shattered. For in place of the accustomed offertory prayers and chants, the bread and wine were simply prepared at the altar. And then the greater shock: instead of the Preface leading into the canon of the mass, it led into the plain Words of Institution (sung aloud!), which was followed by the Sanctus. To cushion the shock a bit, there was an elevation of bread and cup during the second half of the Sanctus. But two of the most important parts of the mass had simply been omitted. Nothing was transplanted in their place; they were simply removed by Luther's scalpel.[2]

The *Deutsche Messe* (1526) was a greater departure from tradition: the Office of the Word was abbreviated; the entire service was in German; chorales replaced the chants assigned to the congregation. But nothing was set forth to fill the void where offertory and canon had been.[3]

Luther's excision of offertory and canon, followed as it was by both families of Church Orders, left the Lutheran rite for the Eucharist something of a curiosity. The Lutherans claimed that they had not abolished the mass. And yet when they celebrated it they omitted two portions which any Christian, eastern or western, would have considered essential.

So far as anyone can tell, the Words of Institution had always been placed within a context of prayer modeled after Jewish blessings. Already by about 200 A.D. we have evidence of such a prayer in the *Apostolic Tradition* of Hippolytus. And if the *Didache* can be dated about 100 A.D., we have even earlier evidence. Though the primitive canon had undergone some modification in the Latin Rite commonly used in the Middle Ages, the Latin canon still reflected the primitive practice shared by the various Eastern Rites.

Luther's objections to the canon were essentially two: (1) He insisted that the Words of Institution should not be said in a low voice (as was the custom), but they should be sung for all to hear. They are proclamatory in nature, and one does not whisper what is to be proclaimed. (2) He could not accept theologically the strong sacrificial emphasis of the Latin canon. He wrote characteristically in the *Formula Missae:*

What I am speaking of is the canon, that abominable concoction drawn from everyone's sewer and cesspool. The mass became a sacrifice . . . [it] began to be a priestly monopoly devouring the wealth of the whole world and engulfing it—as with an apocalyptic plague—with a host of rich, lazy, lascivious, and corrupt celibates.[4]

Both objections were valid. The reforms of Vatican II have already corrected the whispering of the Words of Institution, and it is possible that a sweeping revision of the canon will yet take place, possibly removing the objectionable sacrificial language. But Luther did not follow the way of revision or of new composition. He simply let the institution narrative stand alone, bereft of its context of prayers. And so it stood until Lutheran reforms of the past decades. The *Service Book and Hymnal* restores a canon somewhat reminiscent of that of Hippolytus. *The Liturgy of the Church of Sweden* (1942) and the *German Agende I* (1955) also restore a form of canon.

A proper Eucharistic canon should do several things: (1) express continuity with Jewish forms of blessing, especially those of the Passover; (2) underline the thanksgiving aspect of the sacramental celebration; (3) lessen a mechanistic impact of the Words of Institution as magic formula (in spite of former Roman perversions of the canon) by putting them into a context; (4) give expression to the tension between the assurance of a consecration concept and the imploring of a concept of *epiclesis;* (5) by a proper *anamnesis* give breadth of scope to the ministry of the Lord we here remember, thus hindering a narrow equation of sacrament and cross; and (6) exhibit the manifold nature of the sacrament rather than connecting it solely with the forgiveness of sins. It is true that the *Prayer of Thanksgiving* in the *Service Book and Hymnal* does not do all this as well as it might, but it is an important step toward filling a void of 450 years' duration.

Yet the void left by Luther's surgery on the medieval offertory still wants filling in a satisfactory manner. We do receive monetary offerings and sing a fragment of psalmody now, but that does not satisfy the need. For while we give the monetary offering liturgical importance, we do not really receive it for a cultic reason; and "Create in me" really has little to do either with the offering received or with a more adequate offertory. It is with this problem that the rest of my presentation will concern itself. I hope to be able to suggest why it is a great deal more than merely a problem of liturgical form.

II

THE OFFERTORY TRADITION AND LUTHER'S OBJECTIONS

Luther does not spare the offertory a broadside either. He calls it "that utter abomination . . . which forces all that precedes in the mass into its service. . . . From here on almost everything smacks and savors of sacrifice." [5] Just what is it to which he objects so violently, and how did it get that way?

In the early years of the New Testament church, the Eucharist seems to have been celebrated within the context of a potluck dinner called the *agape* or love-feast. Ideally, people brought gifts of food to be shared, and in this way looked after the poor. From this food was taken enough bread and wine for the sacrament proper. But before the end of the New Testament period a separation was already taking place between the love-feast and the Eucharist. Undoubtedly it was caused by the kind of disorders to which Paul has reference in 1 Corinthians 11.

Apparently, however, the custom of bringing offerings of foodstuffs to the eucharist continued even after the love-feasts had disappeared. Thus a vestige of the corporate meal idea remained. Money was also included. But since only bread and wine were actually consumed during the service, it was natural that attention focused more and more on them.

Around the beginning of the 4th century, in the west, the practice must have been something like this: At the offertory, the people in procession brought all kinds of gifts to be received by the deacons and placed on a table near the altar. Perhaps the name of the giver was spoken and a prayer said over his gift.[6] Or perhaps a collect was said after all the gifts had been offered.[7] At any rate, the gifts were offered to God, apparently often with the intent of procuring a special blessing in return (an indication of the infiltration of sub-Christian concepts). As in any procession, a psalm was sung. From the gifts on the table enough bread and wine for the sacrament was taken to the altar. What remained was used to support the clergy and relieve the poor. No one under discipline was permitted to offer a gift, but it was expected that each communicant do so.

Gradually the concept of sacrifice shifted completely from the offerings of the people and focused upon the sacerdotal act of offering the bread and wine. Werner Elert has noted that with this trend what remained of the idea of a common meal vanished.[8] As would be expected, evangelical and Catholic scholars are not agreed in their description of this process. Many factors were involved: As liturgical forms became more complex, greater ceremony was lavished on the offering of the bread and wine at the altar; as the tradition developed that the elements should be specially prepared and that only unleavened bread should be used, it was no longer possible to take the elements from the offerings of the people, and the two acts were divorced; expecting special blessings in return for offered gifts was open to gross perversion (people requesting the ill fortune of personal enemies, etc.) so that regulations were effected governing that which one might request legitimately. As a result of all this, the offering of gifts other than bread and wine was finally forbidden (except on certain occasions). The other gifts became a sort of tax for the support of the clergy and the relief of the poor. The offertory became a sacerdotal act in which the bread and wine were offered as sacrifice to God with appropriate prayers. Contact with offerings of the people was lost. Though remnants of the old offertory processions remained, they no longer had the same significance.

Never completely lost, however, was the idea that one intending to receive the sacrament should bring an offering. By the Middle Ages it had become an offering of money. Various enforcement measures were taken. In the 11th century obligatory money offerings were received on major feast days (these were the days on which the laity would commune). But such offerings had become only token vestiges. The church and its charitable works were actually supported by income from land holdings, endowments, royal patronage, and fixed taxes.

As the emphasis on the mass as a propitiatory sacrifice increased, the people's money was more often used for "buying" special votive masses than for making offerings within the liturgy. In most European parishes both Sunday and feast-day offerings had disappeared by the 16th century. The church was supported in the ways mentioned, and there was a scandalous traffic in the "selling" of masses. The concept of sacrifice had become tied up with the sacrifice offered by the priest for special intention. Any sense of corporate action had all but vanished. Most masses were solo performances by the priest.

It is against this concept of propitiatory sacrifice that Luther raised his voice, for it struck at the very center of the Christian faith as he understood it. One might speak of Christ's sacrifice present in the Sacrament so that its benefits might be received, but one might never speak of offering the sacrifice of Christ to God.[9] Over against the mass as *sacrificium,* Luther emphasized *beneficium;* against the mass as man's work, he counterposed the concept of *testamentum.* As the Roman Catholic writer Francis Clark has seen clearly, Luther was not merely opposing the popular errors and crass practices on the part of the clergy. "The Reformers . . . made it clear that the object of their attack was not merely 'popular theology' but the doctrine of the Mass as authoritatively maintained by the Roman Church and her approved doctors." [10] The sacrifice of the mass was opposed to the Gospel.

(It is probably true that Luther did not give enough attention to the subtleties of the traditional view, and it is certainly true that Lutherans have tended to overreact, almost ignoring the sacrificial nature of the Sacrament. Roman Catholic theology, however, is involved in a reinterpretation of its post-Tridentine position, recognizing that it is open to question biblically. As both confessions rethink the problem in the light of greater biblical knowledge, there is hope that they can agree on the relationship of the Eucharist to Christ's sacrifice. Hope is not so bright that they will so quickly agree on the function of the Eucharist in God's economy.)

Out of a passion for the Gospel, Luther eliminated those parts of the mass which contained sacrificial language, as we have seen. But it would be wrong to conclude that he had no positive understanding of sacrifice. After all, the burden of proof was with him. He was well aware that the mass had been called a sacrifice by the Fathers since antiquity. In *The Babylonian Captivity* (1520) he recalls the earlier practice of bringing gifts, and makes the point that this is the origin of the sacrificial terminology. It was later misplaced and applied to the Sacrament itself:

> Therefore, let the priests who offer the sacrifice of the mass in these corrupt and most perilous times take heed, first, that they do not refer to the sacrament words of the greater and lesser canon, together with the collects, because they smack too strongly of sacrifice. They should

refer them instead to the bread and the wine to be consecrated, or to their own prayers. For the bread and wine are offered beforehand for blessing in order that they may be sanctified by the word and by prayer . . . but after they have been blessed and consecrated, they are no longer offered, but received as a gift of God.[11]

But it is in another 1520 treatise that he gives fuller attention to the matter: *A Treatise on the New Testament, that is, the Holy Mass.* He begins by pointing out the connection between the nourishment which the Sacrament affords faith, and the good works which result. Among the good works, intercessory prayer and acts of charity are stressed. In the New Testament church these were both closely connected with the eucharistic celebration, and it is in connection with them that the language of offering and sacrifice became attached to the mass. Luther points out that traces of this are still observable in the offertory ceremonies, especially the elevation. But in 1520 there no longer was any connection between the offertory and the people's gifts. What little charity there was had been taken over by the institutions of the church, making the gifts of the people unnecessary.[12] The implication is strong that if the offerings of the people were restored and again connected with the offering of the bread and wine, Luther would not object. To him this would be part of a proper "thanksgiving"—a true sacrifice of praise which would also include hymns, prayers, etc. But since there is no need for the people's offering, it is better to dispense with the sacrificial terms so that they do not detract from the sacrament and testament concepts.[13]

He does not leave it at that, however. Since the external sacrifices are not needed, people should bring "spiritual sacrifices," by which he means themselves:

> What sacrifices, then, are we to offer? Ourselves, and all that we have, with constant prayer. . . . With this we are to yield ourselves to the will of God, that he may make of us what he will, according to his own pleasure. In addition, we are to offer him praise and thanksgiving with our whole heart. . . .[14]

Then, following the imagery of the Epistle to the Hebrews, he speaks of laying these offerings upon Christ who, as a godly priest, makes them pleasing to God.

> From these words we learn that we do not offer Christ as a sacrifice, but that Christ offers us: And in this way it is permissible, yes, profitable, to call the mass a sacrifice; not on its own account, but because we offer ourselves as a sacrifice along with Christ. . . . If the mass were so understood and for this reason called a sacrifice, it would be well.[15]

But then he draws a conclusion which is most consistent for him, but which strikes ears conditioned by the contemporary debate as somewhat disappointing and one-sided:

> . . . For all those who have the faith that Christ is a priest for them in heaven before God, and who lay on him their prayers and praise, their need and their whole selves, presenting them through him, not doubting that he does this very thing, and offers himself for them— these people take the sacrament and testament, outwardly or spiritually, as a token of this, and do not doubt that all sin is there forgiven, that God has become their gracious Father, and that everlasting life is prepared for them. All such, then, wherever they may be, are true priests. They truly observe the mass aright and obtain by it what they desire. For faith must do everything. Faith alone is the true priestly office. . . .[16]

As a corrective polemic the conclusion is admirable. But it illustrates the fact that Luther was not able to transcend the terms of the Reformation debate. He views the Sacrament in terms of the bread and wine alone, not as an action involving bread and wine. He cannot get beyond the western preoccupation with the elements, and so the Sacrament remains a "thing" to be received or offered, rather than an act to be celebrated. And it is for this reason that three years later he had no practical alternative to the offertory which he excised when preparing his *Formula Missae*.

As a sort of postscript to this section, it should be noted that offerings of money were reintroduced in the Lutheran churches. Fredrich Kalb lists the date as 1528.[17] But, as Christhard Mahrenholz points out, these offerings were given no liturgical significance; they were not presented at the altar. They are seldom even mentioned in the agendas of the two families of Church Orders of the 16th century. The money was received either by passing through the congregation with the *Klingelbeutel* during the sermon hymn or the sermon itself, or in a bason at the door.[18] Even in the rare instances where more traditional ceremonies still surrounded the preparation of the elements at the offertory (e.g. Magdeburg Cathedral), no connection existed with the offerings.[19]

At first, Lutherans in America continued this surreptitious type of offering. But it soon became expedient to give it liturgical prominence. Unlike the situation in Luther's day, the Americans needed the money to erect and maintain buildings, pay salaries, and establish the work of the church in general. But it was not until after 1900 that orders of service in English almost uniformly included rubrics dealing with the offering. Even the rubric in the *Service Book and Hymnal* is minimal. It is true that Wilhelm Loehe in his *German Agende* of 1844 tried to restore a sacrificial concept to the offerings of the people, but this had only limited influence upon American practice.

III

PRESENT EVALUATION OF THE OFFERTORY PROBLEM

In this final section, I want to attempt to evaluate where the removal of the offertory and the divorce of the offering from the Sacrament have left us after four and a half centuries. If we include the period of the sacerdotal offertory, the time span is much longer. We noted Werner Elert's observation that with the modification of the offertory into a sacerdotal function, what was left of the idea of meal fellowship vanished. And I think that its recovery has begun only recently. For in spite of Luther's great emphasis on *beneficium*, his insistence on communion at the Eucharist, and his concept of the priesthood of believers, communion for him is primarily for individual comfort and strength. A Lutheran communion has generally been more of a collective action than one which is truly corporate. And this situation will be difficult to remedy until we restore to the eucharistic celebration a proper understanding of the offertory, and an adequate liturgical structure for it.

Three major problems can be traced at least in part to this weakness in our worship. (1) In addition to their monetary worth, the gifts we offer are symbolic of our self-offering. Until the offertory expresses this clearly, it cannot be a satisfactory response to the proclamation which precedes it. In response to the Gospel proclaimed, we offer ourselves, declare ourselves wholly at God's disposal. Symbolically, through money, we offer ourselves upon the altar as our response of love to the love of God which has again been preached to us. Further, until the bread and wine for the Sacrament are obviously a part of the offering we bring, the offertory cannot be a satisfactory first step in the action of the Eucharist proper. Sacrifice includes or leads to communion. It provides the food for the meal. That is involved in the biblical understanding of sacrifice which sees it as God's gift to man, as Marcus Barth so aptly points out.[20] Structurally, the offertory has a pivotal function: it responds to the proclamation and prepares for the Supper. Our offertory tradition cannot do this adequately.

(2) The offertory should be the primary place where one's individual life is focused in the cultic action. The greater part of my most obvious service is done individually, outside the gathered community. This individual life is focused into the cultic life of the community in intercession, but especially when I place it symbolically upon God's altar in company with my fellow–priests. Here it becomes clear that sacrifice really means the bodying forth of love in response to God's love, and as a channel of that love in the world. As H. D. Wendland has observed, divine agape is the content of the New Testament concept of sacrifice.[21]

My sacrifice is shared in that what we offer together will be "returned" to us as heavenly food for our sustenance and joy. In this cultic motion from sacrifice to sacrament the mystery of God's action among men is demonstrated: what we surrender to him he gives to us, and through us to others. Until this finds adequate expression it will be difficult to get beyond the individualistic approach to the Sacrament, and again regard it as a meal of fellowship with God and each other.

(3) Because of the offertory's inability to focus my individual life, it is difficult to see a real continuity between my participation as an individual Christian in the corporate act, and what I do as part of the scattered community. Worship becomes a compartmentalized experience. The only possibility is a holdover from the old sacred-secular dichotomy which I affectionately call a "gas station theory." The corporate act fills me with so much grace, and I am thus strengthened for another week. Of course, there is some truth in that, but it still implies compartmentalization.

My service takes two primary forms: occupational and cultic, and these must remain in balance. The occupational or vocational service we often label *diakonia*. Its theme song, sung by the individuals of the scattered community, is "Brighten the corner where you are." I serve God by doing those things I do as a Christian, and that means being an instrument of God's love in my particular contexts of life. But I also serve God in union with my brother priests in the gathered community where we engage in cultic activity. This is the service often labeled *leiturgia*. These are not two different kinds of service; they are service conditioned by two different sets of circumstances. And these circumstances prevail because as a Christian I am part of a corporate body but also an individual member of it.

In an adequate offertory this polarity would come to more obvious expression than at most other points in the service. And it would also be obvious that man's action and God's action are all bound up together. Ultimately it is not possible to separate sacrifice and sacrament, or to pit them against each other. A proper offertory would make this clear.

By now it may seem as if Luther has been left far behind. But I think not. For it seems to me that the points of contact for everything I have noted in the three problems are there in Luther. It is just that he did not draw the conclusions. But he sees that the proper place to talk about sacrifice is not in connection with the consecration but the offertory. And if his concept of offering one's self as sacrifice is connected to his concept of vocation, the basis for the cultic focusing for which I have been opting is laid. It would only remain to hook it all up to the idea of the congregation as priestly fellowship. If this can be done, then adequate replacement organs would be at hand to transplant in place of the diseased ones Luther cut out so long ago. Perhaps the patient can still be restored to robust health!

10.

Luther, Preaching, and the Reformation

STANLEY D. SCHNEIDER

There is more to the Reformation than Luther. Yet it is of him that most of us think when the word Reformation is mentioned. In him is embodied much of what can be learned and shared from that experience in the life of the church, particularly in the area of preaching. Hence this essay is concerned with Luther, preaching, and the Reformation. The consideration of the topic is under two major headings: Luther, the Reformation of the preacher; and, Luther, the preacher of the Reformation.

I

LUTHER, THE REFORMATION OF THE PREACHER

By his own testimony Luther reluctantly undertook the task of preaching. The procedure in his day seems to have been different from our practice. Preaching was one of the last functions of the ministry of the Word that a man undertook, rather than one of the first.

One day Luther related how hesitantly he undertook preaching. The occasion for his telling this about himself was when he was encouraging a man named Lauterbach to accept the call to be preacher at the Castle Church in Wittenberg, probably in May 1532. Evidently this conversation took place within the precincts of the Wittenberg cloister of the Augustinians in virtually the same spot where Luther's superior, Staupitz, had called on Luther to take up preaching some twenty years before. The comments of Luther to Lauterbach are reported to have been:

Ah my friend, I had the same experience. I feared the pulpit perhaps as greatly as you do; yet I had to do it; I was forced to preach. At first I had to preach to the brethren in the refectory. Ah, how I feared the pulpit! Under this pear tree I advanced fifteen arguments to Dr. Staupitz; with them I declined my call. But they did me no good. When I finally said, "Dr. Staupitz, you are taking my life; I won't be able to endure it three months," he replied, "In God's Name! Our Lord God has many things to do: He is in need of wise people in heaven, too." [1]

Staupitz was able to persuade Luther to preach. And it did not kill Luther to do it. He preached with almost uninterrupted regularity until four days before his death in 1546.

All of the extant remains of Luther's preaching are in some forty different volumes of the Weimar edition of Luther's works. The total number of sermons is over 2,300. The most productive year numerically is the year 1528. From that year there are 195 sermons distributed over 145 preaching days.[2]

The Introduction to Volume 51 of the American Edition of *Luther's Works* contains this observation: "Luther's preaching activity was tremendous by any standards since it was carried out in addition to his proper vocation of lecturing to students." [3] I wonder whether Luther himself would have agreed that his preaching was something other than his "proper vocation." Be that as it may, it is obvious that in Luther there was the reformation of a preacher. From the time of his reluctance under the pear tree he developed into a man who has been described as one who "never failed to strike the archenemy a blow from the pulpit whenever the opportunity came." [4]

What was the situation of preaching in the church at the time of Luther? It was a calling and an activity held in high esteem. That, in part, explains the trepidation and misgiving that Luther experienced when he was called upon to preach. A manual of homiletics written by Jerome Dungersheim in 1514, which Luther probably did not study, but which reflects the thinking of the time, states that a clergyman ought to have received a good education and attained the age of thirty before he be permitted to preach. Luther was two years under thirty when Staupitz spoke to him. He was also about to receive the degree of Doctor of Theology.

The background for preaching in Germany at the time of Luther can be traced to the thirteenth century and the Crusades. It has been observed that preaching is the result as well as the cause of great movements, and so when there are such movements in the church there is also great preaching. The Crusades introduced a new element in the preaching life of the church. That element was the itinerant preacher and the popular outdoor sermon. Originally these men were to recruit the men who were to fight the Crusades. The content of their sermons laid heavy stress on the holy land and its sacred places which had to be taken from the hands of the infidel Moslems. They also came to stress, as additional motivation, the general indulgences which were granted to those who followed the banners into battle.

The slow-minded parish priest was not the man for this task. So the preaching orders came into existence, the learned Dominicans, the popular Franciscans, and the order to which Luther belonged, the Augustinians. These were endowed with a license by the pope himself to preach.

In the late medieval period these monks were also given the privilege of hearing confessions. This became an occasion of conflict with the parochial priesthood. Its abuse also became the object of the satirical pen of Erasmus. In the *Praise of Folly*, which Erasmus wrote in 1517 and dedicated to his friend Thomas More, he wrote of the monks:

> No one, however, even though isolated from public life, will dare to rebuke one of these monks, because through the confessional these men acquire the secrets of everyone. To be sure, they believe it a crime to publish these secrets, but they may accidentally divulge them when drinking heavily or when wishing to promote amusement by relating funny stories. The names, of course, are not revealed, because the stories are told by means of implications in most cases. In other words, if anyone offends the monks, the monks in turn will take revenge against the offender. They will reveal their enemies in public sermons by direct implications, so that everyone will know of whom they speak. And they will continue this malicious chatter until bribed to stop.[5]

As for the preaching itself, Latourette observes,

> Much preaching was heard in Western Europe in the fourteenth and fifteenth centuries. It may even have increased in the period. Some of it was by friars and some by the ordinary parish clergy and bishops. Much of it was routine and quite uninspired, but some of it was profoundly stirring and moved multitudes. It contributed substantially to the groundswell which preceded and in part issued in the forward surge of the tide in the sixteenth century.[6]

Two movements in the life of the church influenced the nature of the sermon during the period which provided Luther's immediate preaching heritage. These were scholasticism and mysticism. Scholasticism provided a way of preparing for preaching and a way of preaching which displaced the old homily style. The old homily was a rather artless running commentary type of exposition. Scholasticism proposed that the preacher must first of all find a *thema* or subject. The sermon was often compared to a tree, such a tree being actually drawn in one of the homiletical manuscripts; the theme, naturally, was the trunk. The whole sermon must grow organically from a theme taken from Holy Scripture, the theme for seasonal sermons at mass being taken usually from the Gospel or the Epistle. To derive a theme from a nonbiblical source would have been a gross error.

If the idea of a sermon being like a tree sounds familiar it may be due to the fact that you have read Grady Davis' book *Design for Preaching* in which he says, "A sermon should be like a tree." [7] Then follows a somewhat poetic development of that idea. Grady Davis wrote that about ten years ago in his book which was published in 1958. The influence of scholasticism made its impact, and still does. That was the first movement which made a lasting impression on the nature of preaching prior to the Reformation.

The second was mysticism. This added the emotional and personal element at a time when preaching tended to become too abstract and pseudo-learned. That element is not missing in Grady Davis' writing either, "It must grow in a warm climate. . . ." [8]

Mysticism led in part to the reintroduction of another element in the content of pre-Reformation preaching which helped set the stage for Reformation preaching, and that was criticism of the church. The well-known names of Wyclif and Hus are associated with this as well as others less well known but nonetheless sharp in their criticism. John Geiler, who occupied the pulpit at Strasbourg Cathedral for over thirty years until his death in 1510 was well known for his satirical sermons on the church. But his sermons, like virtually all of the others, was critical only of the practices, not of the doctrines of the church.

This criticism of the church was synonymous with criticizing the clergy. It led two of the writers of the period, the aforementioned Dungersheim and another named Surgant, to warn against criticizing the clergy before the people. The place for such criticisms was in Latin sermons at synods. This is an indication of the two types of sermons which were preached, those preached to the clergy, and those to the people. Those preached to the clergy were almost always in Latin. But those to the people were almost always in the language of the people. Even in Spain in the early fifteenth century a Dominican friar named Vincent Ferrer spoke only in Spanish and is said to have drawn enormous crowds.[9]

Authorities are in virtual agreement that the medieval sermon was always preached in the language of the people to whom it was addressed.

In spite of the counsel that criticisms of the church should be limited to sermons addressed to the clergy, the people heard a good bit of that. But they heard other things too. The following summary has been given by a Roman Catholic writer, John P. Dolan, on the content of the popular sermon.

> Preachers were preoccupied with the theme of sin and the grim face of death waiting for the moment of merited punishment. There was an emphasis on the horrors of hell and the sufferings of the damned. Their sermons were filled with descriptions of burning trees on which hung the souls of those who did not attend church services, vultures gnawing at men's vitals, venomous serpents stinging the unholy, boiling lakes, frozen fens, heated ovens and vile dungeons. Scripture, when quoted, was completely torn from its living historical context. Its personalities and their sayings were distorted and mutilated into passive conveniences for moral dilation. Everywhere the emphasis was on the negative side of man's salvation, his sins, and punishment.[10]

Preaching probably wasn't all that bad, but there was enough of this kind of content to determine the theological motif which the reformation took. The problem created by such preaching is almost self-evident. How does one avoid such a horrible fate? The official answer was indulgences. The Reformation answer was justification by grace through faith.

Contrary to Dolan's suggestion that Scripture was not used extensively, there is evidence that the late medieval preacher was rather well versed in the Bible. Dr. Reu quotes Dungersheim about the preacher's relation to Holy Writ:

> If they desire to be shepherds of the flock of Christ the Word of God provides them with the only pasture and nourishment of the flock; if

they would be physicians of souls, the Word of God offers the only remedy . . . ; if they would be spiritual leaders of the congregation, God's Word is the sword they must be able to wield. . . . How can they accomplish this task without a thorough knowledge of this same Word and unless they have studiously acquired and practiced the art of using it wisely.[11]

The rub in this heritage is in that last part, practicing the art of using the Scriptures wisely. For the method of using the Scriptures was (1) to quote an authority, chiefly the church fathers, and (2) to apply the fourfold sense, chiefly the allegorical meaning, to scripture texts. Since most of the church fathers were also allegorists, allegorical interpretation was the art that was cultivated.

Broadly speaking, the content of the pre-Reformation sermon was ethical rather than doctrinal. Certain things were generally criticized, Jews and heretics, usury, luxury in clothing, gambling, dancing, drunkenness, and the practice of superstition, except of course that approved by the church.

Though the sermon content was not pointed doctrinally, the dogma of the Catholic Church was nevertheless the foundation stone on which practically every preacher reared the structure of his sermons. It is precisely in doctrine that Luther's sermons differ most radically from those before his time. It was this which reformed him from a reluctant to an eager preacher. He began his preaching as a monk. He developed as a preacher at the town church in Wittenberg, where he was called to be the preacher in 1514 to assist the sickly pastor Simon Heinze. It was in the town church that he restored preaching to its context of a congregational setting. It was there that he was led to the conviction:

When I preach, I sink myself deep down. I regard neither doctors nor magistrates, of whom are here in this church above forty; but I have an eye to the multitude of young people, children and servants, of whom are more than two thousand. I preach to those, directing myself to them that have need thereof. Will not the rest hear me? The door stands open to them; they may begone. I see that the ambition of preachers grows and increases; this will do the utmost mischief in the church and produce great disquietness and discord; for they will needs teach high things touching matters of state, thereby aiming at praise and honour; they will please the worldly wise, and meantime neglect the simple and common multitude.

An upright, godly, and true preacher should direct his preaching to the poor, simple sort of people, like a mother that stills her child. . . .

> In such sort should also preachers carry themselves, teaching and preaching plainly, that the simple and unlearned may conceive and comprehend, and retain what they say. When they come to me, to Melanchthon . . . let them show their cunning, how learned they be. . . . But to sprinkle out Hebrew, Greek, and Latin in their public sermons savours merely of show, according with neither time nor place.[12]

As a result of this conviction Luther developed a style which has been described as neither medieval nor modern, though his style, understandably, has more in common with the medieval. One writer has characterized Luther's homiletical style as "heroic disorder."[13] Most of his early sermons have more of the scholastic style. Later on, particularly in the postils which he wrote to help other preachers, the style is more like the ancient homily in which one verse after another is commented upon. His style may be described as a combination of the expository and topical methods.

Luther's introductions and conclusions are quite abrupt and matter-of-fact. He dispensed with the old *exordium* which came to be much abused. Erasmus, again in the *Praise of Folly*, says of preachers and the introductions of their sermons:

> If charity is to be their topic they commence their sermon with a dissertation on the Nile River in Egypt. Or they are contented to begin with Baal, the Babylonian snake god, if they intend to speak of the mystery of the cross. If fasting is their subject they begin with the twelve signs of the Zodiac; if they wish to expound faith, they initiate their sermon with the problem of squaring the circle.[14]

It is not hard to understand why Luther abandoned that sort of thing. As for conclusions, their abruptness may have a number of causes. One reason is that the announcements came immediately after the sermon, and in fact were considered a part of it. For another, despite some rather long sermons, Luther was aware of time and the fact that he would either preach on this matter again, or had already spoken of it and could refer to the other sermon. There is the further reason that for a while he really spoke twice in the same service, once preaching on the Gospel (or Epistle) for the day, and then having a sort of catechetical sermon following. The original sermons on the Commandments and the Lord's Prayer were spoken in this way. These were done from 1516 through 1518, preceding by ten years another similar series which resulted in the publication of the *Large Catechism*.

In the reformation of the preacher Luther was a man of his times. He used much of the heritage that was his, respecting the sermon as a powerful instrument through which God could speak to his people. The real reformation was in his content in which he went beyond the criticism to the underlying reasons for the conditions which were criticized. The great central topic of justification which brought on the reformation of the church was that which resulted first of all in the reformation of Luther the preacher. That dominated his life, and consequently also his preaching, as we shall see in looking at three sermons of Luther, the preacher of the Reformation.

II
LUTHER, THE PREACHER OF THE REFORMATION

The three sermons which have been selected for a sampling of Luther, the preacher of the Reformation, are all on the same text, Matthew 11:25-30. This is the historic Gospel for the festival of St. Matthias. In the first of these sermons somewhere or other along the line of translation someone has mistakenly translated St. Matthias as St. Matthew. In the American Edition of Luther's Works this sermon is listed as being a sermon on St. Matthew's Day.[15] That is clearly a mistranslation, since the sermon was preached on February 24, 1517, which is St. Matthias' Day, and the text is that historic Gospel. The mistake is older than the American translation, however, since it appears in a 1934 publication and also, surprisingly, in a reference to this sermon in Heinrich Boehmer's *Road to the Reformation*. The Weimar edition is clear, it is St. Matthias' and not St. Matthew's Day.

The reason for selecting these sermons is that they are all in Volume 51 of the American Edition of Luther's Works. Furthermore, they present Luther at three different stages of his preaching career. The first one is on the eve of the Reformation, February, 1517. The second was preached in February of 1525, which was approaching the height of Luther's preaching. The third sermon was preached in February 1546, in Eisleben, and was the last sermon that Luther ever preached.

At the time of the first sermon Luther was serving as the preaching pastor of the congregation at Wittenberg. Although the copies of the sermon from which the translation is made are in Latin, the sermon was probably preached originally in German. The reason that the sermon is printed in Latin is that this was the language in which the notes were taken. There had developed a kind of Latin shorthand which did not exist for German at that time. Those who took the notes were scholars. Furthermore, many of the written works were still printed in Latin rather than German.

This sermon, more than the others, bears the marks of Luther's methodological heritage. He was an Augustinian. Augustine was the man who applied the rules of classical rhetoric concerning the purpose of a sermon and the styles of presentation. Through the influence of Augustine the definition of Cicero regarding the task of the speaker came to be applied also to the sermon. This is to teach *(docere)*, to delight *(delectare)*, and to influence *(flectare)*, in order to appeal to the intellect, feeling, and will. The styles of address that were to be used in achieving this purpose were the restrained *(genus submissum)*, the moderate *(genus temperatum)*, and the grand *(genus grande)*. The purpose of the three styles is to enable the address to be received intelligently *(intelligenter)*, willingly *(libenter)*, and obediently *(obedienter)*. Augustine himself recognized the danger of artistic form getting in the way of the content of a sermon. So he avoided that. So did Luther. Augustine did use pointed word combinations and plays on words. So did Luther, particularly in this sermon.

The text is Matthew 11:25-30:

> At that time Jesus declared, "I thank thee Father, Lord of heaven and earth, that thou hast hidden these things from the wise and understanding and revealed them to babes; yea, Father, for such was thy gracious will." All things have been delivered to me by my Father; and no one knows the Father except the Son and anyone to whom the Son chooses to reveal him. Come to me, all who labor and are heavy-laden, and I will give you rest. Take my yoke upon you, and learn from me; for I am gentle and lowly in heart, and you will find rest for your souls. For my yoke is easy, and my burden is light.

The playing with words begins the sermon. "Man hides what is his own in order to conceal it, but God conceals what is his own in order to reveal it." [17] Then comes an allusion to the text, "he hides it from the wise and great in order that they may be humbled and become fools, and thus reveal it to babes." This also states the purpose or proposition of the sermon. Then comes the division, which he announces, "Two questions should be asked here. Who are the wise and understanding from whom it is hidden, and what is it that is hidden?"

In the development of the sermon the attempts to explain who are the wise ones seem, on reading, to get quite complicated. For example, after explaining who are the wise and who are the apparent fools in the world, he continues the explanation by saying, "Therefore the truly wise—I mean the fools—are always saying. . . ." It becomes clear that he is talking about those to whom revelation is given. But the mixing of the terms "the wise" and "the fools" must have been confusing to his hearers.

He uses the term "fools" rather frequently in the sermon, rather than the term "babes." He picked up the term fools from a reference to 1 Corinthians 3:18, "Let him become a fool that he may become wise."

The use of supporting Scripture is generous. It is his primary source of elaborative material. There are eighteen specific biblical references, from Psalms, Genesis, Romans, 1 Corinthians, Ecclesiastes, Matthew, John, Philippians, and one from an apocryphal book, Baruch.

Evidence of exegetical work finds its way specifically into the sermon when he deals with the verse, "Come unto me, all who labor and are heavy laden." "More fittingly," he says, "the Greek text says: Come to me, all who are *fatigued* and heavy-laden." This does give a fuller connotation of the meaning of the Greek *oi kopiontes* than does either the Latin *laborantes* or the German *mühselig*, or for that matter the English "labor."

It is in this part of the sermon, which really seems to be a third part, not included in the introduction, that Luther, the preacher of the Reformation, begins to come through. For he identifies labor with work-righteousness, saying that those who practice that "seek to extinguish the fire of hell and escape the judgment by all kinds of sanctifications." Then begins the attack on indulgences, for which this sermon is remembered and cited in many biographies of Luther.

> Through these [i.e., indulgences] nothing is accomplished except that the people learn to fear and flee and dread the penalty of sins, but not the sins themselves . . . whereas the people ought rather to be exhorted to love the punishment and embrace the cross. Would that I were a liar when I say that indulgences are rightly so called, for to indulge means

to permit, and indulgence is equivalent to impunity, permission to sin, and license to nullify the cross of Christ.

The justification theme is not explicitly developed in this sermon. The condemnation of indulgences is strong, and just at the point where one might think a specific proclamation of justification could come Luther lapses into a criticism of the clergy. "Oh, the dangers of our time! O you snoring priests! O darkness darker than Egyptian [an allusion to Exodus 10:21-23 and the plague of darkness]! How secure we are in the midst of the worst of all our evils!" And with that the sermon ends, at least as much of it as we have.

This sermon is not unusually long. In fact, as it stands, it surely took less than the usual hour that good preachers took for their sermons, even though Luther was described as a slow speaker. But it was one of two sermons that Luther preached on this particular day, the other one being the final one in the series on the Ten Commandments.

Absent from the sermon is any reference to the festival of St. Matthias. While Luther kept the historic pericopes for these saints' days, it is not often that he makes much of the occasion. As little as there is in Scripture about them, including St. Matthias, this may be understandable. Most of the material about the saints was legendary, and while Luther was not above using legend on occasion, he seems to have avoided it whenever its use would seem to have placed legend on a par with Scripture.

So much for the first sermon. The preacher of the Reformation is evident in the criticism of indulgences on doctrinal grounds. The clear formulation of justification is not yet evident. Yet, as is the case in other sermons, here is a foretaste of something which Luther later put into formal writing. What he preached on February 24, 1517, found more elaborate and more formal expression on October 31, 1517, in the Ninety-five Theses.

The second sermon to be considered was preached in the year 1525. The generally accepted date for it is February 5, but there is some uncertainty about that. It is listed as a "Sermon for St. Matthias' Day." [18] Perhaps subsequent calendar revisions make the date uncertain. Once again there is nothing in the sermon to indicate that it was preached on St. Matthias' Day. The reason for assigning it to St. Matthias' Day is simply Luther's custom of preaching on the Gospel for the day.

This sermon appeared in a sixteenth-century English translation in a collection "of his [i.e., Luther's] writings and preachings for the necessary instruction and edification of such as hunger and seek after the perfect knowledge and inestimable glorie which is in Christ Iesu, to the comfort and salvation of their soules." It can be said of this sermon that it is one of the richest and most thoughtful of all his sermons which sum up his faith in Christ.

It is that. This is Luther preaching at his best. In a sense this could be said to be one of Luther's "heroic disorder" sermons from the point of view of organization. There is no obvious theme. What organization there is is a simple progression through the text, with Luther saying what is suggested to him by the various parts of the text.

The introduction is interesting. One cannot help wondering if a preacher today could be so bold in many of our congregations. Evidently Luther had some problems with miracle texts too, for he begins by saying:

> This Gospel is one of the really genuine Gospels. Other Gospels in which the miracles of Christ are described are not so comforting as those which contain the sermons of Christ in which he so lovingly teaches us and entices us. I am not so certain of the grace which I see in miracles shown to others as when I have before me plain, clear words.

This time Luther says that this Gospel "is nothing else but a knowledge of God the Father and Christ his Son, and the power of this Gospel lies in these two words, 'the wise' and 'babes.'" If there is a theme, that would be it, although it is not very succinctly stated.

He then establishes the relevance of the text by indicating its context, demonstrating that the context indicates that it was originally directed to people who were, or thought themselves to be, the people of God.

There is much less criticism of the papacy in this sermon, but there is some. He says, for example, that worldly wisdom "is always hatching out and devising something new, even in spiritual and divine things." Then, referring to the papacy,

> Thus out of their own wisdom they invented cowls and tonsures and almost everything that is practiced in the whole papacy. There each one chose his own work; one invented this and another that, and when one thing died down or failed to please they soon invented something else, as we, unfortunately, have seen and still see to this day. . . .

But the criticism is not limited to the clergy this time. For, after more gently chastising the papacy than in the other sermon, he continues:

> Now this is not to be understood as applying only to the spirituals [i.e., monks, clergy]; it also applies to the common man, when he does not accept the Word of God. We see citizens dealing in counterfeit wares and merchants who are swindlers, and there is so much trickery and deceit, so much usury and taking advantage that it is hardly possible to enumerate it all. And yet they go on doing it while having masses said and providing candles, thinking that God will allow himself to be propitiated in this way, concerned only that their reputation before the world remain untouched and unsullied, no matter what it is in the sight of God.

So he concludes the part about identifying who the "wise" are, and then continues with a development of who the "babes" are. "Christ here calls foolish, simple people 'babes'; he is not speaking of actual infant children," Luther explains, "nor of people who are childish in the eyes of the world." He had an appreciation of the use of figurative language, recognizing it as a part of the literal sense in which he came to understand Scripture. The babes are all those who let themselves be taught by God. They receive the Gospel. And what is the Gospel? "The Gospel is a good, joyful message which teaches me how to know God, through which knowledge I obtain the forgiveness of sins and eternal life."

Then comes something which one finds frequently in Luther, a slight excursion into a field in which he was doing some work. Just as indulgences got into the 1517 sermon, so something about free will gets into this one which was preached in the same year that he wrote "On the Bondage of the Will." But it's a brief trip, and he soon comes back to contrasting God's grace with the human condition.

One literary device that Luther used, frequently and effectively, was putting words into the mouth of Jesus to interpret an actual quotation. He cites the text: "Learn from me for I am gentle and lowly in heart." This he interprets by saying,

> It is as if he were saying: Flesh and timid natures look upon me as if I were cruel, stern, and severe, but I am not so; I am gentle and lowly in heart. I do not terrify people, as Moses did. I do not preach "do this, do that"; I preach forgiveness of sins. I preach only that you

should receive, not that you should give anything. . . . I am altogether kind and lowly in heart and ready to receive sinners. And even though they fall right back into sin, I still do not cast them away from me. . . .

Then comes the comfort of the Gospel,

> Therefore, even though outwardly everything seems to be against us, as if it would crush and devour us, there is no need to be troubled; for inwardly, in our conscience, we have peace. And this peace of conscience is the first and most immediate fruit of faith, as Paul says in Romans, "Therefore since we are justified by faith, we have peace with God through our Lord Jesus Christ."

The sermon could well have ended right there, but he has not finished with the text. He still has something to say about "Take my yoke upon you." He does so briefly, and ends with a German proverb, "With a good companion the singing is good." Then, "Two can carry a burden easily, though one alone may not carry it well." Thus the sermon ends.

In the sermon there is rich use of supporting Scripture once again, at least 30 references, all of them this time from the New Testament.

Strangely absent from the sermon is any reference to the *Schwärmerei*, the followers of Thomas Muenzer. They were causing problems at this time, even in Wittenberg. But it is also true that some efforts at establishing peace with this group were under way at this time. Perhaps Luther's silence is due to political expedience.

This is a good sermon. If you read only one sermon of Luther's you couldn't do better than to read this one.

The last sermon to be cited is the last one that Luther preached.[19] It was not preached in Wittenberg, as the other two were, but in Eisleben. It is thought that the sermon was preached on Monday, to a large crowd which had come to hear Luther preach. The sermon gives the impression of being one for which no extensive preparation was made on Luther's part. If that is so, it is understandable. He had made this trip to mediate a dispute. He was ill. It was a fatal illness. Three days after preaching this sermon in 1546 Luther died.

Again he begins the sermon with a word of praise for the text. "This is a fine Gospel and has a lot in it. Let us talk about part of it now, covering as much as we can and as God gives us grace."

Again he lashes out at those who think themselves wise, using sarcasm, e.g., ". . . we have the idea that God could not reign if he did not have wise and understanding people to help him." "Everything that God does they must improve, so that there is no poorer, more insignificant and despised disciple on earth than God; he must be everybody's pupil, everyone wants to be his teacher." But the villains have changed, or at least their number have been increased. He doesn't go after the pope alone, but all heretics, "in our time the Anabaptists, and anti–sacramentarians, and all fanatics and rebels; they are not satisfied with what God has done and instituted. . . . They think they have to do something, too." He also goes after the pastors who "hack and snap" at one another, and the people who say, "Ah, our pastor or preacher is nothing; there's the real man, he'll get things done." All these Luther calls by a term that is best translated "wiseacres," who, he says, put the cart before the horse.

The pope gets it too. For he goes on to a recital of the activities of the papacy which led to the Reformation. Then back to the *Schwärmerei,* naming Thomas Muenzer by name in this sermon, and then back to the pope.

But right in the middle of all this is a prayer that Luther says we ought to say: "Dear heavenly Father, speak thou, I am willing to be a fool and a child and be silent; for if I were to rule with my own understanding, wisdom, and reason, the cart would long since have been stuck in the mire and the ship long since have been wrecked. Therefore, dear God, do thou rule and guide it thyself; I will gladly put out my eyes, and my reason besides, and let thee alone rule through thy word."

Other content of this sermon that is different is at least one, and, perhaps two, liturgical references. St. Agnes, who is commemorated by the Roman Church in January, is mentioned by name. There is an allusion to St. Vincentius, who is also commemorated in January. Since this sermon was preached in February the possibility of these two persons being relatively fresh in the minds of the people is strong. The biblical references are much fewer in this sermon, only eight. But the Old Testament got back into the picture.

It seems as though Luther himself was aware of the largely negative nature of this sermon. For the last sentence in the sermon proper comes to a positive point.

> Lo, this means that the wise of the world are rejected, that we may learn not to think ourselves wise and to put away from our eyes all great personages, indeed shut our eyes altogether, and cling only to

Christ's Word and come to him, as he so lovingly invites us to do, and say: Thou alone art my beloved Lord and Master, I am thy disciple.

The text was not exhausted in this sermon. But Luther was. After ending on the prayer note he says, "This and much more might be said concerning this Gospel, but I am too weak, and we shall let it go at that."

Luther, the preacher of the Reformation, was not at his best in this sermon. But an understandable lack of specific preparation, a strange congregation, and a fatal illness shed more than enough light on the situation to know why that is the case.

His utter reliance on God and his grace is here, however, and that was Luther's faith. In his preaching this treasure of the Gospel was shared with the people of his time. In the preaching that has been preserved for us we can still share in that same Gospel.

11.

Luther as *Seelsorger*

ARTHUR H. BECKER

Many have observed that one of the principal motivations for Luther's reforming activity was his pastoral concern. What aroused him was that simple people were being deceived by the extravagant claims of the indulgence peddler with his "medicine show." Luther was one of a considerable line of theologians and parish priests who had severe theological reservations about the efficacy or even the justice of the indulgences, but what seems to have been the last straw for him was not a theological but a pastoral concern. In his letter to the archbishop, Tetzel's employer, he writes:

> I grieve over the utterly false notions the people have conceived . . . unhappy souls . . . O Good God! I could keep silence no longer. . . . Works of piety and love are infinitely better than indulgences.

In the complex professional identity which was his, as theologian, exegete, translator, pamphleteer, social activist, politician, that of parish priest was certainly one of the central elements. Yet, strangely enough, while this central element of Luther's concern is frequently mentioned, little is written of Luther as pastor. I have been able to find one book in English by August Nebe, translated from the German in 1894, *Luther as Spiritual Adviser*. Dr. Hans Schwarz informs me there is one in German which I have not seen, and there is one doctoral dissertation by Charles Bachman, written in 1948, which has one chapter on Luther as pastor.

Because of a growing conviction that modern ministry of pastoral care must recover as well as establish its own unique role, distinct from psychotherapist or social worker or community organizer, I have felt that an examination of Luther's pastoral care, as one of the sources of our ministry, is in order.

I
HISTORICAL CONTEXT FOR REFORMATION "SEELSORGE"

In understanding both Luther as *Seelsorger* and the cure of souls in the Reformation, one must of course guard against judging his mode against the norms of today; rather one must attempt to see the matter in its own historical context and setting. Except for the parish priests who largely pass unnoticed, save for John Gailer of Kaisersburg and the parish priest of Chaucer's tale, pastoral care as we know it today was largely absent during the Middle Ages.

The care of souls had deteriorated from the integrity of a St. Francis or a St. Dominic, and had fallen to the peripatetic "pardon-ners," hearers of confession, wandering purveyors of lurid *exemplae* [1] and sellers of indulgences. "For long centuries the emphasis had been not on sin as a state of the soul from which repentance and divine grace would emancipate it, but upon sins in the plural, that swarmed in great numbers and must be confessed in great detail." [2] The New Testament inner renovation of the spirit gave way to an anxiously filled routine of confessions, penances, and uneasily accepted absolutions which simply started the cycle all over again. This "despotism and extortion of the pontiffs" raised Luther's pastoral ire and was one of the important elements of the setting in which Reformation *Seelsorge* develops.

Two other patterns of church life also set the context for Luther's pastoral work. Consistent with the nature of the Holy Roman Empire and the twin symbols of power in pope and emperor, the cure of souls in the late medieval period centered on the formal power of the church to heal both the inherent and accidental ills of men. If the church is accepted as the primary repository of the "power of the keys," particularly in an autocratic sense, as the decrees of both Innocent III and Gregory IX attested, then cure of souls, particularly penance and absolution, become a simple matter of the exercise of that power through verbal decree. The indulgences which Tetzel sold were certifications of such power. Thus, a primary reliance on *word* or *decree* in pastoral care results. The medium of pastoral care is then simply the *"official language"* of admonition and confession and the decree of absolution.[3] This is the pastoral heritage of Luther, only partially modified through his experience of the personal pastoral relationship with Staupitz in the monastery, which preconditions Luther to a primary verbal and proclamatory mode in pastoral care. I hope to show that Luther's understanding of the Word of God occasioned a change not only in the theological understanding of the nature and force of that Word but, in addition, brought about the beginnings of a fundamental change in the nature of the pastoral relationship itself.

In addition to the "official" relationship and language of the confessional, pastoral guidance for troubled souls during the 14th and 15th centuries was given via the medium of pastoral writings of various kinds. A first group was directed toward maintaining personal piety and included *exemplae* for education in morality. In these, through various stories, the Seven Virtues and Vices, and the Twice-Seven Works of Mercy were detailed. Gerard Groote's *Imitatio Christi* (often ascribed to Thomas à Kempis) is the most famous modern remnant. Various ladders of devotion were also written, as well as books of consolation for troubled souls. One of Luther's first pastoral works is one of these: his *Fourteen of Consolation* written to Elector Frederick the Wise of Saxony in 1520.

Pastoral writings during this era were also directed toward the "art of holy writing and holy dying." One by Gerson, *De Arte Moriendi,* purposed to provide material by which one friend might support another in death.[4] A similar work in England is Caxton's *Arte and Crafte to Knowe Well to Dye.* The interesting thing about many of these manuals is that they provide no particular role for the priest or pastor to fill during the hour of death, perhaps on the presumption that, during the time of plague, no priest would be available. So every good Christian man can provide his brother with help in this hour. This stressed what Luther was to recover and stress even further, the pastoral ministry of every Christian for his brother, the *consolatio fratrum.*

If often escapes our attention that a sizable portion of the population, particularly of the cities, had learned to read and could profit by such works already before Luther's time.[5] It is not surprising then that Luther should make use of this medium of pastoral care. Many of the major papers of the Reformation (apart from the confessional writings) are literature of this sort.[6] One of Luther's most beautiful pastoral letters *On the Freedom of the Christian Man* is perhaps in itself a rather audacious attempt to give pastoral care even to the pope himself!

II

THE TYPES OF PASTORAL CARE
AS LUTHER PRACTICED IT

Seelsorge, or the "concern for souls" which Luther practiced extensively through his writings and in his direct personal pastoral ministry, falls into two broad classifications: *für die Seele sorgen—* the concern for souls—and *die Seele weiden,* or guidance of souls (or if it does not fall too unkindly on Protestant ears) "spiritual guidance," though not in the traditional Roman sense [7] of achieving a beatific vision of God, but rather spiritual guidance in loving service to the neighbor.

The first—concern for souls—Luther carries out through his sermons, his *Postillen,* his several papers on Confession and, somewhat more indirectly, through confessional writings as they relate to confession and absolution, and through his personal ministry.[8] Shepherding, or guidance of souls, is carried out largely through his personal letters and through his direct pastoral ministry, especially visiting the sick. He felt this to be a particularly important responsibility. During the time of the plague, in 1527 in Wittenberg, he urged parish priests not to flee the plague but to stay for

> we must and are in duty bound to deal with our neighbor in all times of need and danger whatever. If his house is burning, love bids me run thither and help to put out the fire; if there are enough other people there to put it out, I may return home or remain there, as I please. . . . He who will not help and assist another until he can do it without danger or injury to his own person or property will never help his neighbor.[9]

Luther's shepherding, concerned as it was with giving guidance in living out the consequences of faith (that man will love his neighbor in all the complexities of life), brought him to deal with all manner of human issues and social problems. The range of issues touched on in his letters and pastoral work would do justice to a modern inner city minister. He gave guidance in ethical situations that "trouble the conscience of men"—the letter *Whether Soldiers Too Can Be Saved* is an example here, as is his extensive correspondence on marriage and family problems.

In dealing with these problems, Luther emphasizes that his pastoral care has only an advisory function; he advises people how they may act, he does not command them as to what they must do. He is also unwilling to represent any form of casuistry, which is the application of specific commandments to specific situations with the exceptions involved. Rather he intends simply to apply the commandment of love to specific situations where Scripture has given no definitive command.[10] In giving this ethical guidance, Luther did not believe one could simply look up what the Bible has to say about a situation and apply that as a rule for every case. He is surprisingly "situational," except that his emphasis is not on what is "right" or "allowable for me," but rather what is "good for the neighbor." The individualistic sense of modern situationism is entirely foreign to Luther. His pastoral care was not "client centered" it was *neighbor centered,* addressing itself always to the question as to what serves the neighbor in Christian love.

III
LUTHER'S THEOLOGY OF THE WORD AND ITS IMPLICATIONS FOR "SEELSORGE"

The overpowering impression one gains from reading any of Luther's letters, whether written to the sick and dying, the doubting, the persecuted and imprisoned, letters of advice to preacher or prince, is that in him there is complete integration of faith and theology with pastoral practice and human compassion. He "is his theology." He did not separate his theology from experience,[11] nor did he make his experience the sole source of his theology.

Luther's study of the Word and his life in it was not just a "soaking up of sacred information" to be expelled later at the stimulation of some theological issue or personal crisis. Something deeper is involved, more than an intellectual process. To formulate this accurately is difficult and perhaps treacherous, but one has the feeling, in reading Luther's letters and papers, that he is sharing or expressing his "love affair" with us; it is his love affair with the Word of God and the gracious Savior cradled in that Word. He describes himself, as it were, in *The Freedom of the Christian Man*:

> The soul which clings to them [the promises of God] with firm faith is so united with them, altogether taken up into them, that it not only shares in all their power, but is saturated and made drunken with it.[12]

Life in the Word for Luther is expressed in the "theology of the cross"—the life of a sinner being graciously befriended by Christ of the cross, even while the rebellious spirit within the sinner which alienates him from God is being crucified with the same friend.

> In every word of the Law which humbles us and reduces us to nothing, God is uniting us with the crucified Christ; and in every word of the Gospel, which gives us Christ our righteousness, God is uniting us with the risen Christ.[13]

So intimate is this communion that Luther resorts to the intimacy of the marriage relationship itself to portray it in his essay on the *Freedom of the Christian Man*: "Faith . . . unites the soul with Christ as a bride is united with her bridegroom. . . . Christ and the soul became one flesh."

Luther's participation in the Gospel, furthermore, like all personal relationships, was a growing and ambivalent relationship. There were "ups and downs," and part of Luther's uniqueness and strength certainly lies in both his acute consciousness of these oscillations and the heights and depths to which he rose. And Luther believed wholeheartedly, even as he doubted manfully, as he writes of the period during his *Anfechtung* in 1527:

> For more than a week I was close to the gates of death and hell. I trembled in all my members. Christ was wholly lost. I was shaken by desperation and blasphemy of God.[14]

Bainton notes that Luther once said, "I would like to write a book about *Anfechtungen*," and I dare say all of us would be most eager to have been able to read that book. His experience of the full range of human ecstasy and despair enabled him to empathize with those who looked to him for pastoral help, to enter into their sufferings and their fears, as well as into their hopes. From Luther's own autobiographical theology we find the "thin line" which preserved him from being overwhelmed by his *Anfechtungen*. It was the neighbor (often his wife Katy) who was and spoke the Gospel, the objective Word of God in which he trusted, to him—the neighbor whose need enticed him away from his self-contemplation. Modern ministers are so often misled into thinking that pastoral stability, which is important in effective ministry, is a sort of static well-being, putting them a cut or two above the suffering man. Luther teaches us that one's strength does not lie alone in one's own stability, but in the Person and the persons in whom you trust and for whom you are concerned.

If we are to take seriously his word about the nuptial character of the faith relationship, a figure Luther uses often, and apply it to him as well as to ourselves, then we must say that in this intimate relation, not only was Luther the minister of the Word, but the Word was in him; he becomes a form of the Word, just as does every ministering Christian who lives in the Word. This is Luther's concept of the "Living Word."

This is the core of his theology of preaching and of pastoral care. In the *Kirchenpostille* of 1522 he says:

> The Church is not a pen house, but a mouth house . . . thus it is the manner of the New Testament and of the Gospel that it must be preached and performed by word of mouth and a living voice.[15]

Through speaking and performing the Gospel, the minister becomes the instrument of God. In the tract on the *Babylonian Captivity* Luther develops the concept that while man may baptize by performing the work of immersing, he does not baptize, he acts not on his own account, but in God's stead:

> Look upon the person administering it [baptism] as simply the vicarious instrument of God by which the Lord sitting in heaven thrusts you under the water with his own hands, and promises you forgiveness of your sins, speaking to you on earth with a human voice, by the mouth of the minister.[16]

This concept is applied again and again by Luther to preaching, and particularly also to confession (both public and private), which the well known passage from *Babylonian Captivity* will here suffice to demonstrate:

> When we have laid bare our conscience to our brother and privately made known to him the evil that lurked within, we receive from our brother's lips the word of comfort spoken by God himself. And if we accept this in faith, we find peace in the mercy of God speaking to us through our brother.[17]

So important was the personal encounter, "the living Word" of the servant of Christ, that some interpreters of Luther have even held that for him the forgiveness of sins was not certain unless it was verbally pronounced as in private absolution,[18] but Pelikan goes on to caution that this is an exaggeration. The emphasis of Luther on the "spoken" or perhaps *"personalized"* Word, however, bears close examination.

The issue here is closely related to the Law-Gospel character of the Word of God in Luther's thinking, clearly pointed out in *The Freedom of the Christian Man*. The humbling process of Law takes place more fully in a personal encounter with another; only in the presence of another person are we really humbled. Even when we read Scriptures to ourselves the humiliation amounts (psychologically speaking) only to a kind of "self-humiliation" which tends to be either shallow or sick (too severe-masochistic); one which, because of our self-centeredness, we are quick to rationalize ourselves out of. To a degree this happens even in the vivid general confrontation by the Word through preaching; but in the face-to-face pastoral conversation (in its confessional forms, for example) we do not let ourselves off so easily, and there is always the "other" who is objectively there, and through him the "Law" is objectified more realistically.

So also with the promises of the Gospel; to read them without the living *presence* of another is to be subject to delusion. We doubt or undercut the promises because they are "just too good to be true"; we feel we are kidding ourselves. But when another announces it to us we may still doubt, but it will no longer be the doubt of self-distrust or delusion which again because of our self-centeredness is especially destructive of the promise. The doubt is more easily dispensed because of the objective presence and proclamation of the "brother." When we discover that the Christian brother (whether he is pastor-priest or lay-priest) finds the same promise in the Word that we do, then through the experience of consensual validation by the community of faith, the words in a double sense carry life-giving, hope-generating force.

Consistent with this we find Luther occasionally (particularly the early Luther) expressing the viewpoint that both preaching and penance and absolution are Sacraments, or at least sacramental in character. In this case, the Christian brother or minister is the "visible element." At one point he says the voice of the minister is analogous to the water in Baptism, or the bread and wine of the Eucharist. In his *Instructions for the Visitors of Parish Pastors* Luther writes: "Penance also is to be reckoned as a sacrament—all sacraments are a kind of penance." [19] In the *Apology* he declared that "the genuine sacraments are Baptism, the Lord's Supper, and Absolution (which is the sacrament of Penance)." [20] Pelikan observes that Luther remained constantly willing to speak of absolution as a sacrament.[21]

I do not intend here to argue for a reinstatement of Confession or Penance as a Protestant sacrament—even assuming that were a remote possibility. But Luther's high regard for Penance and the reasons for thinking of it as a sacrament or at least as having sacramental character not only gives us deeper insight into Luther's own pastoral concern, but it says something very significant about modern pastoral care, particularly the pastoral conversation.

Luther wants to emphasize the "spoken" or "living" character of the Word through the presence of the brother in faith, as a "means of grace." But it is not simply the *audible* character of the Word that is important here—though that, psychologically at least, has its importance by providing objectivity—as we have seen. It also symbolically emphasizes the fact that our help or salvation comes from *outside* ourselves. What is also important here is the character of personal relationship which the "living Word" in the presence of the brother emphasizes. Faith in the Word is not merely propositional; the Gospel is not merely "sacred information," but a *living relationship with the living God* which in the economy of God is to be expressed in the fellowship or personal relationship of the saints. Historically one cannot but wonder how very significant for Luther the brotherly relationship with Staupitz was for Luther's own personal "discovery of the Gospel." I would contend that this is of most critical import and forms part of the seed-bed for this theological insight. Also we should not overlook the monastic brotherhood in Luther's experience.

From the other side of the dialogue in pastoral conversation, the spoken Word is of equal importance, particularly when the conversation becomes confessional. It has frequently been noted, and I believe it is an accurate appraisal, that by far the largest share of what transpires in "pastoral counseling" is in fact confessional in nature. When this hidden, guilt-laden material is brought to the surface—more fully in open aloud conversation than in any other way—the confrontation with the reality of one's sin is greater, and the continued hearing and presence of the confessor who is there in the name of Christ, who is not repulsed by what has been confessed, symbolizes the double force of the Word as promise and demand. Without the presence of the brother, the auricular confession might well lead to despair over one's utter unworthiness; but in the presence of the priest the gracious character of even the Law is sustained until the clear light of the Gospel in the crystallizing form of the absolution shines forth.[22] Luther himself felt that a very strong faith was necessary to sustain "confession to God alone."

All of what has been said here regarding the pastoral conversation must be understood against the background of Luther's theology of the ministry, particularly in its relation to the community of saints. The relationship of the community (the "priesthood of all believers," correctly understood) has a double significance. First: the pastor is frequently a less effective expression of the "living Word" (in Luther's sense) than he might be simply because for present-day Protestants particularly his presence is simply "his professional duty." This is *true,* of course, in the double sense that as a professing Christian he is concerned to heal the troubled conscience of his brother, and he is "paid to do it" by a concerned community who puts the pastor at the place where he must listen to a troubled person and communicate the Word. Second: the pastoral responsibility to "hear the confession" should, in Luther's thinking, under no circumstances be limited to the pastor, but is a shared responsibility emerging out of the baptismal covenant. Repeatedly Luther argues that Baptism is every Christian's "ordination" for hearing confession, or in the larger sense to be minister to his neighbor,[23] though he agrees that simply for the sake of effective administration the community must exercise selectivity in the *public expressions* of the offices. When every baptized Christian in the community of faith may hear confession and pronounce the absolution, then the entire community is involved, by covenant and profession, in the absolution declared by one man, whether pastor-priest or lay-priest. Then it is not just the "private opinion" of the confessor who declares the absolution that is being expressed, but the judgment of all.[24] And all, as "forgiving community," are necessarily involved in being the "living Word" in the sense of the continuing forgiving personal relationship. So concerned was Luther about pastoral care for troubled consciences that he takes great pains to emphasize its almost universal availability in the church by a large number of confessors.

In his sermons he is evidently concerned to "equip the saints" for this ministry.

In these days of awakened consciousness of the ministry of the layman, the modern pastor can, as Luther did, alert and prepare the entire congregation for its ministry in this significant area. There are obvious dangers, particularly in the matter of responsibility, good judgment, and sensitivity which the wise pastor will take into account as he "equips the saints" for the work of the ministry, but this should not deter us. It would seem that this is by far the wiser means to deal with the troubled spirits of our time than to attempt a repristination of the formal private confessional on a large scale. There is, however, a special ministry of the pastor that could be recovered and a wider use of a more formalized private confession to the pastor that could be advocated.

IV

THE PASTORAL RELATIONSHIP IN LUTHER'S "SEELSORGE"

It has already been implied that the pastoral relationship, that between the minister (ordained or lay priest) and the parishioner, is of critical importance for Luther. In the context of the church it has a sacramental character, it is the "instrument of God," the medium of the living voice of the Gospel.

We can penetrate further into the dynamic of this relationship. In rather sharp contrast to the individualism that is sometimes ascribed to Luther, he sees the minister not at all as an isolated individual but as a *symbolic person*. He makes the distinction between the private person and the public person in a sermon preached on Palm Sunday in 1518 or 1519 on Phil. 2:5-6. While he is here not speaking directly of the ministry, but rather of the public "official" in the usual sense, it does not do violence to his thinking to apply this to the pastoral person.

The pastor is obviously a public person, particularly in his preaching (which Luther theoretically allowed was possible for any private individual, but which, for the sake of order, was to be a delegated function). A public person is one who "has been placed in a responsible office by God" and who in this capacity speaks for God. By virtue of having been called by the Gospel into the community of faith through Baptism, as Luther pointed out in the *Babylonian Captivity of the Church*, every Christian must stand ready in his

ministry of consolation to proclaim the Gospel to his troubled brother. This is also peculiarly true of the pastor who has a special call
from the congregation to serve God as the servant to "the brethren"
—the church.[25] The public person, furthermore, is directed by his
"calling" to his neighbor: "For no man acts in God's place for the
sake of himself and his own things, but for the sake of others." [26]
Bonhoeffer makes this distinction contemporary with his concept of
"the deputy" in his *Ethics*. The deputy is one who acts in the place
of other men, and thus is not an isolated individual but one who
combines in himself a number of human beings.[27] This is an accurate
portrayal of the minister in Luther's understanding. The minister
does not merely speak his "own" word of absolution, nor even the
"corporate word" of the human fellowship in which complete
acceptance is the characteristic, but he speaks the Word of God—
the Gospel which has been given to the human fellowship, making
it the church, which in turn empowers the minister to speak the living Word which it has received.[28]

Those who are familiar with the literature in pastoral care will
immediately recognize the words "empathy" and "acceptance" as
key concepts in the process of the pastoral relationship. These, of
course, would be strange words for Luther, but when he describes
the inevitable outgrowth of faith, love for the neighbor, he moves
far beyond what these modern words convey. In the following passages Luther does not have the pastor (the ordained priest) solely
in mind, but rather all priests (the "brotherhood" of the Christians)
—the human relations of the Christian toward the troubled neighbor. What does it mean for Luther to be concerned about the sinner and his sin and to share it with him? He thinks primarily of
what is decisive in Christ's dealing with sinners: Christ covers our
sin and intercedes for us with his righteousness. In a very colorful
and powerful message he writes:

> This is what you must do, the virgin must place her wreath upon a
> prostitute, a virtuous wife must give her veil to an adulteress, and we
> must let everything we have be a covering for the sinners.[29]
> These are the genuinely Christian works, that we fall into and get as
> deeply involved in the quicksand in which the sinner finds himself, and
> that we take his sins upon ourselves and work our way out with them,
> acting as though they were our own. We should admonish him and
> deal with him most seriously, but we should not despise him, rather
> we should love him most heartily.[30]

Even the most daring psychiatrist would hesitate to go this far! Such treading out into the quicksand of the sinning brother's life is possible without peril only for the man who does so in the righteousness of Christ ("It is God and not my merit that protects me when I fall into my neighbor's sin" [31]) and the fellowship of the church which sustains the minister to thus take his neighbor's sins into his own life. The movement here is that the Christian man or minister takes his brother into the grace of God by joining himself with the neighbor, or brings the grace of God with him when he steps out into the quicksand of the brother's life. Empathy and acceptance pale in comparison. There is no psychological distance between Luther and the neighbor. This is far more bold and active than the "acceptance" of the modern psychotherapist or pastoral counselor who remains where he is and is ready to "accept" the person who comes to him. Luther would reach out to the person who needs the Gospel. "I will therefore give myself as a Christ to my neighbor, just as Christ offered himself to me." [32] For Luther the Christian man who is concerned for sinners enters into solidarity with them as Christ has entered into solidarity with him. This too is an expression of Luther's *theologia crucis.*

There is one more dynamic in the "helping" or ministering relationship. It is expressed in the introduction to Luther's *Fourteen of Consolation* (and elsewhere) written to Frederick, Duke of Saxony:

> Since then, most noble Prince, I perceive that your Lordship has been smitten . . . and that Christ has thus fallen sick in you [the reference here is to Matt. 28], I have counted it my duty to visit your Lordship with a little writing of mine. For I cannot pretend to be deaf to the voice of Christ crying to me out of your Lordship's flesh and blood.[33]

The Christ to be served presents himself to us in the suffering neighbor; but we perceive him only because the Christ who redeems dwells in us and has opened the seeing eyes of faith.

Some additional implications for contemporary *Seelsorge* should be drawn. *First:* The critical importance of the office and ministry of the pastoral conversation correlative to the ministry of preaching and the ministry of the sacraments. Not only does this highly personalized form of the living Word of God have profound significance for *Seelsorge,* but it is a ministry that must take place in the context of a total ministry of preaching and the administration of the sacraments. There is important psychological, if not also theological, significance in the fact that the minister, who publicly proclaims the Word as the double "public person" or deputy of God and the congregation, also now personally speaks the living Word of the Gospel to the troubled soul. To be separated from this total ministry renders the pastor spiritually sterile, for then the Word of the Gospel is only his private and personal word, not the commissioned word spoken on behalf of God and having force as one of the "masks" of God. The detached "pastoral counselor" who is engaged in a form of private pastoral ministry is a modern counterpart of the friar of the 1300's who was "licensed" to hear confession and who pursued his task wandering from village to village, free from episcopal control and with little regard for church order.[34]

The pastoral conversation, particularly when it is of confessional nature, has a sacramental character which distinguishes it sharply from all other forms of psychotherapy or counseling. This distinction and sacramental character, however, depends upon the vital "connection" with the Word of God, just as do the chief Sacraments (Baptism, Lord's Supper). Only when this pastoral conversation is conducted in the "name of Christ" on his behalf, and on behalf of and at the behest of the church, does it have this sacramental character. The "Word of God" which is involved must be both implicit and explicit in this conversation, at least in Luther's judgment. This is clear from the development of Luther's thought as well as from his pastoral practice reflected in his letters of counsel to troubled and guilt-burdened souls. He writes and speaks always from within the church and is, as I have tried to show, "in" the Word as the Word is "in" him. One is tempted to apply the traditional descriptive formula applied by Luther in the *Catechism* to the Sacraments, the word of the Gospel is "in, with, and under" the pastoral presence and the pastoral conversation. Particularly in confessional pastoral conversations it is important to make explicit that the absolution directly spoken or implied by the pastoral relationship does not just involve the relationship of pastor to person, but is a symbolic relationship in which, by commission, the pastor speaks for God and proclaims the very Word of God. This can ultimately be made explicit by reference to the Scriptures where this commission is clearly stated.

In a recent article Pelikan observes that one of the differences between theological thinking in Luther's time and our own is the manner of speaking and thinking about the transcendent reality which the means of grace mediate to men. In Reformation times theological thinking began with the transcendent reality (*sola gratia*) itself. It may now "be the task of Reformation theology to begin with the immanent reality—the historical reality of the Person of Christ and the immanent sacramental reality of the means of grace . . . and to find ways of speaking about their transcendence." [35] This is particularly true in the area of the pastoral conversation and the "mutual consolation of the brethren," it seems to me. We have, for about two decades now, been preoccupied with the immanent reality—the human, psychological processes in pastoral care in a very fruitful way—but at times to the near obscuring of the transcendent reality. We need now to come to an even more complete understanding of these immanent processes which we have developed, and perhaps discovered, and rediscover the transcendent without losing what we have gained. The implications of this are not yet fully clear, and there are theological problems. I do not by any means here imply a return to wooden traditional patterns of *Seelsorge* with their mechanical "use" of the Word. But perhaps it is time for us to reconsecrate pastoral counseling, pastoral care, and group processes within the church to their truly sacramental character by realizing more fully their sacramental nature, and by making more explicit their intimate connection with the Word of God and the ultimate purpose of that connection, namely to communicate the Gospel in Luther's sense—the forgiveness of sins, life, and salvation.

12.

Martin Luther—
Parish Educator

GERHARD H. DOERMANN

Whatever Martin Luther, the monk of Wittenberg, was or was not, it cannot be denied that he was a many-faceted man. This is attested to by the many viewpoints expressed in countless books and articles during these four and a half centuries, whether by playwrights like Osborne, psychoanalysts like Erikson, protagonists on the Protestant and Lutheran side, or even (in these later days) the Roman Catholic side, or antagonists, usually Roman Catholic but also Protestant and non-religious. It is not easy to assess a many-faceted personality who looms so large in history, and I make no pretense of scholarly completeness in this survey of Luther as a parish educator.

Luther, as has often been pointed out, was not a systematician. In theology he was a biblical theologian, well-versed, to be sure, in almost all branches of theology, but his purpose, in most of his endeavors, was to meet existing needs. His writings, therefore, with perhaps the exception of his studies of biblical theology (which were prepared for university students) arose out of his concern for people and their needs. Naturally, in view of his intense feeling that the great need of people was for the Gospel, he stressed not his own opinions in answer to needs, but the Scriptures. These were always the basic source of his writings. A second source was the event, situation, or need which he tried to meet. The third was his own burning desire to fulfill or meet the needs of others. This made Luther the many-faceted man he was, and it also accounts

151

for his stress on education, which he felt was totally inadequate for the needs of the people and the church.

I
THE EDUCATIONAL SITUATION IN LUTHER'S DAY

In a sense the educational efforts of the medieval and Reformation times can trace their origin to the educational reforms of Charlemagne. In 787 he issued an order directing that abbots give more earnest attention to education and that this directive be transmitted to all the monasteries in the jurisdiction. In 789 a directive was issued for the establishment of schools, and as late as 802 he issued an order commanding all men to learn the Creed and the Lord's Prayer thoroughly. After great initial success, the effort lapsed, because his successor failed to share his views and churchmen had never espoused them except under duress.

The Crusades, providing contact with other cultures and art forms, and stimulating trade, led to the establishment of burgher schools where the three "r's" were taught.

Scholasticism, although it contributed a great deal to the educational enterprise, often veered off into speculative thinking, unending analysis, hairsplitting distinctions, and discussions about the most insignificant matters.

The religious orders, like the Franciscans, Dominicans, and Augustinians, while not primarily educational in purpose, were the repositories of culture and learning, as well as the reservoir of well-trained men. Some of them did, indeed, provide schools, the convent schools of those days, but this effort was limited and sporadic. These orders also provided the staffing for the universities which grew out of convent and cathedral schools during the 12th century.

The Renaissance of the 13th century revived interest in classical and ancient literature and culture, and along with greatly improved tools in the graphic arts, should have resulted in a steadily growing, universal education.

Roman Catholic writers emphasize the wealth of educational opportunities that existed. Thus the Catholic scholar Johannes Janssen writes in his *History of the German People:*

> The period of German reform, which began in the middle of the 15th century, produced the most splendid intellectual results. It was a time when culture penetrated to all classes of society, spreading its ramifica-

tions deep and wide, a time of extraordinary activity in art and learning by catechetical teaching, by sermons, by the translation of the Holy Scriptures, by instructional and devotional publications of all sorts. Religious knowledge was zealously diffused and the development of the religious life abundantly fostered. In the lower elementary schools and the advanced middle schools a sound basis of popular education was established. The universities attained a height of excellence undreamt-of before and became the burning centers of all intellectual activities. And more even than learning, art was seen to blossom and develop on the soil of national religious life, beautifying all departments of life, public and private, secular and ecclesiastical, in the worthiest manner, while in its many grand and comprehensive works, inspired by the then prevailing sense of Christian brotherhood, it manifested the real core of German genius and character.[1]

Patrick J. McCormick, an American Catholic scholar, seems to ascribe the educational fruits of the Reformation and Counter-Reformation to the Roman Church when he writes in his *History of Education:*

In addition to the cathedral and monastic institutions, other types of elementary schools flourished in the countries of Europe in the later Middle Ages. Chief among them were the parish, chantry, town, and guild schools, and these were so numerous and widely extended that we must conclude elementary education was then well provided for in cities and rural districts, and not only for boys but also for girls. The Church was solicitous for the education of all. This is clear from the councils and general legislative actions of her officials. As in the earlier Middle Ages there is notable provision for free schools for the poor.[2]

Several observations are in order. While it is natural to emphasize the fact that there was education prior to the Reformation, it is misleading to overemphasize and generalize. These writers ascribe a particularly favorable educational program, existing in a specific place, to all situations. This is done, not by direct assertion, but by implication. It is even more misleading to ignore so completely the obstacles Rome continuously tried to place in the way of lay education in the Scriptures.

What the situation was in far too many communities, and probably in most communities in Luther's day, is made abundantly clear in many of Luther's writings. One of the earliest of these, the *Address to the German Nobility,* 1520, gives a vivid portrayal of the religious, social, and educational conditions prevailing at that time.

The purpose of this writing was to level the walls behind which Rome had entrenched itself. These walls were: (1) that the church is superior to the secular government in all things; (2) that the pope alone has the right to interpret Scripture; and (3) that the pope alone has the authority to call church councils. Of the twenty-eight sections that offer a constructive program, Section 25 deals specifically with educational reforms.

A second such writing, issued in 1524, is Luther's *A Letter to the Mayors and Councilmen of the German Cities*. It portrays a condition of education that had grown out of the Reformation, now seven years old. The people had been compelled to support the cathedral and convent schools, such as they were, but now had been freed of that ecclesiastical compulsion. So they felt no particular obligation toward education since in their opinion schools had been intended to prepare for monkhood and priesthood, now no longer in existence among them. Thus Luther appeals to the rulers of cities to establish schools.

A third important writing is the *Sermon on Keeping Children in School* of 1530. In its two main divisions Luther discusses the necessity of maintaining adequate instruction for the spiritual and the temporal welfare of the people.

Perhaps the best known of the writings portraying the educational conditions of that day is Luther's introduction to his *Small Catechism*. In describing the conditions he encountered on a tour of visitation he cries out:

> Dear God, help! What misery I encountered! That common men know nothing of Christian teaching, particularly in the villages, and sad to say many pastors completely unable to teach; yet all are called Christians, are baptized, and partake of Holy Communion; but they do not know the Lord's Prayer, nor the Creed, nor the Ten Commandments; they exist like contented cows and irrational hogs.[3]

A quotation or two like the above may help us taste the flavor of Luther's earnest concern, but to be truly appreciated he must be read. For he abounds in such allusions to prevailing conditions, not only in these and similar booklets, but in his table talks, his sermons, and other writings. Hear him as he rants against rulers and people for not being willing to found adequate schools: *"Pfui,* and again *pfui,* and *pfui* again to our blind and disgraceful thanklessness."[4]

Luther is often accused of using language that was unbecoming his position. It is true that his language was pungent, full of barnyard allusions and illustrations, often by today's standards pretty "straight from the shoulder." It must be further admitted that in his polemical writings his language was at times even vitriolic and caustic. We need to remember, however, that this was not "unbecoming" in that day. Luther's enemies were just as vitriolic as he. His barnyard language and allusions were illustrative and informative to all alike, the peasant as well as the priest. They knew what he was talking about! I believe both Osborne in his play *Luther* and Erikson in his psychiatric study *Young Man Luther,* miss this point. Luther's use of down-to-earth, even caustic language, reveals his deep concern for the welfare of his beloved people—and of all people.

II
LUTHER THE PASTOR-EDUCATOR

I am convinced that it is this pastoral concern that marks the greatness of Luther. It breathes through all of his writings, and today it must breathe through every activity of the minister—his counseling, his calling, his preaching, and surely his teaching.

In his letter to the mayors and councilmen he says:

> Dear gentlemen, since we must annually spend so much on arms, highways, dams, and the like, in order that a city may enjoy earthly peace and prosperity; why should we not spend just as much, yes much more, on our needy youth, and that a skilled man or two might become teachers!
>
> Every citizen ought to be moved and influenced by the fact that in the past he lost money and property on indulgences, masses, vigils, foundations, testaments, holy days, begging monks, brotherhoods, pilgrimages, and all the rest of these bleeding ulcers, and are now by God's grace free from such robbery and forced giving, we ought to be moved in thankfulness to God to share some of this for schools, to train our poor children.[5]

The same spirit of concern breathes through his *Address to the German Nobility* and particularly through the fifty-three pages of his "sermon" that parents should keep their children in school.

Since Luther speaks and writes out of a heart full of concern for existing situations and problems, it is often difficult to pinpoint quotations, for the same thoughts will recur in other writings in similar if not identical words: in his table talks, his volumes of sermons, his exegetical writings. In his table talks he urges that, while schools are not held in high esteem, they yet have genuine usefulness since they do uphold the churches by instructing and guiding youth and preparing them for godliness and for all honorable and all Christian callings.

In a letter to the Bishop of Mainz, urging more attention to education, he thanks God that at Wittenberg, which he terms "the lone corner," education was still flourishing, and he predicts that in time "the papists" will want to build the barn of education after the sheep have been destroyed. The implication is strong that Wittenberg was an exception in its educational program.

So his writings and his life breathe concern for the people, primarily for their eternal or spiritual welfare, but certainly also for their temporal well-being. Consider the fact that his *Sermon on Keeping Children in School* has two almost equal parts, the first devoted to the spiritual, and the second to the temporal benefits of education.

This concern arose, in my opinion, out of his own struggle for identity as a child of God. In Act 2, Scene 2 of Osborne's play, Staupitz is talking to Luther about his obsession with the *rule:*

"You're obsessed with the Rule because it serves very nicely as protection for you." Luther: "What protection?" Staupitz: "You know perfectly well what I mean, Brother Martin, so don't pretend to look innocent. Protection against the demands of your own instincts, that's what. You see you think you admire authority, and so you do, but unfortunately, you can't submit to it. So what you do, by your exaggerated attention to the Rule, you make the authority ridiculous. And the reason you do that is because you're determined to substitute that authority with something else—yourself. Oh, come along, Martin. I've been Vicar General too long not to have made that little discovery." [6]

While there are some valid insights in the above it is still misleading because Osborne never gets to the heart of the matter—namely, Luther's struggle to find peace with God. This is further aggravated in the play by leaving Luther still vacillating in almost every scene of the play. Staupitz did help Luther; he helped him to an understanding of the central truth in Christ—salvation by grace through faith. And this truth, which possessed Luther in increasing measure as the years went by, was the driving force behind his pastoral, educational concern.

Luther's concern was for people and it fostered understanding of people because he had come up the "hard way." He had come up the "hard way" educationally, economically, and spiritually. He could understand the resistance and stubbornness of the German peasants, and he could sympathize with them, even though he was often so impatient that he called them contented cattle, ignorant pigs, and even "Rotzlöffel" (a German idiom for our inelegant "snot nose"). He knew their aspirations and their needs, which they themselves often did not recognize. He understood their failure to see life as a whole and in its fullest aspect, and not merely from the short, temporal viewpoint.

Yet with all his learning and advancement, he never lost touch with the common people, impatient as he often became with them. Perhaps he was trying to help them come through this difficult period which caused him so many years of soul-searching struggle, in too short a time, trying to save them some of the struggle he had to go through.

This concern further reveals itself in his emphasis on Scripture. It was his study of the Scriptures that helped him come through from darkness to light. Even the word " 'righteousness' so nauseated me when I heard it, that I would not have been sorry if someone had done away with me." Then when God in the Scriptures revealed to him the true meaning of righteousness, it was as if he were born again, as indeed he was. And it became his concern to share with others the wonder of God's righteousness, not the righteousness demanded by God, but first that offered by God in Christ. It is for this reason that his table talks, introductions, monographs, and letters, as well as his Scripture expositions and sermons, are so filled with scriptural quotations and illustrations.

This concern for people centered not in mere knowledge of the Scriptures but in trust. His concern was for commitment of the entire person to God. In writing on the Apostles' Creed in 1520, Luther speaks of two "ways" of believing,

the first *about* God, that is when I believe that what is said concerning God is true. A faith of this kind is more knowledge or information than faith. The second way of believing is this, that I not only believe it to be true what is said concerning God, but I put my trust in him, commit

myself to him in a personal relationship. Such faith which ventures
everything upon what it has heard of God, be it in life or death, consti-
tutes the Christian man, and it receives everything it desires from God.
Such a faith cannot tolerate a false and wicked heart; it is a living faith,
such as the First Commandment enjoins. . . .[7]

Such was the burning, consuming concern of Luther, which made
him, not a systematic theologian, nor a systematic educator expound-
ing a list of half-intelligible educational principles, but a warm,
trusting, sometimes overzealous, pastor-educator.

III
LUTHER THE EDUCATIONAL THEORIST

To call Luther an educational theorist in any modern sense of the
word is, of course, inappropriate. As he was no systematician in
theology, so he was not systematic in his educational approach. He
formulated no laws of learning or teaching. He wrote no books on
education in any technical sense and no educational psychologies.
Yet, because he wrote from the depth of his heart and out of his
understanding of the needs of people to the situation of the day,
his writings abound in educational directives. He identified with
the people, and this empathy gave him a deep understanding of
them and their needs. We pick out just a few of his directives and
insights.

The first of these insights is the idea of joy and pleasure in learning. This is a "principle" that too often we moderns believe we have
invented. Often it is attributed to John Dewey, and in its modern
form perhaps does find its origin in the Dewey school of thought.
Luther put it this way: "We must strive to make learning a joy for
our children." Somewhere in the centuries between Luther and
today this was lost sight of or buried under the pressure of the
"much" learning considered essential at any age and stage.

Luther, however, did not go to the extreme of some followers of
Dewey, the extreme progressivists. They not only espoused the
valid idea that youngsters should be guided to learn at their own
pace, but went to the extreme of letting them do as they please and
learn what they please. As a result the chorework in education, the
learning of basics and basic tools, was, and too often still is, neglected. Luther emphasized basics as necessary and vital to all

other learning, whether in religion or the arts. But he also stressed the need to make it a cheerful, satisfying experience.

> It is a bad thing if children lose their spirit on account of parents and teachers. There have been many bungling masters who have destroyed splendid talents by their blustering, storming, striking, and pounding. . . . Good method in teaching should note differences of character in pupils.[8]
>
> Since young people must run and jump or have something to do which they enjoy, and you can't stop it (nor would it be good to try), why shouldn't that type of school be provided and such arts and skills be offered them? This is especially so since it is ordered by God's grace that children can learn with joy and play, whether it be language, other skills, or even history.[9]

Without question his opposition to the browbeating type of education was a reaction against his own childhood when he was severely beaten by his mother for stealing a nut, and when he was struck fifteen times at school for not being able to define a word which the teacher had not yet explained.

A second principle of Luther was the importance of the home in education. We need not belabor this point in view of the fact that his *Sermon on Keeping Children in School* consists of fifty-three pages of parental duties to their children. While this is stressed, the burden of the *Sermon* repeats the demand made previously in the *Address to the German Nobility* and the *Letter to Mayors* that if parents do not keep their children in school the state should make sure they attend.

His emphasis on the home is further brought out by his own stated purpose in producing the Catechisms. For these were intended not only for pastors but for the use of parents in the home, to help them answer their children's questions concerning the meaning of the Commandments, the Articles, the Petitions, etc. Modern research has compiled impressive scientific evidence to show that true Christian character cannot be attained effectively without the cooperation of the home. Luther knew it by observation, by intuition, and from intimate knowledge of the Old Testament emphasis on the family.

A third principle in Luther is his stress on compulsory education. In the post-Reformation era this principle was often lost sight of. We need only recall the work of Robert Raikes in England who started Sunday schools for underprivileged slum-dwellers, not to teach them religion but the three R's, since no provision was made for their education either by private concerns or the state. We need only think of the struggle in our own country for compulsory education. While many schools existed in the Colonies, no provision was made by government itself, and thus those who could not afford private schools and tutors had to do without.

It is interesting to note that Luther compares the work accomplished by the schools of that day (1530) with the achievements of the convent or cathedral schools:

> Isn't it evident that now we can accomplish more in three years, by the time the lad is fifteen or eighteen, than heretofore all the high schools and convents could accomplish? What did they learn there in past times but to be jackasses, blockheads? For twenty, forty years they were instructed and when they finished they still didn't know either Latin or German. I'll not even mention the despicable, blasphemous life they were steeped in.[10]

This, of course, also reinforces what was said in the first part of the paper, concerning educational conditions in Luther's day.

IV
LUTHER'S CATECHETICAL WRITINGS

While we usually consider Luther's catechetical writings to be two in number, we must also recall that he has commentaries on the parts of the Catechism, particularly in his sermons, both before and after the appearance of the Catechisms themselves.

Since most of us are familiar with the two Catechisms, I shall not belabor the obvious but rather give some estimates of the Catechisms by others than Luther. He himself did not seem to realize what gems he had produced, for he said that pastors should choose whichever one of the many available catechisms they preferred to use—whether his or another's—and should stick by it, lest they confuse the learners by jumping from one to another.

Dr. J. Michael Reu called the *Small Catechism* "the crowning consummation of the evangelical endeavors put forth by the church during the course of fifteen centuries" [11] and admired its deeply evangelical interpretation of the constituent parts, all relating to justification. He further stressed its pedagogic excellence: the consummate linguistic style, the absence of polemics, its limitation to the essentials of faith and life, and the fact that it does not try to combine the five parts into a dogmatic whole.

Many of these points are mentioned by non-Lutheran writers such as Philip Schaff, A. C. McGiffert, and even the Catholic Hartmann Grisar. I shall not quote them at length, but merely recall that Gustav Bruce's *Luther as an Educator*,[12] published in observance of the 400th anniversary of the Catechism in 1929, contains many quotations from such sources, as does Franklin Painter's earlier *Luther on Education*.[13] Both are still very much worth reading but should always be followed up or preceded by reading Luther himself.

I quote just one reference from McGiffert. He calls the *Small Catechism* "the little gem of the Reformation," and says that "the versatility of the reformer in adapting himself with such success to the needs of the young and immature is no less than extraordinary. Such a little book as this it is that reveals most clearly the genius of the man." [14]

In all of these evaluations I miss a point of commendation that has impressed itself upon me in increasing measure over the years. *The objective wholeness and completeness of the Catechism coupled with the subjective warmth*—a continual personal appropriation and therefore a constant living witness to the truth. This is for me the genius of the *Small Catechism*. It is obvious in his explanation of the Second Article:

> *I* believe that Jesus Christ, Son of the Father from eternity, and also true man, born of the virgin Mary, is *my* Lord.

Again we recognize it in the Third Article explanation:

> *I* believe that *I* cannot by my own reason or strength believe in Jesus Christ, my Lord, or come to Him; but the Holy Ghost has called *me* by the Gospel, enlightened *me* with his gifts, sanctified and kept *me* in the true faith, etc.

In conclusion, recall with me these words of Luther on the chart for congregational use published by Augsburg Publishing House in 1967:

> We can engage in no greater work on earth than educating others by preaching and teaching.

13.

Luther, Man of Prayer

LEONHARD LUDWIG

There are probably as many images of Luther as there are students of his career. Everyone who occupies himself with the Reformer's life carries away his own impression. These impressions vary according to the beholder's temperament, background, and specific point of interest. To one Luther is the cantankerous rebel and archschismatic. To another he is the rediscoverer of Gospel truth and its infallible interpreter. To a third he is the stern authoritarian who presumes to speak the last word on any subject placed before him. A fourth finds him the sympathetic counselor of all who are perplexed and the congenial housefather who welcomes yet another guest to his table. The Monk of Wittenberg is many-faceted. His life and character can be painted in many hues.

As Luther is being assessed, it is good occasionally to leave the realm of controversy and to seek to know him simply as a man among men and as a fellow Christian. This is the intent as we concentrate on Luther, man of prayer.

I
LUTHER'S THEOLOGY OF PRAYER

Men have ever undertaken to systematize the unsystematic Luther by writing volumes entitled "The Theology of Luther." None of these volumes carries a longer section with the subtitle "Luther's Theology of Prayer." The recent *Accents in Luther's Theology*[1] places no accent on his theological thought on prayer. Julius Köstlin dwells on the futility in prayer which Luther experienced as a monk, as well as on echoes from the prayer life of the Reformer.[2] Paul Althaus, *The*

Theology of Luther,[3] translated into English in 1966, devotes one page to gathering together in Köstlin's fashion many of the Reformer's expressions concerning prayer. When Heinrich Bornkamm, *Luther's World of Thought,*[4] characterizes Luther's faith as a belief in reality, he substantiates his assertion with a page and a half of text in the down-to-earthness of Luther's prayer life. Roland Bainton, *Here I Stand,* devotes page 358 to "Prayer" but is content with six lines of introductory text and the reprinting of two prayers. The introductory statement reads:

> Luther was above all else a man of prayer, and yet of his prayers we have less than of his sermons and conversations because he succeeded in keeping his students out of the secret chamber. There are the excellent collects which he composed for the liturgy, the prayer for the sacristy, and a prayer reported to have been overheard by his roommate in Worms. We are on safer ground in the following excerpts from his exposition of the Lord's Prayer.[5]

No one even slightly acquainted with Luther would conclude from the sparsity of his treatment of the subject in a deeply theological way that prayer played a secondary role in the Reformer's life. For him prayer was so natural, so self-evident, so much part and parcel of his daily existence, that he had neither time nor inclination to engage in an abstract discussion of the theology of prayer or in any other speculative treatment of the subject. As he pondered on *deus absconditus,* the God hidden and beyond us, he might indeed for a moment wonder whether such a God could or should be bothered by the cries of frail men. But the exhortations to and the promises in connection with prayer were so numerous in Scripture that theoretical aspects of the question never lived in Luther's soul.

II
LUTHER'S PRAYER PRACTICE

When it comes to prayer, Luther was not a theoretician, but a practitioner. He does not furnish a speculative treatment of a topic but the powerful demonstration of a life steeped in prayer.

Doubtless he had expected that when he had decided to become a full-time religious by entering the monastery he would spend many undisturbed hours in prayer communication with God. Little did he know what problems he would encounter on this very score. In one of his table talks we hear him report:

Prayer under the papacy was pure torture *(Stockmeisterei)* of the poor conscience and only blabbering and making of words; no praying, but a work of obedience. The pope commands a threefold manner of praying. The material prayer, in which a person recites words he does not understand, as the nuns do with the psalter [probably recited in Latin]. This was merely a prayer to satisfy the pope. The other, the formal prayer, in which one does understand the words. The third, the effectual prayer, the prayer of devotion and meaning. The third is the right essence and quality of prayer. But on this there is no insistence, but only on the material prayer, that the words were recited and read, as a parrot talks. From this sprang a desolate ocean full of hours of prayer, the howling and shouting in convents and monasteries in which the psalms and lections were sung and read without spirit, in a manner that a person neither understood nor retained either words or sentences of meaning.[6]

Luther goes on to confess that even after the Gospel insight had begun to work in him, he still was troubled about the canonical hours which, because of being busy, he had not kept. On Saturday he would lock himself up in his cell until he had fulfilled his prayer obligations. Finally he became completely bogged down. When Amsdorf and others derided this kind of mechanical and coerced prayer, Luther dropped it.

In fairness it should probably be added that here Luther remembers the worst features of the compulsory prayer life of the monks, and that it does not do justice to the fine prayers and devotional helps to which he had access as a member of the Augustinian Order and which proved food for his soul.

Bainton traces Luther's insomnia to his irrational way of trying to catch up on the saying of the canonical hours.

All through his controversy with Rome he was still a monk, obligated to say matins, tierce, nones, vespers, and complin. But when he became a professor at the university, a preacher in the village church, and the director of eleven monasteries, he was simply too busy to keep up. He would stack his prayers for a week, two weeks, even three weeks, and then would take off a Sunday, or, on one occasion, three whole days without food or drink until he was "prayed up." After such an orgy in 1520 his head reeled. For five days he could get no sleep, and lay on his bed as one dead, until the doctor gave him a sedative. During convalescence the prayer book revolted him, and he fell in arrears a quarter of a year. Then he gave up. This was one of the stages in his weaning from monasticism. The permanent residue of the experience was insomnia.[7]

But on to a more positive aspect of Luther's prayer practice. Herbert F. Brokering, *Luther's Prayers*, 1967, rightly summarizes and characterizes:

There was no monotony to the prayer salutations of Luther. Some are lengthy. More often this man breaks into prayer as abruptly as some one addressing a friend. He is as one in continued conversation with God. To him the name of God is the presence of God. Many of the prayers end as abruptly as they begin. Some close with several "Amens," like a hallelujah chorus.

The prayers show Luther as one deeply dependent upon grace and mercy. Mercy, mercy, was his plea, and he trusted that mercy was always present in Christ. Mercy was Luther's plea. Mercy was God's promise in prayer.[8]

Luther recommended and practiced praying in a standing or a kneeling position, preferably at an open window. This man could never do anything by halves. He had to throw himself also into the practice of prayer with all that he had. That open window doubtless symbolized for Luther open access to God and he felt that his cry was ascending straight to the throne on high.

Köstlin reports that one day when the little household dog patiently awaited a morsel from his master's hand, Luther cried out: "Oh, that I might be able to pray with the intensity with which this little dog looks for his morsel of meat!"[9] Luther doubtless came closer to praying with that kind of intensity than many another Christian. This is the prayer attributed to him as spoken during the days he was on trial at Worms:

Almighty, eternal God! How strange this world! How it makes the mouths of people gape! How little is the trust of people in God! How quickly it withdraws its hand from a matter, flits on, and follows the common track and broad road toward hell; and looks only on what is pompous and imposing and on what makes an impression! If I should turn my eyes in that direction, I am undone, then the bell is already cast, the sentence already spoken. O God, my God, come to my aid against the mind and wisdom of all the world. You must do it; it is not my, but your cause. I for my person have no business here with these big lords of the world. Don't you hear? Oh, my God, are you dead? No, you cannot die; you are only hiding. Did you predestinate me unto this? I ask you, as indeed I know. God's will be done; for never in my life did I expect to confront such lords. Come, come, I am ready even to give up my life as a patient lamb. For the cause is just, and it is yours, and to eternity I will not separate myself from you.

This be resolved in your name. The world will needs have to leave me in conscience free; and if my body, the work of your hand, should be crushed for this cause, the soul is yours and belongs to you and will remain with you eternally. Amen! God, help me! Amen.[10]

Or hear him pray amid bodily affliction, as he did at Smalcald in 1537. When seized by a vomiting spell, he pleaded: "Oh, dear Father, take this little soul *(Seelchen)* of mine into your hands. I will thank you for it, and all creatures shall praise you. Grant, that soon I may be gathered to my fathers." After the attack had abated: "Pass on, little soul of mine, pass on in God's name! How frail we men are. I scarcely have any strength in me. And yet the little that is left is being tormented so miserably by the devil. Therefore, my Father, make me steadfast and patient in faith toward you, that I may overcome." [11]

Veit Dietrich, Luther's companion at Coburg Castle, wrote Melanchthon, who was doing battle for the evangelical cause at Augsburg:

I cannot sufficiently admire the singular steadfastness, the happy attitude *(Heiterkeit)*, the faith and hope of this man in serious times. But he nurtures this without surcease by diligent occupation with the divine Word. There is not a day on which he does not devote at least three hours, the very ones most suitable for studying, to prayer. Once I was fortunate to overhear his prayer. Good God, what faith in his words! He speaks with the great reverence of one who speaks to his God, and with the trust and hope of one who speaks with his father and friend. He said: "I know you are our God and Father. Therefore I am certain that you will confound the persecutors of your children. If you do not do it, the danger is yours and ours. Yours is the cause. We went at it, because we knew this. Therefore be pleased to defend him" [probably Melanchthon]. Standing at a distance I heard him pray thus with a clear voice. My heart burned mightily within me when he prayed so intimately, so earnestly, so reverently to God, and in his prayer appealed to the promises in the psalms as one who is sure what he asks will come to pass.[12]

Luther could pray with a boldness to which few attain. December 21, 1525, he wrote to Duke George, who was so very hostile to the Gospel. The letter, respectful in itself, pledged obedience in all things, save in the matter of the biblical teaching, and begged the Duke to give free course to the Word of Christ. But this was followed up with a warning not to drive Luther and his followers to prayer against the prince. The climax:

Your princely grace might perchance discover that it is not one and the same thing to move against Münzer and against Luther. I would prefer if your princely grace might not experience this. I consider my and my followers' prayer mightier than the devil himself. Were this not the case, Luther's cause were in different circumstances.[13]

What pastor of today would dare imitate Luther's language in a congregational prayer of Sunday, March 2, 1539:

> Dear Lord, preserve us from war which devastates the country and all classes of society (*Stände*). . . . Send us rather a mighty pestilence that the people may be God-fearing and that church and secular government and homes may not be destroyed.[14]

What presumption to prescribe to God the more desirable form of wrathful visitation!

It is refreshing to find the dour author of the Smalcald Articles break into prayer at the end of his preface.

> Dear Lord Jesus Christ, assemble a council of thine own, and by thy glorious advent deliver thy servants. . . . Help us poor and wretched souls who cry unto Thee and earnestly seek Thee according to the grace which Thou hast given us by Thy Holy Spirit, who with Thee and the Father livest and reignest, blessed forever. Amen.

Contention for the truth of the Gospel is mingled with childlike prayer. But there is another portion, a portion fierce and devastating. It reads, "The pope and his adherents are lost. They will have nothing to do with Thee." This man speaks the mood of his soul, even when it goes too far.

A different kind of boldness is manifested in the prayer for the recovery of Melanchthon from grievous illness. Melanchthon had sunk into deep despondency over the aftermath of the bigamous marriage of Philip of Hesse in 1540. Physician Sturz was at his wits' end. The professor's eyes were already glazed; consciousness, speech, hearing were gone. "Heaven help us!" exclaimed Luther, "how has the devil maltreated this *Organon* (instrument)!" Luther turned to the window and prayed, at a later time recalling: "There God had to take it. I cast the whole sack at his door and rubbed His ears with all the promises I could recount from Scripture that He would hear prayer; that He would have to answer my prayer, if I were to trust

His promises." Then Luther took hold af Melanchthon's hand and spoke earnestly to him, saying among other things that God did not wish the death of a sinner, but that he live; that Melanchthon should not become a suicide, but should trust the Lord. The sick man began to breathe again. After intently looking at Luther he asked him to let him depart. But Luther answered, "By no means! You have to serve the Lord some more. . . . Philip, eat, or I'll excommunicate you!" [16] Melanchthon lived twenty more years.

How Luther felt about prayer is also revealed in his letters. There is scarcely a letter to a friend that does not embody the refrain, "Pray for me!" It becomes a "pray for poor me" in the May 30, 1519, letter to Martin Glaser.[17] Spalatin is urged, June 10, 1521, "Be sure to pray for me," and November 1, "Do pray that Christ does not desert me in the end." [18] In a letter to Philip Melanchthon, May 12, 1521, Luther wonders, "Are you not praying for me that this retreat [the Wartburg], to which I unwillingly consented, may result in something great for God's glory?" [19] Two months later, to the same Philip, "I ask all of you to pray for me, since in this seclusion I am drowning in sins." [20] With regard to his intended return to Wittenberg he requests Philip, January 13, 1522, "Pray the Lord that this may be done in agreement with his will." [21] In turn, Luther assures Melanchthon, May 12, 1521, "I pray for you as for no one else, if my prayer can accomplish something—which I do not doubt." [22] In a long letter two weeks later, "As much as I am able, I shall also remember you in my prayer." [23]

That Luther's prayer life did not always proceed smoothly, even apart from reciting the canonical hours, becomes apparent from a letter to Melanchthon under date of July 13, 1521:

> Your high opinion of me shames and tortures me, since—unfortunately—I sit here like a fool and hardened in leisure, pray little, do not sigh for the church of God, yet burn in a big fire of my untamed body. In short, I should be ardent in spirit, but I am ardent in the flesh, in lust, laziness, leisure, and sleepiness. I do not know whether God has turned away from me since you all do not pray for me. You are already replacing me; because of the gifts you have from God, you have attained greater authority and popularity than I had.
>
> Already eight days have passed in which I have written nothing, in which I have not prayed or studied. This is partly because of temptations of the flesh, partly because I am tortured by other burdens [his chronic constipation].[24]

While the plague rages at Wittenberg in 1527 Luther writes Hausmann:

> I pray you for Christ's sake that you stand by me with your prayers against the devil and his angels, who are exceedingly hostile to me; that Christ, who so far has selected me for the furtherance of His Gospel, may not depart from me, but glorify His name in my weakness, be it through death or through life. I do not ask you without reason, for I stand in need of the prayer and help of the brethren, in whom I adore and worship my Christ. Farewell in this Jesus Christ, the dearest Savior.[25]

III

LUTHER'S INSTRUCTION CONCERNING PRAYER

Luther's thoughts about prayer are set forth extensively in the instructions he has written concerning this subject. The material is voluminous.

Having finished an exposition of the Ten Commandments during Lent of 1517, Luther next preached a series of sermons on the Our Father. This became the first of many subsequent explanations of the Lord's Prayer to appear in print. A 1519 version bears the curious title, "A Short and Good Interpretation of the Lord's Prayer Forward and Backward." [26] To pray it forward is recommended as being the right way, for it puts the things of God first; to put one's own honor and affairs first is spoken of as praying the Lord's Prayer backward.

In 1520 Luther published a sermon on good works. A very sizable portion thereof was prayer instruction and exhortation, of which the following is a sample.

> Oh, would to God that every congregation of people would conduct Mass and pray on this wise that a joint, earnest cry of the heart of the whole people ascend to God! What immeasurable virtue and help would follow upon this prayer! What more terrible thing could come upon all evil spirits? What greater thing could happen on earth? Many believers would thereby be preserved, many sinners converted! [27]

Luther's *Small Catechism* of 1529 not only contained his masterly exposition of the Lord's Prayer, but had attached to it a section on "How the head of the family shall teach his household to say morning and evening prayers," and another on "How the head of the family shall teach his household to offer blessing and thanksgiving at table." The material for these two sections was adapted from the

Roman Breviary, proving that there were precious values resident in the church that had excommunicated him. The prayers themselves can easily be read in the *Book of Concord* [28] or other editions of the Catechism; but it may be worth while to reprint a few of Luther's directions.

> In the morning, when you rise, make the sign of the cross and say, "In the name of God the Father, the Son and the Holy Ghost. Amen." Then, kneeling or standing, say the Apostles' Creed and the Lord's Prayer. Then you may say this prayer: 'I give Thee thanks, heavenly Father, through thy dear Son Jesus." After singing a hymn (possibly a hymn on the Ten Commandments) or whatever your devotion may suggest, you should go to your work joyfully. [29]

The similar instructions for evening prayers conclude, "Then quickly lie down and sleep in peace."

The preface to the *Large Catechism*, also of 1529, contains some strong language as to how parents and children and servants should practice forms of the devotional life. Pastors are jolted out of complacency by a sentence like this, "Such shameful gluttons and servants of their bellies would make better swineherds or dogkeepers than spiritual guides and pastors." Luther confesses concerning his personal need,

> As for myself, let me say that I, too, am a doctor and a preacher— yes, and as learned and experienced as any of those who act so high and mighty. Yet I do as a child who is being taught the Catechism. Every morning, and whenever else I have time, I read and recite word for word the Lord's Prayer, the Ten Commandments, the Creed, the Psalms, etc. I must still read and study the Catechism daily, yet I cannot master it as I wish, but must remain a child and pupil of the Catechism, and I do it gladly.

Then there is a comment about those who think they have outgrown such childish exercises,

> These dainty, fastidious fellows would like quickly, with one reading, to become doctors above all doctors, to know all there is to be known. Well, this, too, is a sure sign that they despise both their office and the people's souls, yes, even God and his Word. [30]

Since the material is so well known, it is not necessary to refer to the classic exposition of the Lord's Prayer constituting Part III of the *Small Catechism*. But those who handle it in catechetical instruction are advised from time to time to read the fifteen pages that constitute Part III of the *Large Catechism*. Five of these pages are on prayer in general.[31]

One of the most interesting writings is the one dedicated to *Master Peter, the Barber, How We Should Pray*. It was published in 1534. In the second paragraph Luther states how he works himself into the spirit of prayer.

When I feel that through strange dealings and thoughts I have become cold and undisposed to prayer—as flesh and the devil always resist and hinder prayer—I take my little psalter, proceed to my room, or, if it is during the day and the proper time, I go to church and to the congregation and begin to say to myself orally, just as the children do, the Ten Commandments, the Creed, and, as I have time, some sayings of Christ or Paul or the Psalter. For that reason it is a good thing to permit prayer to be the first thing in the morning and the last thing in the evening and diligently to guard against these false, deceptive thoughts that say, "Wait a while. An hour from now I'll pray. I have first to attend to this or that." With such thoughts one is diverted from prayer into activities, which then keep and embrace you, that nothing comes of the prayer of the day.[32]

Luther grants that there might be a few things which are as good or better than prayer, especially when necessity demands; but he advises that we be on our guard so that we do not become lax and lazy in prayer. He would have us make the "Amen" strong, to say the "Yes" to our prayers, never to doubt that God hears.

Luther does not want Master Peter to think that he must use all the words which his instructor has just put into the expanded paraphrase of the seven Petitions. That would become babbling and idle loose talk, like rattling off the rosary.

I don't tie myself to such words and syllables; but speak the words today on this wise, tomorrow otherwise, as I have a mood to. But I stay as close as I am able to the same thought and meaning. It happens, however, that in one petition I ambulate about in such prolific thoughts, that I have to pass up the other six petitions. And when such rich, good thoughts come, a person should surrender the other prayers and give room to such thoughts and quietly listen to them and not interrupt; for then the Holy Spirit Himself preaches. And one word of His sermon is worth more than a thousand words of our prayers. In this way I have learned more from one prayer than I could have gotten out of much reading and contemplation.

But Luther would have Master Peter to concentrate on his words
and thoughts,

> as a good diligent barber must concentrate his thoughts, senses, eyes,
> accurately on his scissors and on the hair and not forget where he is
> with his comb and trim.[33]

Luther further tells how he at times prays his way through the
Commandments. To a later edition of this tract is added the portion,
"A Way to Meditate on the Creed." [34]

It is impossible to consider how frequently and effectively Luther
treated the prayer theme in his sermons. We must be content with
an excerpt from the sermon on the healing of the blind man on the
road near Jericho, Luke 18:31-43.

> Such a brazen prayer that does not let up and is not scared away
> from blaring at God, pleases God well. . . . Under the papacy we de-
> spised our own prayers and thought if others do not intercede for us,
> we obtain nothing. But, by his life, no Christian should do such a
> thing. On the contrary, as soon as the need arises, quick into the
> chamber and down on your knees and say: "Lord, here I am, I need
> this and that, though I am unworthy. You, Lord, told us, Call upon
> me in trouble. That is why I ask that you would consider my great need
> and misery and deliver me for the sake of your honor." [35]

IV

COLLECTS AND HYMNS

Luther manifests himself as man of prayer also in his liturgical
labors. As he revised and provided liturgical forms for congregational
worship, as also for the so-called occasional services, he had to deal
with the prayers contained therein. He freely drew on material that
was available, adapting it as he saw fit. Even the expert is at a loss
at times to determine to what extent the material that passed
through Luther's hands is original with him or is adapted from the
earlier liturgical treasure of the church.

We are on more certain ground when it comes to the hymns that
are attributed to Luther, though even here he often translated or
paraphrased Latin hymns of earlier centuries. Our concern is not
with the details of original authorship, but with the prayer aspect
of Luther's hymns. That aspect is prominent throughout, even
though in rendering the hymn into English it is difficult fully to

retain the fragrance of the worshipful attitude that pervades the original.

Penitent souls readily plead with Luther:

> Out of the depths I cry to thee,
> O Lord, my sins bewailing!
> Bow down thy gracious ear to me,
> Make thou my prayer availing.[36]

Three mighty prayer stanzas constitute the great hymn of Pentecost,

> Come, Holy Spirit, God and Lord;
> Be all thy gifts in plenty poured
> To save, to strengthen and make whole
> Each ready mind, each waiting soul.[37]

The hymn which in its original text prays for preservation amid the murderous intent of pope and Turk *(Und steur des Papsts und Türken Mord)*, yet concludes with the precious prayer for unity:

> O Comforter of priceless worth,
> Send peace and unity on earth;
> Support us in our final strife,
> And lead us out of death to life.[38]

In the fifteen stanzas of his Christmas hymn, "From heaven above to earth I come," Luther narrates the Bethlehem story in simple fashion, and becomes almost a child himself as he prays in stanzas nine and thirteen:

> Ah Lord! the maker of us all!
> How hast thou grown so poor and small,
> That there thou liest on withered grass,
> The supper of the ox and ass?

> Dear little Jesus! in my shed,
> Make thee a soft, white little bed,
> And rest thee in my heart's low shrine,
> That so my heart be always thine.[39]

Of course, the original German of that last stanza is even more child-like than any attempted translation:

"Ach, mein herzliebes Jesulein,
Mach dir ein rein sanft Bettelein,
Zu ruhn in mein'm Herzensschrein,
Dasz ich nimmer vergesse dein."

Whoever can pray thus is indeed a praying soul.

V

Luther Dies as a Man of Prayer

As a man of prayer Luther lived, as a man of prayer he died. In our age of massively applied sedation, a conscious, prayerful departure from this earthly scene is granted to but a few. It might serve more than one purpose to give an account in condensed form of Luther's dying hours in the night from February 17 to 18, 1546, in his native city of Eisleben. The account of Köstlin is summarized here.[40]

The reconciliation of the Counts von Mansfeld had been brought to a successful conclusion, but the ailing Luther suffered increasing distress from chest pains. Jonas, Coelius, Rudtfeld, and sons Martin and Paul were with him that last night. They had conversed with him a while and then he dozed in the living room. On waking, he decided to go to bed. As he made for the door to the bedroom he prayed: "If it please God, I'll go to bed. Into Thy hands I commend my spirit; Thou hast redeemed me, my faithful God." He slept till about one o'clock, when he awoke with more pain. Unaided he made his way back into the living room, repeating: "Into Thy hands I commend my spirit." Others were being summoned, also the physicians. They tried to give him relief, but he said, "Dear God, I have pain and anxiety, I am departing." After a further interval he prayed at some length:

O my heavenly Father, the God and Father of our Lord Jesus Christ, Thou God of all consolation, I thank Thee that Thou hast made Thy Son Jesus Christ known to me. Him I believed, Him I preached and confessed, Him I loved and praised, the One whom the sorry pope and all the godless disgrace, persecute and blaspheme. I pray Thee, my Lord Jesus Christ, let my wee soul (Seelchen) be commended to Thee. O heavenly Father, though I must leave this body and must be taken out of this life, I know for certain that I will be eternally with Thee and that no one can tear me out of Thy hands.

Three times he distinctly repeated John 3:16, "God so loved the world," and then Psalm 68:20, "Our God is a God of salvation; and to God, the Lord, belongs escape from death."

As they were still trying to give him strengthening medicine, he said once more, "I am departing, I will give up my spirit." Then three times in rapid succession, "Father, into Thy hands I commend my spirit. Thou hast redeemed me, my faithful God." Then he grew quiet and made no more response until Jonas and Coelius shouted into his ear, "Reverend Father, will you abide firmly on Christ and on the doctrine you have preached?" He answered with an audible "Yes," dozed off for another 15 minutes or so, until his dazed friends had to realize that the great leader had slept away.

NOTES

Abbreviations

BC   —   *The Book of Concord: The Confessions of the Evangelical Lutheran Church,* translated and edited by Theodore G. Tappert, in collaboration with Jaroslav Pelikan, Robert H. Fischer, and Arthur C. Piepkorn (Philadelphia: Fortress Press, 1959).

LW   —   *Luther's Works,* American Edition (Philadelphia and St. Louis: Fortress Press and Concordia Publishing House, 1955-).

WA   —   *D. Martin Luthers Werke.* Kritische Gesamtausgabe (Weimar, 1883-).

1. Luther and the First Commandment

1. *BC*, p. 112.
2. Heinrich Bornkamm, *Luther und das Alte Testament* (Tübingen, 1948), p. 122.
3. *Deuteronomion Mosi cum annotationibus* (1525), WA 14, 499, 19. *Von den letzten Worten Davids* (1543), WA 54, 77, 24.
4. Bornkamm, *Luther,* p. 140.
5. *Ibid.,* p. 151.
6. *Wider die himmlischen Propheten, von den Bildern und Sakrament* (1525), WA 18, 80, 18-19.
7. *Ibid.,* 18, 81, 19-20.
8. *BC*, p. 409.
9. *Ibid.,* p. 114.
10. Bornkamm, *Luther,* p. 114.
11. *Unterrichtung wie sich die Christen in Mosen sollen schicken* (1525), WA 16, 373, 12 and 375, 14.
12. *Predigten über das 2. Buch Mose* (1525), WA 16, 394, 4-5.
13. Bornkamm, *Luther,* pp. 107.
14. *Ibid.,* p. 108.
15. *Die zweite Disputation gegen die Antinomer* (1538), WA 39 I, 454, 4 and 15.
16. Bornkamm, *Luther,* p. 116.
17. *Ibid.,* p. 151.
18. *Glossen zum Dekalog* (1530), WA 30 II, 358, 5-6.
19. WA TR 1, No. 369. p. 160, 5-6.
20. Bornkamm, *Luther,* pp. 141-142.
21. *Predigten über das 2. Buch Mose* (1525), WA 16, 434, 24-31.
22. Julius Köstlin, *The Theology of Luther in Its Historical Development and Inner Harmony* (Philadelphia: Philadelphia Publication Society, 1897), II, 232.
23. Bornkamm, *Luther,* p. 151.
24. WA TR 1, No. 868. p. 432, 19-20 and p. 433, 1-2.
25. Bornkamm, *Luther,* p. 143.
26. *Ibid.,* Cf. *Deuteronomion Mosi cum annotationibus* (1525), WA 14, 640, 30.
27. *Vorrede auf die Propheten* (1532), E.A. 63. 44. The translation is that of the Holman Edition, *Works of Martin Luther* (Philadelphia: Muhlenberg, 1932), VI, 396.

28. Bornkamm, *Luther,* p. 151.
29. *Ibid.,* p. 144.
30. *Ibid.*
31. *Ein Sermon von dem Sakrament der Busse* (1519), WA 2, 717, 36-39.
32. *Operationes in Psalmos* (1519-21), WA 5, 398, 27-34.
33. Bornkamm, *Luther,* pp. 146-147.
34. Karl Holl, *Gesammelte Aufsätze zur Kirchengeschichte* (Tübingen, 1928), III, 248.
35. Paul Althaus, "Gottes Gottheit als Sinn der Rechtfertigungslehre Luthers," *Luther-Jahrbuch 13, (1931),* p. 10.
36. Bornkamm, *Luther,* p. 147.
37. *Ibid.*
38. *Ibid.*
39. *Ibid.,* p. 148.
40. *Ibid.*
41. *Predigten über das 5. Buch Mose* (1529), WA 28, 722, 23-25.
42. *Kirchenpostille* (1522), WA 10 I 1, 675, 6-15.
43. WA TR 1, No. 369, p. 160, 21-23.
44. *Ibid.,* p. 160, 24-27.
45. Bornkamm, *Luther,* p. 150.
46. *Predigten des Jahres 1532. No. 2 (1. Januar),* WA 36, 25, 21-26.
47. *Ibid.,* 25, 29-34 and 29, 32-35.
48. Paul Althaus, *The Divine Command. A New Perspective on Law and Gospel,* trans. by Franklin Sherman (Philadelphia: Fortress, 1966), p. 38.
49. *Von den guten Werken* (1520), WA 6, 209, 24-27.
50. Bornkamm, *Luther,* p. 140.
51. Karl Barth, "Gospel and Law," *God, Grace and Gospel* (Edinburgh: Oliver & Boyd, 1959), p. 10.
52. *Ibid.,* pp. 3.
53. *Ibid.,* pp. 3-4.
54. *Barmen Declaration* II, 1. Arthur C. Cochrane, *The Church's Confession under Hitler* (Philadelphia: Westminster, 1962), p. 239.
55. Barth, "Gospel and Law," pp. 5-6.
56. *Ibid.,* pp. 8-12.
57. *Ibid.,* pp. 16-17.
58. *Ibid.,* pp. 18-19.
59. *Ibid.,* pp. 20-22.
60. *Ibid.,* pp. 24-25.
61. *Ibid.,* p. 26.
62. Cf. Note 24 above.
63. *In epistolam S. Pauli ad Galatas Commentarius* (1535), WA 40 I, 527, 23-26. The translation is that of L.W. 26, 343.
64. *Predigten über das 2. Buch Mose* (1525), WA 16, 384, 13-14 and 385, 7-9, 12-16.

2. Luther's Principles of Biblical Interpretation

1. *Theology Today,* 21 (April 1964), 34-46.
2. *Luther the Expositor* (St. Louis: Concordia, 1959), p. 141.
3. B. Gerrish, "Biblical Authority and the Continental Reformation," *Scottish Journal of Theology,* 10 (Dec. 1957), 339.
4. William Kooiman, *Luther and the Bible* (Philadelphia: Muhlenberg, 1961), pp. 29 ff.
5. LW 34, 325-338.
6. WA 54, 185f.
7. Cf. Pelikan, *Luther the Expositor,* ch. 3 passim.
8. Heinrich Bornkamm, *Luther und das Alte Testament* (Tübingen, 1948), pp. 139-151.
9. WA 10¹, 181f.
10. WA 21, 235-236.
11. WA 12, 259; 37, 207.
12. W. G. Kümmel, "The Continuing Significance of Luther's Prefaces to the New Testament," *Concordia Theological Monthly,* 37 (Oct. 1966), 574 f.
13. WA 48, 31.
14. WA 1, 648.
15. WA 26, 450.
16. WA 56, 249.
17. WA 39¹, 47.

18. *WA* 3, 19.
19. *LW* 35, 362.
20. *LW* 35, 396.
21. *WA*, TR 5, No. 5533.
22. Pelikan, *Luther the Expositor*, pp. 126 f.
23. *LW* 1, 233.
24. Pelikan, *Luther the Expositor*, pp. 95ff.
25. *LW* 35, 274.
26. *WA* 6, 301.
27. *WA* 8, 239.
28. Kooiman, *Luther and the Bible*, pp. 233 f.
29. *WA* 45, 22.
30. *The Christian Doctrine of God* (Philadelphia: Westminster, 1950), p. 111.
31. "Luther as Exegete," *Expository Times, 69* (Nov., Dec. 1957), 48.
32. "Biblical Authority," 357.

3. Scripture and Tradition, in Luther and in Our Day

1. Paul Verghese, "Authority in the Church," *McCormick Quarterly,* 21 (Nov. 1967), p. 150.
2. Quoted from J. Michael Reu, *Luther and the Scriptures* (Columbus: Wartburg Press, 1944), p. 14.
3. Yves M-J. Congar, *Tradition and Traditions* (New York: Macmillan, 1967), pp. 107-118.
4. *Ibid.,* p. 114.
5. *Ibid.,* p. 140.
6. Jaroslav Pelikan, *Obedient Rebels* (New York: Harper & Row, 1964), p. 21.
7. *Commentary on Psalm 90, LW,* 13, 99.
8. *Luther the Expositor* (St. Louis: Concordia, 1959), p. 51.
9. *On the Abuse of the Mass,* WA, 8, 597.
10. *Tradition and Traditions,* p. 480.
11. *WA,* 10, I, 2, 48.
12. *Leipzig Disputation* (1519), WA 2, 286.
13. *Confession on the Lord's Supper* (1528), WA 26, 313.
14. *Commentary on Psalm 37* (1521), WA 8, 237.
15. *To the Christian Nobility* (1520), WA 6, 461.
16. *Large Catechism,* Part II, par. 56, *BC,* p. 418.
17. *Ibid.,* par. 45, p. 416.
18. Congar, *Tradition and Traditions,* pp. 285-286.
19. *Ibid.,* p. 300.
20. *Ibid.,* p. 301.
21. *Ibid.,* p. 87.
22. *Ibid.,* p. 88.
23. *Ibid.,* p. 113.
24. *Ibid.,* pp. 100 f.
25. *Ibid.,* p. 145, or J. Pelikan, *Obedient Rebels,* pp. 50 f.
26. Congar, *ibid.,* pp. 145 f.
27. *Augsburg Confession* XV, 4, *BC,* p. 37.
28. See Edgar Carlson, *The Reinterpretation of Luther* (Philadelphia: Westminster, 1948), p. 158.
29. See W. M. Abbott & Joseph Gallagher: *The Documents of Vatican II* (New York: Guild Press, 1966).
30. *Ibid.,* p. 125.
31. Report published in *Unity Trends,* 1 (Jan. 1968), 2.
32. Typescript working paper, Report to the Commission on Faith and Order, World Council of Churches, Division of Studies.
33. Oscar Cullmann, *The Early Church* (London: SCM, 1956), p. 98.
34. Ernst Kinder, in K. E. Skydsgaard, "Interim Report, Faith and Order Commission, August, 1960," pp. 16-17 (transcript).

4. The Changing Catholic View of Luther

1. John Sheerin, "Canonize Martin Luther?" *The Catholic World,* 197 (May 1963), 84-87, takes note of the sentiment but is very skeptical about the possibility.
2. *Commentaria de actis et scriptis Martini Lutheri,* 1549. For a good summary of Catho-

lic attitudes to the Reformation see Walter von Loewenich, *Modern Catholicism*, trans. by Reginald H. Fuller (New York: St. Martin's, 1959), pp. 265-292.

3. *Anatomiae Lutheri* (2 vols.; Cologne, 1595-1598).
4. Heinrich Boehmer, *Luther in the Light of Recent Research* (New York: Christian Herald, 1916), p. 26.
5. *Geschichte des deutschen Volkes seit dem Ausgang des Mittelalters* (8 vols.; Freibourg, 1879-1894). English translation by M. A. Mitchell and A. M. Christie, *History of the German People at the Close of the Middle Ages* (12 vols.; London, 1896-1907).
6. Hubert Jedin, "Wandlungen des Lutherbildes in der katholischen Kirchengeschichtsschreibung," in *Wandlungen des Lutherbildes*, Karl Forster, ed. (Würzburg, 1966), p. 88.
7. J. Michael Reu, *Thirty-Five Years of Luther Research* (Chicago: Wartburg, 1916), pp. 35 f.
8. *Luther und Luthertum in der ersten Entwickelung quellenmässig dargestellt* (2 vols.; Mainz, 1904-1907).
9. *Luther* (Freibourg, 1911-1912).
10. Richard Stauffer cites with approval the comment of Walter Köhler that the brutality of the Dominican is better than the smoothness of the Jesuit. *Luther as Seen by Catholics*, trans. by Mary Parker and T. H. L. Parker (Richmond, Va.: John Knox, 1967), p. 15.
11. *Martin Luthers Leben und sein Werk* (Freiburg, 1926), p. viii.
12: (New York: Frederick Pustet, 1916). Somewhat similar to O'Hare but much more temperate is Christiani's *Luther wie er wirklich war* (Stuttgart, 1955). The book is recommended in a foreword by the Lutheran Hans Asmussen as one which can show evangelicals "how good-willed Roman Catholics see the start of the evangelical affair." [!]
13. O'Hare, *The Facts about Luther*, p. 350.
14. *Ibid.*, p. 357.
15. *Ibid.*, pp. 16, 286, 271.
16. *Three Reformers* (New York: Scribners, 1942). The 1st edition appeared in 1928.
17. *Ibid.*, p. 34.
18. Stauffer, *Luther as Seen by Catholics*, p. 71, summarizes Weijenborg's "Miraculum a Martino Luthere confictum explicante eius reformationem?" *Antonianum* 31 (Rome, 1956), 247-300.
19. "Martin Luthers Religiöse Psyche," *Hochland: Monatsschrift für alle Gebeite des Wissens, der Literatur, und der Kunst*, 15 (Oct. 1917-Mar. 1918), 7-28. I rely on the summary by Stauffer, *Luther as Seen by Catholics*, pp. 27 f.
20. See Walter von Loewenich's summary of Kiefl in "Evangelische und katholische Lutherdeutung der Gegenwart im Dialog," *Luther Jahrbuch*, 34, ed. by Franz Lau (Hamburg, 1967), 65.
21. *Luther as Seen by Catholics*, p. 38.
22. Alfred von Martin, ed. (Stuttgart, 1929). See summary of the articles in Leonard Swidler, "Catholic Reformation Scholarship in Germany," *Journal of Ecumenical Studies*, 2 (1965), 192-194.
23. Jedin, "Wandlungen," p. 93.
24. (2 vols.; Freibourg, 1939-1940). English translation by Ronald Walls, *The Reformation in Germany* (2 vols.; New York: Herder & Herder, 1968). Ecumenical implications of Lortz's reformation studies are sketched by him in *The Reformation: a Problem for Today* (Westminster, Md.: Newman, 1964).
25. *Die Reformation in Deutschland* I, 11.
26. *Ibid.*, 408.
27. *Ibid.*, pp. 162 ff. Karl Adam, *One and Holy* (New York: Sheed & Ward, 1951), shares many of Lortz's views but has much less appreciation than Lortz for Luther's theology and emphases.
28. Jèdin, "Wandlungen," p. 96, comments that Lortz's book might well have been suppressed if it had been translated into Italian or French when it first appeared. The Romance countries, as well as the Catholics in England and the U.S.A., were not yet ready for this kind of re-evaluation of Luther and the Reformation. In any case, Lortz was never censured.
29. (3 vols.; Münster, 1943).
30. Stauffer probably overstates Herte's position when he says that Cochlæus' "polemical work . . . in its animosity, takes no account of truth." *Luther as Seen by Catholics*, p. 43. Jedin says that Herte has proved Cochlæus to be guilty of much carelessness and many errors, but not of conscious falsification of evidence through deliberately misleading quotations or fabricated additions. "Wandlungen," p. 82.
31. Von Loewenich notes that Catholics seemed to be strangely silent about Herte after World War II. "Evangelische und katholische Lutherdeutung," p. 63.
32. Subtitle: *Zur Worttheologie in Luthers ersten Psalmenvorlesung* (Paderborn, 1960).

33. *Luther and Thomas on Salvation,* trans. by Edward Quinn (New York: Sheed & Ward, 1965).
34. One of the most profound recent theological analyses is by an American Paulist, Harry McSorley, *Luthers Lehre vom unfreien Willen nach seiner Hauptschrift de servo arbitrio im Lichte der biblischen und kirchlichen Tradition* (München, 1967). It has just been published in English by Augsburg under the title *Luther: Right or Wrong?* See the review by Eduard Stakemeier, "Luthers *de servo arbitrio,*" *Catholica,* 22 (1968), 132-135.
35. *True and False Reformation in the Church.* See Per Erik Persson, "The Reformation in Recent Roman Catholic Theology," *Dialog,* 2 (Winter 1963), 27-29.
36. *The Spirit and Forms of Protestantism,* trans. by A. V. Littledale (Westminster, Md.: Newman, 1957).
37. Subtitle: *Grundlegung eines ökumenischen Gespräches* (Bonn, 1947). Stauffler, *Luther as Seen by Catholics,* p. 44, regards it as "the most noteworthy attempt to understand Luther's real motives."
38. Hessen, *Luther in katholischer Sicht,* pp. 9-17, 20-23.
39. *Ibid.,* pp. 26-34.
40. *Ibid.,* 35-38.
41. Examples of what Hessen regards as "extremes" are: (1) that Luther in his stress on the forensic nature of justification failed to do justice to the fact that God's justifying act achieves a real change in man's soul, and (2) that Luther's fear of man's innate desire to rely upon himself virtually blinded him to the Pauline teaching about the conquest of sin in the believer. *Ibid.,* pp. 54-58.
42. On the tendency to moralism, Hessen says that Catholicism in its desire to be "Volks- und Weltkirche" tends to tailor its message to the level that appeals to the average man. Therefore it stresses the moral demands of faith rather than "living out of the heart of God." *Ibid.,* p. 68.
43. *Ibid.,* p. 67. Karl Adam gives the same idea a much more Roman turn—"It is only a determined return to Luther himself which will make it possible for our separated brethren to come home to their Mother, the Church." *One and Holy,* p. 68.
44. "Luther in katholischer Sicht," *Una Sancta: Zeitschrift für Interkonfessionelle Begegnung,* 16 (Mar. 1961), 38-54.
45. *Ibid.,* p. 42.
46. *Ibid.,* p. 48.
47. *Ibid.,* p. 50.
48. *Ibid.,* p. 52.
49. *Ibid.,* p. 54.
50. (Westminster, Md.: Newman, 1964.)
51. *Ibid.,* p. xvi.
52. *Ibid.,* pp. 219 ff.
53. *Ibid.,* pp. 133-193, Part IV: The Public Figure.
54. *Ibid.,* p. 204.
55. *Ibid.,* p. 253.
56. *Ibid.,* p. 184, n. 2.
57. *Ibid.,* pp. 271 f.
58. *Ibid.,* p. 276.
59. *Ibid.,* p. 216.
60. Von Loewenich accepts the Catholic invitation and indicates the outlines of a possible answer from the Lutheran perspective in "Evangelische und katholische Lutherdeutung," pp. 86-89.

5. A Positive Response to Erik Erikson's *Young Man Luther*

1. Erik H. Erikson, *Young Man Luther* (New York: W. W. Norton, 1958), pp. 223 f.
2. *Ibid.,* pp. 9 f.
3. Philip Woolcott, Jr., "Erikson's Luther: A Psychiatrist's View," *Journal for the Scientific Study of Religion,* 2 (Spring 1963), 243-248.
4. Erikson, *Young Man Luther,* p. 249.
5. Roland H. Bainton, *Studies on the Reformation* (Boston: Beacon Press, 1963), pp. 86-92.
6. Erik H. Erikson, *Childhood and Society* (2nd ed.; New York: W. W. Norton, 1963), p. 16.
7. Bainton, *Studies,* p. 92.
8. Erik H. Erikson, *Insight and Responsibility* (New York: W. W. Norton, 1964), pp. 201-202.
9. *Ibid.,* p. 207.

10. John Osborne, *Luther* (New York: New American Library, 1963).
11. Erikson, *Young Man Luther*, p. 149.
12. *Ibid.*, p. 245.
13. Conversation at Evangelical Lutheran Theological Seminary, April 1967.
14. Quoted by Erikson, *Young Man Luther*, p. 162.
15. Martin Luther, *The Letters of Martin Luther*, sel. and trans. by Margaret A. Currie (London: Macmillan & Co., 1908), p. 456. See also the series of letters pp. 416-420.
16. Erikson, *Insight and Responsibility*, pp. 146-147.
17. Bainton, *Studies*, pp. 86-87.
18. George R. Collingwood, *The Idea of History* (New York: Oxford U. Press, 1957).
19. Quoted by Erikson, *Young Man Luther*, pp. 30-31.
20. Philip Rieff, *The Mind of the Moralist* (New York: Doubleday, 1961), pp. 361-392.
21. Bainton, *Studies*, p. 87.
22. Erikson, *Young Man Luther*, p. 28.
23. Erik Erikson, review of *Thomas Woodrow Wilson: Twenty-eighth President of the United States—A Psychological Study*, by Sigmund Freud and William C. Bullitt, in *The New York Review of Books*, Feb. 9, 1967, pp. 3-8.
24. Erikson, *Insight and Responsibility*, pp. 209-212.
25. Erikson, *Young Man Luther*, p. 140.
26. *Ibid.*
27. Paul Tillich, *The Courage to Be* (New Haven: Yale U. Press, 1952), pp. 186-190.

6. The Smalcald Articles and Their Significance

1. *BC*, p. 289.
2. E. G. Schwiebert, *Luther and His Times: The Reformation from a New Perspective* (St. Louis: Concordia, 1950), p. 741: "The Smalkald Articles are a declaration of independence on the part of Luther from the compromising *Leisetreterei* of Melanchthon at the Diet of Augsburg."
3. *Die symbolischen Bücher der evangelisch-lutherischen Kirche, deutsch und lateinisch*, ed. by J. T. Müller (Stuttgart: Samuel Gottlieb Liesching, 1848).
4. *Die Bekenntnisschriften der evangelisch-lutherischen Kirche herausgegeben im Gedenkjahr der Augsburgischen Konfession 1930* (5th ed.; Göttingen: Vandenhoeck & Ruprecht, 1964).
5. *Ibid.*, pp. lxxxii-lxxxiii; quoted in Charles P. Krauth, *The Conservative Reformation and Its Theology* (reprint ed.; Minneapolis: Augsburg [1963]), pp. 283-284.
6. *BC*, p. 300.
7. *BC*, p. 291.
8. *BC*, pp. 26 f.
9. *Documents Illustrative of the Continental Reformation*, ed. by B. J. Kidd (Oxford: Clarendon, 1911), p. 300.
10. *Urkunden und Aktenstücke zur Geschichte von Martin Luthers Schmalkaldischen Artikeln (1535-1574)*, ed. by Hans Volz in collaboration with Heinrich Ulbrich (Berlin: Walter de Gruyter & Co., 1957), hereafter abbreviated *UuA*.
11. Julius Köstlin, *Martin Luther: Sein Leben und seine Schriften*, ed. by Gustav Kawerau (2 vols.; 5th ed.; Berlin: Alexander Duncker, 1903), II, 376.
12. *Ibid.*
13. F. Bente, *Historical Introductions to the Book of Concord* (St. Louis: Concordia, 1965), p. 49.
14. *Ibid.*, p. 48.
15. *UuA*, p. 25.
16. Bente, *Historical Introductions*, p. 50.
17. *Ibid.*
18. *Ibid.*
19. *UuA*, p. 19.
20. *Ibid.*
21. *Ibid.*
22. Ernst Bizer, "Zum geschichtlichen Verständnis von Luthers Schmalkaldischen Artikeln," *Zeitschrift für Kirchengeschichte*, 67 (1955-56), 61-92; Hans Volz, "Luthers Schmalkaldische Artikel," *ZK* 68 (1957), 259-286; Ernst Bizer, "Noch einmal: Die Schmalkaldischen Artikel," *ZK* 68 (1957), 287-294.
23. *UuA*, p. 27.
24. *UuA*, pp. 22-24; translated in Bente, *Historical Introductions*, p. 52.
25. The articles, however, were prepared only in German. They were first translated into Latin by Petrus Generanus in 1541. *UuA*, pp. 188 f.
26. *UuA*, p. 81.

27. *Ibid.*
28. *UuA*, pp. 26-29.
29. Heidelberg, Universitäts-Bibliothek, Cod. Pal. Germ. 423, 4°; printed in *UuA*, pp. 35-69.
30. *UuA*, pp. 35 f.
31. Volz, "Luthers Schmalkaldische Artikel," p. 260.
32. *UuA*, p. 20.
33. *UuA*, p. 35.
34. *BC*, p. 316.
35. *BC*, p. 291.
36. *BC*, p. 292.
37. *BC*, p. 302.
38. *BC*, p. 292.
39. *UuA*, pp. 69 f.
40. *UuA*, p. 70.
41. *UuA*, pp. 70 f.
42. *UuA*, pp. 71-73.
43. *UuA*, pp. 73-75.
44. *UuA*, pp. 76 f.
45. *UuA*, pp. 83-87; translated in Bente, *Historical Introductions*, pp. 58 f.
46. *UuA*, p. 88.
47. *BC*, pp. 316 f.
48. Volz, "Luthers Schmalkaldische Artikel," p. 274.
49. *UuA*, pp. 145-175.
50. Volz, "Luthers Schmalkaldische Artikel," pp. 279 f.
51. Köstlin, *Martin Luther*, II, 390.
52. Bente, *Historical Introductions*, p. 60.
53. *BC*, p. 319.
54. *UuA*, p. 116.
55. *BC*, pp. 334 f.
56. *UuA*, pp. 137-139.
57. *UuA*, pp. 176-178.
58. *UuA*, pp. 178-183; translated in *BC*, pp. 288-291.
59. *UuA*, pp. 174 f.
60. *BC*, pp. 291-316.
61. *UuA*, pp. 188-190.
62. *UuA*, p. 209.
63. Johann Friedrich der Mittlere.
64. *UuA*, p. 212.
65. Volz, "Luthers Schmalkaldische Artikel," pp. 285 f.
66. *BC*, p. 505.
67. *BC*, p. 292.
68. *BC*, p. 293.
69. *BC*, p. 297.
70. *BC*, p. 298.
71. *BC*, pp. 298-300.

7. Luther's Understanding of Heaven and Hell

1. Cf. *WA* 42, 329, 29-34.
2. *WA* 25, 139, 36 ff.
3. *WA* 42, 24, 3-7.
4. *WA* 42, 22, 33 ff.
5. Cf. for the following *WA TR* 2, 619, 16-22.
6. Cf. *WA* 18, 687, 20-27.
7. Cf. *WA* 5, 263, 28-38.
8. *WA* 16, 204, 1 f.: "Our heaven, which we see, has a different dimension from the one heaven above all."
9. *WA* 8, 32, 33- 33, 7.
10. Cf. *WA* 26, 346, 347, 19 ff.
11. *WA* 26, 422, 26 ff.
12. Cf. for the following, *WA* 23, 135, 26-33.
13. Cf. E. Metzke, *Sakrament und Metaphysik. Eine Lutherstudie über das Verhältnis des christlichen Denkens zum Leiblich-Materiellen* (Stuttgart: 1948), p. 27.
14. *WA* 19, 219, 31 ff.
15. Cf. *WA* 26, 318, 10-18.

16. *WA* 18, 689, 22: "That he dwells in an inaccessible light as Paul testifies."
17. Cf. *WA* 19, 423, 8-13.
18. *WA* 26, 344, 31 f.: "Because what is in heaven is in and before God, similar to the angels that are at the same time in heaven and on earth."
19. Cf. F. Heidler, *Christi Gegenwart beim Abendmahl. Eine Frage an die Evangelisch-Lutherische Kirche* (Berlin: 1949), p. 31.
20. Cf. *WA* 2, 98, 37 f.
21. Cf. for the following, *WA* 26, 422, 20-25.
22. *WA* 43, 599, 14-17.
23. Cf. *WA* 26, 425, 31-35.
24. Cf. for the following, *WA* 25, 387, 25-29.
25. *WA* 3, 262, 13 ff.: "Finally, the Father in heaven himself will talk to us, he will reveal his Word to us without any medium so that we may hear him, see him, and be happy."
26. *WA* 5, 310, 13-17: "In heaven, where all will see the glory of God, they will not need a preacher. But on earth, where the glory of God is by no means understood, as long as it appears under such a disadvantageous form that it seems to be more obscured than understood, it is necessary that the glory is at least entrusted to the Word and understood by faith."
27. See W. Elert, "Wirkungen der Abendmahlslehre in der Geschichte der Weltanschauung," *Allgemeine evangelische-lutherische Kirchenzeitung*, 60 (1927), col. 746-752, 770-773, 794-798.
28. *WA* 15, 749, 5 ff.
29. For the following cf. *WA* 12, 562, 15-24.
30. Cf. Heidler, *Christi Gegenwart*, 30 f.
31. Cf. Heidler, *ibid.*, 21.
32. *WA* 12, 562, 24-27.
33. Cf. *WA* 23, 723, 11 f.—724, 1.
34. *WA* 12, 562, 28-24: "Therefore, it is an article of faith; there you have to close your eyes and not follow your reason but grasp it by faith."
35. Cf. *WA* 44, 285, 33 f.
36. Cf. *WA* 19, 225, 20-25.
37. *WA* 19, 225, 7-11.
38. Cf. E. Vogelsang, *Der angefochtene Christus bei Luther* (Berlin and Leipzig 1932), p. 35.
39. Cf. E. Vogelsang, "Weltbild und Kreuzestheologie in den Höllenfahrtsstreitigkeiten der Reformationszeit," *Archiv für Reformationsgeschichte*, 38 (1941), 96 f.
40. See Vogelsang, *Der angefochtene Christus*, 35.
41. See E. Hirsch, *Luthers Gottesanschauung* (Göttingen: 1918), p. 7.
42. *WA* 1, 162, 22-26.
43. *WA* 1, 162, 22-26. In his earlier years Luther, following the "devotio moderna," emphasized love towards God as a means of overcoming temptation and the wrath of God. Later on, he put more stress on God's promise of salvation in Christ's redemptive act, i.e., in Word and Sacrament (cf. *WA* 49, 206, 14-20; *WA* 49, 208, 15-23; *WA* 23, 23, 32—24, 5).
44. *WA* 19, 225, 12-16.
45. *WA* 19, 225, 26-29.
46. *WA* 1, 161, 35-162, 2.
47. *WA* 5, 497, 16-19: "Death is the bitter separation from life, but hell means that death is accompanied by the feeling that the punishment is, at once, unchangeable and eternal. Here the soul is captured and surrounded so that it cannot think anything else except that it is to be eternally damned."
48. *WA* 31 I, 517, 15 f.
49. *WA* 10 III, 69, 30 ff.
50. *WA* 11, 432, 21 ff.
51. For the following cf. *WA* 19, 225, 34—226, 5.
52. For the following cf. *WA* 44, 811, 22-26, and 813, 22-29.
53. See *WA* 10 III, 191, 13ff., where Luther says that except in the Word of God man's soul has no rest until judgment day.
54. For the following cf. *WA* 43, 361, 9-16.
55. *WA* 44, 811, 29-32.
56. *WA* 43, 359, 24 ff.: "As the bosom of Abraham was destroyed after Christ's resurrection, a better bosom followed, that of Christ: thus when we go away from that life, we are received into Christ's bosom."
57. Cf. *WA* 43, 359, 11-17.
58. Cf. Vogelsang, *Der angefochtene Christus*, 91 f.
59. Cf. *WA* 4, 23, 2-6.

60. *WA* 25, 243, 14 f. "The Hebrews call hell the grave and even the Scriptures do not mention a place to which the dead will go."
61. *WA* 25, 144, 12 ff.: "Furthermore, in Hebrew hell is usually called the place to which the body and the soul are brought after death, but especially to which the body is brought."
62. See I. Ludolphy, *Die Natur bei Luther* (Leipzig, 1960), 83 f., who observes that Luther is here opposed to Augustine's view.
63. Cf. especially Luther's writing *"Widerruf vom Fegfeuer"* (1530), *WA* 30 II, 371, 13-16, and cf. *WA* 50, 204, 29 ff.
64. *WA* 1, 558, 12-15.
65. *WA* 1, 557, 15-18.
66. *WA* 7, 450, 13-16: "I find in the Scriptures that Christ, Abraham, Jacob, Moses, David, Ezekiel, and some others have tasted hell in their lives, but I think this means purgatory and this is not unbelievable."
67. *WA* 1, 555, 29-33. Luther here probably claims Augustine for himself. Augustine, *Enchiridion*, Ch. CIX: "In the time, however, that lies between the death of man and the final resurrection, the souls are contained in hidden receptacles." Cf. *WA* 44, 516, 22 f., where Luther explicitly refers to this passage. Luther is here opposed to Thomas Aquinas, who says that the receptacle of the dead is deep down there (cf., for instance, *Summa Theologiae* Suppl. quaest. 69, 2). Of course, here we have to take into consideration that though this last part of the *Summa* renders his thoughts, it was not written by Thomas.
68. *WA* 11, 451, 28-31.
69. See, for instance, Vogelsang, *Der angefochtene Christus*, 44 ff., in this otherwise very profound study.
70. *WA* 30 II, 300, 8-11 and cf. Duns Scotus *Opera Omnia I* (Rome: 1950), *distinctiones quaestiones* 1, 5 to which Luther refers here: "Concerning this kind of reasoning about the Gospel, I say that 'Christ descended into hell' is not taught in the Gospel. But it has to be kept as an article of faith, because it is contained in the apostolic symbol." The question must remain open here, whether Luther had a greater confidence in the scriptural basis of the "descent into hell" than Duns Scotus, or whether he succumbed to the tradition as Duns Scotus did. I am inclined to assume the former.
71. Thus, for instance, P. Althaus, *The Theology of Martin Luther*, trans. by R. C. Schultz (Philadelphia: Fortress, 1966), pp. 207 f., and his extensive investigation "Niedergefahren zur Hölle," *Zeitschrift für Systematische Theologie*, XIX (1942), 365-385, especially pp. 371 ff.
72. *WA* 46, 311, 14 f.: "Others say that he had suffered after death. But I say that descent into hell means that he is Lord of hell."
73. *WA* 46, 305, 8 f.: "We have to believe that he descended into hell, because the article [of the creed] says it."
74. Cf. *WA* 46, 310, 6 f., and *WA* 12, 367, 29-368, 4.
75. Cf. *WA* 5, 463, 17 ff.
76. *WA* 46, 312, 7 f.
77. Cf. *WA* 46, 307, 4 f.
78. *WA* 46, 310, 12 f.: "Therefore, he went into hell, took the thief with him, and redeemed the fathers."
79. *WA* 31 I, 517, 16-19. Beyond that, we have to consider that the conviction of the omnipresence and ubiquity of Christ does not leave room for a "descent" of Christ. Thus Luther even said once that if one wants to speak with real precision, one would have to say that Christ did not descend to any place. "Er ist wohl am Kreuz, Grab vel im Himmel blieben" (*WA* 36, 161, 16 f.). Descent into hell, therefore, cannot mean that Christ went to a specific place. In the same way he did not go to earth when he was incarnated. However, it means that he shows his power in a certain way at a certain place or rather in a certain dimension of being.
80. Cf. *WA* 36, 161, 4-8.
81. *WA* 31 I, 517, 19-22: "But these questions about the descent according to the substance or to the efficacy are worth nothing, because these are considerations about a different world. Look at Paul: 'What does it mean that he ascended unless he descended?' He has ascended, therefore he descended into the interior parts of the earth, i.e. beyond this world below the earth."
82. Cf. Metzke, *Sakrament und Metaphysik*, p. 42.
83. Cf. W. v. Loewenich, *Luther als Ausleger der Synoptiker* (München, 1954), 239.
84. Cf. further P. Althaus, *Unsterblichkeit und ewiges Sterben bei Luther. Zur Auseinandersetzung mit Carl Stange*. Studien des apologetischen Seminars, Vol. 30 (Gütersloh, 1930); p. 36. See also the excellent investigation of P. Althaus "Luthers Gedanken über die letzten Dinge," *Luther-Jahrbuch* 23 (1941), 9-34. He justifiedly emphasizes that Luther, in contrast to the Middle Ages, was not interested in a comprehensive

topography of the beyond. His view was directed only to Christ and the Word of God (Althaus, *loc. cit.* p. 14). This cannot be understood as a privatisation of piety which then developed further in the 17th century (*loc. cit.*, 33), but Luther desired the coming of Christ, and of judgment day. Luther's strictly theocentric thinking was never without a God-given ontological foundation, in spite of its steady existential involvement.

85. See further F. Hildebrandt, *Est: Das lutherische Prinzip.* Studien zur systematischen Theologie, Vol. 7 (Göttingen, 1931), p. 73, who points out here some affinity between Luther and Kant.
86. For the following cf. *WA* 37, 65, 29-38, and the extensive analysis of these Torgau Sermons by E. Vogelsang: "Luthers Torgauer Predigt von Jesu Christo vom Jahre 1532," *Luther-Jahrbuch*, 13 (1931), 114-130. Cf. further the justified critique of this analysis by Althaus, "Niedergefahren zur Hölle," 337, n. 2, and 379, n. 1.
87. *WA* 37, 66, 1-9.
88. For instance, W. Elert, *The Structure of Lutheranism*, trans. by W. A. Hansen, Vol. I. (St. Louis: Concordia, 1962), p. 415, shows this optimism. But he is concerned only with Luther's doctrine of the Lord's Supper.
89. Cf., for instance, John A. T. Robinson, *Honest to God* (Philadelphia: Westminster, 1963), pp. 13 ff. Regarding God's acting in space, Robinson attacks exactly the same thing that Luther had already attacked 400 years ago. However, the results are entirely different.

8. Concern for the Person in the Reformation

1. *WA, Br.* V, 409.
2. *Dr. Martin Luthers Sämmtliche Schriften*, hrsg. von Dr. Joh. Georg Walch XII (St. Louis: Concordia, 1881-1904), 1225 f.
3. *WA* 40a, 289.
4. *Sermons on Exodus, 1524-27, WA*, 16, 548.
5. *WA, TR* 5, No. 5494.

9. Luther's Liturgical Surgery

1. The instructions are not clear: cf. *LW* 53, p. 23 f.
2. *An Order of Mass and Communion, LW* 53, pp. 19-40.
3. *The German Mass, LW* 53, pp. 61-90.
4. *LW* 53, pp. 21-22.
5. *LW* 53, pp. 25 f.
6. Cf. Wetter, *Das christliche Opfer* (Göttingen, 1922), pp. 100 ff.
7. Cf. Kalb, *Grundriss der Liturgik* (Munich, 1965), p. 132. Luther was of the opinion that such a prayer gave the "collect" its name. Cf. *The Babylonian Captivity of the Church, LW* 36, p. 53
8. *Eucharist and Church Fellowship in the First Four Centuries* (St. Louis: Concordia, 1966), p. 27.
9. *The Babylonian Captivity of the Church, LW* 36. Cf. Meinhold, *Abendmahl und Opfer* (Stuttgart, 1960), pp. 46 f., 70 f.
10. Francis Clark, *Eucharistic Sacrifice and the Reformation* (Westminster, Md.: Newman, 1960), p. 225
11. *LW* 36, p. 54, cf. p. 53.
12. *LW* 35, pp. 94 ff.
13. *Ibid.*, p. 97.
14. *Ibid.*, p. 98.
15. *Ibid.*, p. 99.
16. *Ibid.*, pp. 100 f. For the entire section, cf. Vilmos Vajta, *Luther on Worship* (Philadelphia: Muhlenberg, 1958), pp. 149 f.
17. *Grundriss*, p. 133.
18. "Kompendium der Liturgik zur Lutherischen Agende I," *Musicologica et Liturgica* (Kassel, 1960), p. 386.
19. Graff, *Geschichte der Auflösung der alten gottesdienstlichen Formen in der ev. Kirche Deutschlands*, I (Göttingen, 1937), p. 182. Cf. Julius Smend, *Die evangelischen deutschen Messen* . . . (Göttingen, 1896), pp. 241 ff.
20. *Was Christ's Death a Sacrifice?* (Edinburgh: Oliver & Boyd, 1961), p. 26.
21. "Opfer: III, Im NT," *RGG*, IV (Tübingen, 1959), c. 1649.

10. Luther, Preaching, and the Reformation

1. *WA TR* 3, No. 3143b.
2. Elmer Carl Kiessling, *The Early Sermons of Luther and Their Relation to the Pre-Reformation Sermon* (Grand Rapids: n.p., 1935), p. 43.
3. *LW* 51, 9.
4. Kiessling, *Early Sermons,* p. 45.
5. John P. Dolan, ed., *The Essential Erasmus* (New York: The New American Library, 1964), p. 150.
6. Kenneth Scott Latourette, *A History of Christianity* (New York: Harper, 1953), p. 652.
7. H. Grady Davis, *Design for Preaching* (Philadelphia: Muhlenberg, 1958), p. 15.
8. *Ibid.,* p. 16.
9. Latourette, *History of Christianity,* p. 652.
10. John P. Dolan, *History of the Reformation* (New York: The New American Library, 1965), p. 186.
11. J. Michael Reu, *Luther's German Bible* (Columbus, n.p., n.d.), p. 57.
12. William Hazlitt, ed., *Luther's Table Talk* (London, 1872), pp. 191, 192.
13. Kiessling, *Early Sermons,* p. 60.
14. *The Essential Erasmus,* p. 150.
15. *LW* 51, 26.
16. Cf. Yngve T. Brilioth, *A Brief History of Preaching* (Philadelphia: Fortress, 1965), p. 51.
17. The entire sermon is found in *LW* 51, pp. 26-31. This, and all other quotations from this sermon, come from this source.
18. The entire sermon is found in *LW* 51, pp. 121-132.
19. The entire sermon is found in *LW* 51, pp. 383-392.

11. Luther as *Seelsorger*

1. J. T. McNeill, *The History of the Cure of Souls* (New York: Harper, 1951), pp. 136, ff., 163.
2. *Ibid.,* p. 160.
3. Hans J. Hildebrand, *The Reformation* (New York: Harper & Row, 1964), p. 44, reproduces some indulgence documents.
4. Noted by J. T. McNeill, *History,* p. 158.
5. *Ibid.,* p. 161. He estimates that "50% of the towns folk, and some other layfolk, had learned to read."
6. *The Fourteen of Consolation,* the *Small Catechism, Whether Soldiers Too Can Be Saved, On Secular Authority: To What Extent It Should Be Obeyed,* to mention only a few.
7. It should be pointed out that this was a tradition not strange to the young Luther as a monk. He himself describes his own "spiritual exercises" and was a superior in spiritual calisthenics. Also, Ignatius Loyola, whose *Spiritual Exercises* are still a classic and much used in Roman Catholicism, was a contemporary of Luther (d. 1556), though he had no direct contact with Luther.
8. For example, at dawn on April 17, 1521, in Worms—between his first and second appearance before the Diet—he was at the bedside of Hans von Minckwitz, a dying knight, to hear his confession and administer the sacrament (McNeill, *History,* p. 170).
9. Letter in response to request from Johann Hess, "Whether One May Flee from Death," quoted in August Nebe, *Luther as Spiritual Advisor,* trans. by Charles A. Hay (Philadelphia: Lutheran Publication Society, 1894), p. 32.
10. Henrik Ivarsson, "The Principles of Pastoral Care According to Martin Luther." *Pastoral Psychology,* XIII (Feb. 1962), pp. 19-25.
11. For an interesting and somewhat humorous example of this see his letter written to his wife after the successful completion of his mission to Mansfeld, one week before his death, Feb. 10, 1546: "Yesterday, doubtless as a consequence of your anxiety, a stone almost fell on our heads and might have crushed us. . . . I fear that if you do not stop worrying, the earth will swallow us up and all the elements will fall upon us. Is this the way in which you have learned the Catechism. . . . I beg you to pray and leave the worrying to God."
12. *Three Treatises* (Philadelphia: Muhlenberg, 1947), p. 251.
13. Regin Prenter, "The Living Word," in *More About Luther* (Decorah, Iowa: Luther College Press, 1958), p. 72.
14. Roland H. Bainton, *Here I Stand* (New York and Nashville: Abingdon, 1950), p. 361. Luther writes: "I would like to write a book about *Anfechtungen,* for without them no

man can understand Scripture, faith, the fear or the love of God. He does not know the meaning of hope who has never been subject to temptations."

15. *WA* 10 I 2, 48.

16. *The Babylonian Captivity of the Church*, in *Three Treatises* (Philadelphia: Muhlenberg, 1947), p. 174 f.

17. *Ibid.*, p. 201.

18. Jaroslav Pelikan, "The Theology of the Means of Grace," in Heino O. Kadai, *Accents in Luther's Theology* (St. Louis: Concordia, 1967), p. 140.

19. *LW*, 40, 293.

20. *Apology*, XIII, 4. See also the *Sermon on the Sacrament of Penance*, 1519.

21. Pelikan, "Theology of the Means of Grace," p. 139.

22. "We must have many absolutions, so that we may strengthen our timid consciences and despairing hearts against the devil and against God [I] . . . And if any one wrestles with his sins, is eager to be rid of them and looks for some assurances from the Scriptures, let him go and confess to another in secret, and receive what is said to him there as if it came directly from God's own lips. Whoever has the strong and firm faith that his sins are forgiven, may ignore this confession and confess to God alone. But how many have such strong faith? Therefore, as I have said, I will not let this private confession be taken away from me." *The Eighth Wittenberg Sermon*, in Charles Anderson, ed., *Readings in Luther for Laymen* (Minneapolis: Augsburg, 1967), p. 67.

23. See *An Open Letter to the Christian Nobility, Three Treatises*, pp. 14-16: "Whoever comes out of the water of baptism can boast that he is already consecrated priest, bishop, and pope, though it is not seemly that everyone should exercise the office." See also the letter to the Christians in Prague, "On the Ministry" where a more radical statement of the thesis is developed. *LW* 40, 26.

24. Luther, of course, makes it very clear always when speaking of the Absolution that is proclaimed that it is the Word of God, and not a human word. In the *Eighth Wittenberg Sermon*, he speaks of Private Confession: "After that we have private confession when I go and receive a sure absolution as if God Himself spake it, so that I may be assured that my sins are forgiven." This is but one of many similar statements. See also in this connection Luther's concept of the public and private persons expressed in the sermon *Two Kinds of Righteousness*, in the essay *On Secular Authority*, and elsewhere. The "public person" is one of "those who have been placed in a responsible office by God." These persons are not to act in God's place for the sake of themselves, but only for the sake of the neighbor. This would tend further to necessitate the Word spoken to us (on God's behalf) by another, rather than our applying the Word to ourselves (on God's behalf) as we hear and read it privately. Anderson, *Readings*, pp 67, 93 ff., 145 ff.

25. "The brethren" is Luther's synonym for the church in the Smalcald Articles.

26. *Two Kinds of Righteousness*, in Anderson, *Readings in Luther*, p. 102.

27. Dietrich Bonhoeffer, *Ethics* (New York: Macmillan, 1962), p. 194.

28. One of the difficulties here is that this symbolic character of the pastoral office often passes unnoticed because of its "low visibility"; the pastor is "simply another human being." To deal with this the medieval church ritualized the conversation and the person of the pastor. This avenue is open only to a limited extent for the modern pastor because of our modern distrust of rigid rituals and because rigidifying this in a ritualized form also tends to destroy the dynamics of the process. What may seem a more appropriate solution is to ensure a very close organic and human relationship between the minister and the congregation so that the Word of the Gospel is reflected or reciprocated by a human fellowship in Luther's sense of the church, where the means of grace are alive in the believers in the "mutual conversation and consolation of the brethren" (cf. Pelikan, "The Theology of the Means of Grace," pp. 143 f.). This "mutual conversation and consolation" is not to be understood in the purely verbal sense but is rather the total style of interpersonal life in the congregation where human forgiving is a real fact and "visible" to anyone. Congregations may need some education in this direction, and this surely is what Paul would include in "building up the body of Christ" or "equipping the saints" for their ministries.

29. *LW* 31: 368-371.

30. *WA* 10 III, 218.

31. *WA* 15, 674.

32. *Freedom of the Christian Man, Three Treatises*, p. 304.

33. *The Fourteen of Consolation, Works of Martin Luther* I (Philadelphia: Muhlenberg, 1943), p. 111.

34. Cf. McNeill, *History*, p. 150.

35. Pelikan, "The Theology of the Means of Grace," p. 145.